3D COMPUTER GRAPHICS
A User's Guide for Artists and Designers

SECOND EDITION

3D COMPUTER GRAPHICS
A User's Guide for Artists and Designers

SECOND EDITION

Andrew S. Glassner

Design Press

Second Edition, First Printing

Copyright © 1989 by Andrew S. Glassner

Printed in the United States of America

Library of Congress Cataloging-in-Publication Data

Glassner, Andrew S.
   3 D computer graphics : a user's guide for artists and designers /
Andrew S. Glassner. — 2nd ed.
     p.   cm.
   Rev. ed. of: Computer graphics user's guide. 1st ed. c1984.
   Bibliography: p.
   Includes index.
   ISBN 0-8306-1003-0 (pbk.)
   1. Computer graphics.   I. Glassner, Andrew S. Computer graphics
user's guide. II. Title. III. Title:Three D computer graphics.
T385.G577 1989
006.6—dc20   89-33109
                                              CIP

Design Press offers posters and The Cropper, a device for cropping artwork, for sale. For information, contact Mail-order Department. Design Press books are available at special discounts for bulk purchases for sales promotions, fund raisers, or premiums. For details contact Special Sales Manager. Questions regarding the content of the book should be addressed to:
   Design Press
   Division of TAB BOOKS Inc.
   10 East 21st Street
   New York, NY 10010

CONTENTS

Preface   vii

1   Basic Concepts and Hardware   1
2   Geometry and Color   15
3   Computer Graphics Hardware   35
4   Surfaces and Materials   49
5   Lighting and Shading   61
    Color Plates follow page 70
6   Polygons and Polygonal Models   71
7   Textures   87
8   Fractals   99
9   Curved Surfaces   107
10   Basic Modeling   115
11   Principles of Rendering   127
12   Rendering Algorithms   139
13   Advanced Modeling   159
14   Computer-Assisted Animation   177
15   Production Techniques   195

Bibliography   210
Index   211

Preface

The field of computer graphics is a wonderful blend of traditional art techniques, programming, geometry, physics, and creative invention. It is a diverse and exciting discipline that keeps changing and growing as new ideas are contributed from universities, art studios, research labs, and animation houses.

There is so much happening in the field that just the term "computer graphics" can have a different meaning for each person encountering it. So I am going to narrow the scope of that term right from the start: For this book, "computer graphics" means the art and science of creating images of three-dimensional objects. These images should suggest that the objects being viewed really existed and were photographed with a camera. Pictures can convey much more than words, so I invite you to flip through the pages of this book and look at the pictures; they are examples of the kinds of images users of computer graphics are interested in creating.

Why is there such a field at all? After all, a good artist can create any of the pictures in this book using traditional materials. There are at least four reasons why computer graphics were invented in the first place, and they are the same reasons the field continues to flourish.

One reason is scientific visualization. Scientists are not artists, but they do need to draw pictures. A meteorologist might have a theory about how rain clouds form; it would be very useful to see the clouds predicted by the theory. An aeronautics engineer might want to study the flow of air around an airplane's wing by looking at pictures of colored bits of air. A biologist might want to simulate the flapping wing of a bird that may or may not have ever existed. There are many other scientific fields where researchers want to see the results of their theories and experiments presented as pictures. Using a computer to make the images is very attractive, since the data are often on a computer anyway. These images can then be used for communication in professional papers or used for education.

Another use of computer graphics is in commercial and industrial design. An industrial designer might be working on a new type of car. It is important to understand the way the car looks from all angles, so car designers often build clay models. But suppose they want to make a little change here, or a big change there? Making a new clay model is not a trivial process. But if the model is in the computer, they can make a change and see the results immediately, from any point of view. Or suppose you were a designer who wanted to make a reflective teapot with interchangeable handles, and you chose to render this design with felt-tip markers. The reflections are an important part of the design, so you would probably have to draw the teapot once for each handle, and that could be a lot of work if there were a lot of handles! Using the computer you could easily render the teapot with one handle, tell the computer to switch in another handle, and then render the teapot again.

Another popular use of computer graphics is for commercial art. Computer graphics offers enormous flexibility for animation. You can create almost any effect you want, and then change it easily. Just as you can easily create a dozen different renderings of a shiny teapot, you can create a dozen sequences of animation, each with slightly different objects or motion. Once you have the basic pieces in place, the computer can save you a great deal of work and offer you a flexible environment in which to experiment. Commercial animation is used for everything from television commercials to feature films. There have even been feature films in which entire scenes were created with computer graphics, not as a special effect, but as an integral part of the film.

Computer graphics is increasingly used for fine art. Artists are a creative and experimental group, and computer graphics is a new medium ripe for exploring. This area is just getting off the ground.

One reason that computer graphics is attractive to people in all of these different fields is because the computer can be programmed to do an amazing variety of tasks. Almost anything that you need done and you don't want to do yourself can be turned over to the computer. If you want to build a wonderful model and see it from all angles, you build the model and describe it to the computer. It will allow you to rotate the model in space, move the lights, and otherwise play with the model and its appearance on the screen. If you want to make a film, but don't have the budget to hire a gaffer, and a grip, and a set designer, and a carpenter, and all the other personnel important on a set, then you can design your set yourself and describe it to the computer. It will draw the set and animate it for you if you wish. If you want to add characters moving around on the screen, but you don't want to draw every frame yourself, just create the characters and describe some of the frames, and the computer will fill in the empty frames for you.

The power of the computer is that it can help you do your work more quickly and with more flexibility. It frees you from much of the mechanical, uncreative work involved in traditional image and film-making, and lets you focus your energies on creativity. The price you must pay (today, at least) is that you must be familiar enough with computer concepts and techniques to be able to work with this tool. As an analogy, you won't get very far in a stick-shift automobile until you learn that higher gears are for faster speeds, that the lever on the left side is for turn signals, that the horn is in the middle of the wheel, and so on. You need to speak the language and know a little about what's going on inside to use the machine properly.

Likewise, to use the programs and hardware of computer graphics effectively, you have to know something about what's going on inside the equipment. Then you'll know the limitations and the problems. You'll know what you can do (signal a left turn) and what you cannot do (drive straight up into the air).

This book is for anyone who wants to make pictures using a computer: artists, scientists, designers or anyone else with a need to make pictures. I assume that you are interested in the subject, and that you are willing to learn some new language in order to master this new medium. That is really what this book is all about: new words and the meaning of those words. If you can understand the concepts and you know how to talk about them, then you can use almost any computer graphics equipment anywhere after learning its idiosyncrasies. I present the basic ideas here, not the details (unless they are necessary for a complete understanding of the big picture).

This is not a book for programmers or mathematicians. I do not tell you how to write computer programs to make pictures. I assume you already have those programs, and you just want to use them wisely and creatively.

Computer graphics is really a new medium for creative expression and communication. It is as versatile as paper and pencil, but you do not work directly with your image as with a pencil. Instead of using the pencil yourself, you have a genie living inside your pencil; you tell the genie what to draw, and the picture will appear before you. This book tells you how to command your genie to draw the pictures you want to see.

This book is a substantial revision of my previous book entitled *Computer Graphics Users Guide*. To bring the text up to date, entirely new material has been added in many places. Specifically, there is new discussion of some hardware, several color systems, gamma correction, and material properties. The chapter on texture mapping has been revised and expanded to include several new techniques. Rendering has been separated into two chapters, one discussing principles such as aliasing and shadows, and the other discussing techniques such as radiosity. Chapter 13, which covers advanced modeling techniques, is completely new to this version. There are new discussions of dynamics and procedural motion, and the discussion of image composition and matting has been considerably expanded.

The result of these changes is a longer book than the first edition, but a much more comprehensive and practical one. I believe that much of the material from the first edition has been improved through changes in presentation and approach. I hope that this new material will help the reader stay current in this quickly changing field.

But I would like to repeat my admonition from the first edition that you should not take the material in this book as the last word on anything. Computer graphics is a rapidly changing field, and new contributions are made constantly. I hope that through this book you'll be able to join in and participate, and perhaps invent some new techniques of your own.

Much of this manuscript was written using the Tioga editor/typesetter at Xerox PARC, which is part of the Cedar operating system running on the PARC-designed Dorado computer. The rest of the text was prepared on an Apple Macintosh Plus and Macintosh II, using Microsoft Word 3.01. New line diagrams were created using the Gargoyle electronic drafting tool at PARC, and printed on the Platemaker prototype phototypesetter. The two-dimensional fractals in Chapter 8 were created with the combination of Gargoyle and the MatchTool graphical editor. Many of the shaded illustrations from the first edition were created on an IBM 370 using a rendering system I wrote especially for the book in the APL programming language.

I could never have written this book without help from a great many people. I would like to thank Bill Maher for the original inspiration; my mother, Roberta Glassner, for editorial help; Anne Beekman, Eric Braun, Bruce Glassner, Mark Howard, Chris Jones, David Labuda, and Barak Pearlmutter for reviewing the first edition; Chuck Rose for early access to equipment; Frederick Way III for support and encouragement while writing the original text; Dave Bantz for help and support while creating the images; Alan Norton and Paul Sholtz for discussion about the presentation of graphics; Claire Albahae for the illustrations in Chapter 14; Paula Sweeney for extensive help with the first edition; Duane Palyka for ideas about how to revise the first edition; Larry Bergman, John Gauch, Marc Levoy, Chuck Mosher, Doug Turner, Lee Westover, and the other members of the University of North Carolina at Chapel Hill Computer Graphics Lab for discussions and ideas; and all the artists, programmers, and designers who contributed images used in this book.

Many of the new images in this edition were created at Digital Arts in San Diego, using their fine computer graphics software. Shelly Liebman of Digital Arts was a prime motivator behind getting me to start this new edition. Shelly then volunteered his equipment and staff to make many new pictures from my rough drawings. I am indebted to Shelly, Ed Chmiel, and Ron Deutsch for their time and efforts in making these images, under very tight time constraints. We used a variety of their software packages to build the models, design the lighting, and render the images. That we were able to create over forty final images in just three days is testament to the quality and convenience of their products. Their programs performed flawlessly and the resulting images greatly contribute to the book.

I started work on the new manuscript for this edition not long after I joined the research staff of the Electronic Documents Lab,which is part of the Xerox Palo Alto Research Laboratory (PARC). The excellent facilities and people at PARC helped make this project a pleasure.

Particular thanks to Jules Bloomenthal and Frank Crow, who helped me use existing software and write new programs to generate several new images, and Brian Tramontana for photographic support.

This new edition would have not have been possible without the encouragement and support I received from Lakshmi Dasari, who also helped me with many of the technical and creative facets of writing this book.

And thank you, too, to the readers of the first edition, for letting me know what was good and bad about the original book. I hope I have corrected all the old errors and not introduced too many new ones!

1 BASIC CONCEPTS AND HARDWARE

Three-dimensional computer graphics involves creating images with a computer, and for most people a computer is a very strange sort of device, far different than most of the tools used every day. Consider that an understanding of cameras, lenses, and photographic paper is important to creative photographers who want to get the most out of their medium. The same principle applies to the use of a computer: a good understanding of the equipment will help you use it in efficient and creative ways. Think of a computer as something like a remote-control servant; you issue commands, and it carries them out. Just how you issue instructions to the machine is an important part of your daily work.

Consider a home stereo system. To use it, you need to know what the various knobs and buttons do. If you encounter a system at a friend's house that differs from yours, everything might be labeled differently, and you could be stumped momentarily about its use. But the basic machine is the same—you still put on a record and the tonearm lowers a needle that rides in the groove. If you know this fact, then your friend can simply tell you which button performs what operation, and you'll know how to run the record player. Your knowledge of the principles behind the hardware helps you adapt to a new device.

The same situation holds true in the computer field. There appear to be an incredible number of devices out there, all different. In fact, there are a small number of general ideas on which all these different devices are based. If you understand these ideas, then you can adapt to whatever hardware you happen to encounter.

In this chapter I first describe some of the basics of creating objects on a computer, then discuss the devices used to create and manipulate the desired objects.

WHAT IS A COMPUTER MODEL?

One of the most essential concepts in computer graphics is the idea of a model. In this book I use the word *model* in two different ways.

A *scale model* is a scaled up (or down) copy of some object, usually built up from many smaller pieces, or *surfaces*. Anyone who has ever built a plane or car from a plastic hobby kit is familiar with the idea of a scale model. A scale model is a copy of some object, recreated either larger or smaller than the original.

A *mathematical model*, though widely used in scientific work, is less familiar than a scale model. A mathematical model is a description of physical laws that models, or describes, the behavior of something (as opposed to a scale model that describes its shape). For example, engineers planning the flight path for the space shuttle use a mathematical model. They supply the model with various data called *input*, such as the earth's size, its motion around the sun, its gravity, and so on. The model then supplies them with *output*, or new information derived from the given information; in this case, specifics on the flight path of the shuttle. The model itself is usually considered a set of mathematical equations that are organized into a whole.

When applied to computer graphics from the point of view of an artist or designer who wants to represent a real object (such as a person or a spaceship) on a computer screen, with the freedom to manipulate that object as if it were real, the person would be a scale model, and a description of how that person walks would be a mathematical model.

PREPARED AND INTERACTIVE MODELING

Once you have an object in mind, there are two popular approaches for getting your vision into the computer.

In one technique, you plan your model meticulously before you describe it, like creating a detailed drawing of a sculpture before picking up a tool. The other technique allows you to invent your model directly on the computer, like starting a sculpture with a rough idea, and immediately carving. Both approaches have their merits.

The first method, called *prepared modeling*, begins with accurate engineering drawings of your scale model. You then measure the drawings themselves for the sizes of the different shapes that make up the model and enter that information into the computer in terms of three-dimensional points, lines, spheres, and other shapes and surfaces. The computer assembles these shapes into a complete scale model, which it stores in its memory. Fig. C-1 shows an image composed of several pieces, each of which was created independently as a prepared model.

The advantage of prepared modeling is that you can get a very precise model; the disadvantage is that your model must be completely prepared in advance.

The second design technique is called *interactive modeling*. Using this technique you manipulate the computer's various switches, knobs, and joysticks to juggle shapes around on the screen, create new shapes and change old ones, put shapes together and take them apart, until you have built a satisfactory model. One advantage of this technique over prepared modeling is that it requires less preparation. Another advantage is that interactive modeling allows you to work *with* the computer when making your design; in a sense, the computer itself is acting as your medium. Fig. C-2 shows a scene created using an interactive modeling system.

The main advantage of interactive modeling is that you are free to explore while you design your model; the main drawback is that it is a difficult technique to master.

SUBTRACTIVE AND ADDITIVE MODELING

There is an old joke about a hobby kit that claims to be a complete kit for an elephant. Inside the box is a block of wood and a knife, with the instructions, "To make an elephant, just carve away everything that doesn't look like an elephant!" That technique is called *subtractive modeling*, and in general it means you start off with too much material and gradually take away pieces until the shape you desire emerges. Carving is a subtractive process because it is accomplished by cutting away chunks of the material to reveal a sculpture.

A more popular modeling technique is called *additive modeling*, and it involves building up a model by assembling many simple pieces. This method, used in traditional plastic model kits, is the technique of choice in this book. An example of additive modeling is a circus clown's creation of a dog made out of long, thin balloons. By assembling the right balloons the right way, the complete dog appears. Sometimes the phrases *solid modeling* or *constructive modeling* are used to mean the same thing as additive modeling. Either subtractive or additive modeling may be communicated to the computer with a prepared model or interactively.

LINE DRAWINGS AND SHADED DRAWINGS

Computer graphics mainly produce two kinds of drawings: *line drawings* and *shaded drawings*. They are compared side-by-side in Fig. 1-1. A line drawing simply represents an object with lines and is, consequently, not a lifelike representation. Usually line drawings are only meant to indicate the structure of an object, not to convince you that you are looking at the object itself. Shaded drawings, on the other hand, can look very much like photographs of real objects, but there are subtleties in the appearance of the real world that most computer programs cannot account for. Most shaded images suffer from some kind of inaccuracy, however inconspicuous: the objects are too metallic, or crisp edged, or otherwise unreal. This look is not necessarily a drawback because such computer-generated images appear unique. Nevertheless, many people are working on improving the realism that shaded graphics can produce. This book concentrates on methods that produce realistic pictures, where "realistic" means as close as possible to a photographic image.

Line drawings are faster and cheaper to generate than shaded drawings and sometimes are all you need. They are well-suited for charts and graphs, engineering drawings, and other precise line-oriented images, and are often used when setting up or previewing an image or animation. When you know a lot about your scene, a line drawing can usually provide detail needed to make sure things are in the right place. Once you are satisfied with the line-drawing version of a still or animation, you can start the more time-consuming process of generating the shaded pictures.

STATIC AND DYNAMIC DISPLAY

The purpose of computer graphics is to draw pictures. You may hear that the computer *renders* a picture, under the control of a program called the *renderer*. These rendered images might be used as single photographs or slides, or to make an animation. When making a high-quality computer-generated image, you want it to look as good as possible. In general, the better a picture

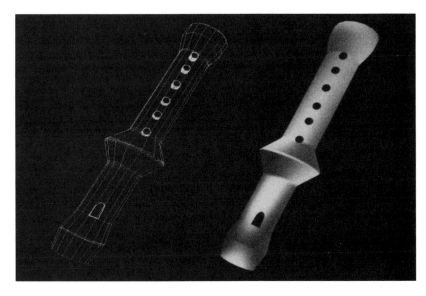

1-1. Two images of a simple recorder. The left-hand drawing is a wireframe representation, the right-hand drawing a shaded image.

looks, the longer it takes to draw, so making high-quality images can mean waiting a long time for each picture to be made. To achieve high quality in an image, the computer must perform many complex operations, and the effect of that effort is the time required for the picture to be drawn. This kind of operation produces *static images*, or pictures that take so long to generate that there is no illusion of movement from one picture to the next as you watch them being drawn.

In addition to creating high-quality slides or video, another popular use of computer graphics is for simulation and testing. An example of simulation is training a pilot to fly a new kind of airplane. The control panel is physically constructed just as it is in the airplane, but the windows of the cockpit look out onto the screens of computer graphics equipment, TV tubes, or projection-TV displays, as shown in Fig. 1-2. As the pilot flies the airplane, the view out the windows should look as if the plane really were surrounded by the countryside, buildings, water, and so on. The aesthetic purity of the individual images is not as essential as having the images come out, one after the other, fast enough to move and react to the pilot's control of the airplane.

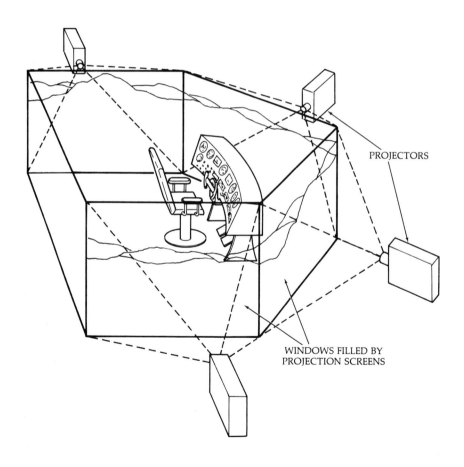

PROJECTORS

WINDOWS FILLED BY
PROJECTION SCREENS

1-2. A schematic illustration of a flight simulator.

To get that kind of speed requires shortcuts in making the pictures, and the resulting images are less realistic, containing different kinds of errors. However, no single image remains visible for very long. If you carefully choose speedup techniques so that the errors are small, then they will not be noticed during the moment when the picture is visible. This kind of operation is called *dynamic* (or *moving*) *image generation*.

When discussing motion you sometimes hear the phrase *real time*. This term refers to something happening at a rate consistent with events in the outside world.

Suppose you were working with a system that takes two minutes to render an image. If you wanted to make a change to the picture, you would have to specify your change, and then wait two minutes to see the result. This is not real-time response, since you are not getting a completely new picture immediately after asking for one. A flight simulator by necessity is real time, since the images must always accurately display what the pilot would see in a real plane. In general, a program is said to have real-time response if it can react to your changes and present you with a new, updated image immediately.

STATIC AND DYNAMIC MODELS

Just as the images on a display can be called static or dynamic, so can these words be used to classify scale models. A model in which there are no moving parts (such as a canoe) is called a *static model*; a model with moving parts (such as a sailboat with working rudder and moving sail) is a *dynamic model*.

The distinction between static and dynamic becomes important if you want to animate your model. A static model cannot change its shape. Because of its mathematical description, a static model can only be moved around within a scene; typically, you can change its position, orientation, and size. If you want a sequence of several planets orbiting a sun, then a static model of each planet would be sufficient because the planets do not change in any way (Fig. 1-3). But a view of the entire solar system as a single model would require a dynamic model, because the pieces inside the model move with respect to each other.

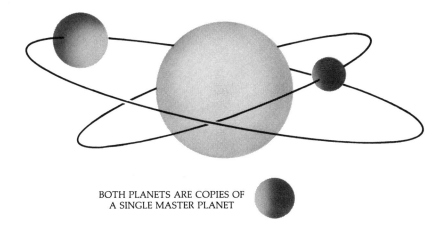

BOTH PLANETS ARE COPIES OF
A SINGLE MASTER PLANET

1-3. Each planet is a static model. Together, they form a dynamic model of the solar system.

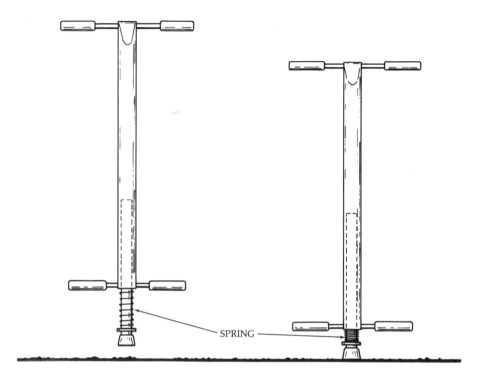

1-4. The spring must be created in such a way that it is able to compress when the pogo stick hits the ground.

Although dynamic models require more work to create, they are often necessary. For example, to simulate a pogo stick, the spring must compress when the foot bar comes down (Fig. 1-4). Just how you tell the computer to do this compression is covered in later chapters, but the *capability* for that spring to compress must be part of the model description when it is originally entered into the computer. This ability to move or actually change the shape of all or some of the pieces within a model is what distinguishes static from dynamic models.

PHYSICAL SYSTEMS (HARDWARE)

The act of generating computer graphics places an artist in direct contact with the computer. Most artists and programmers alike want this contact to be as pleasant as possible. Over the years, a number of popular techniques have been developed to assist the communication between user and computer.

Some of these techniques are more closely linked with the physical equipment (*hardware*) that the computer offers to the artist than with the programs (*software*) that the hardware executes. Computers are not the only instruments that constrain you with their hardware. Consider your car: The way you drive and interact with your car will differ depending on whether you have a manual or automatic transmission.

The next few sections of this chapter discuss the various pieces of equipment that you are likely to find around a computer graphics installation. It is not possible to describe all of the many available devices in just one chapter, nor will every site have all the hardware that is discussed.

But a general idea of the most common hardware can help you feel more comfortable when you sit down to use a new computer for the first time.

The imaginary computer graphics workstation described is shown in Fig. 1-5, which represents much of the equipment covered in this chapter.

Text CRT and Keyboard

The *text CRT* and *keyboard* make up a standard computer terminal. (CRT stands for cathode-ray tube, the formal name for a television picture tube.) A text-only CRT can display only *text*, that is, letters, numbers, and punctuation, or anything that might come out of a standard office typewriter. The display is usually *monochrome* (meaning black and white). The keyboard looks like a regular typewriter keyboard, although there are often some additional, special-purpose keys. The computer terminal provides the physical means for you to log on to the computer, run programs, and type in data.

Color Raster CRT

The *color raster CRT* (or sometimes just *color CRT* or *color monitor*) is another TV tube, but it is usually much larger than the text CRT, has the ability to display color, and, in general, is capable of high precision in color intensity and positioning of the image. Shaded pictures drawn by the computer are shown on this monitor.

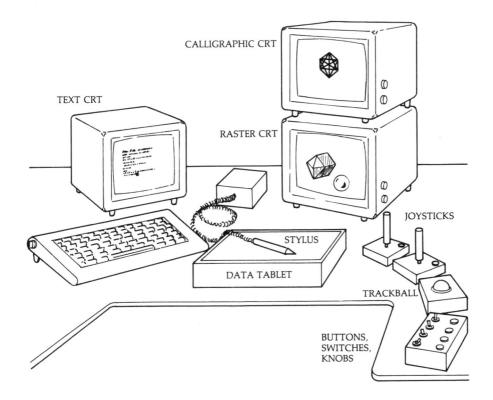

1-5. A well-equipped computer-graphics workstation.

Since a color monitor can display any image, it can also display text, just like a text CRT. Sometimes a color monitor is used to display both graphics and text, either superimposed or in separate regions on the screen.

When a color CRT is showing an image, the information that makes up the image is often coming to the monitor from a device called a *frame buffer*. This is a piece of memory of just the right shape and size to hold a picture. It is discussed in detail in Chapter 4.

Calligraphic CRT

The *calligraphic* (or *vector*) *CRT* is yet another TV tube, but it only draws lines, which can sometimes be in color. The advantage is that these lines are drawn with much greater precision than the color CRT can offer. Because the calligraphic CRT is constructed to draw lines only, the hardware can be tuned to the task; usually a calligraphic CRT can draw a line picture faster than a color CRT. This speed makes calligraphic CRTs useful when previewing animation.

Image Digitizer

A color CRT is good for displaying a picture, but to get a picture into the machine in the first place requires an *image digitizer*. This unit is basically a television camera connected to the computer. When you give the signal, the computer takes the image seen by the camera and turns it into a digital signal that is fit for display, storage, and manipulation on the computer. Many image digitizers have the ability to record color signals in addition to black and white. Some image digitizers work in a slightly different way; they look more like small photocopiers. You place the image you want to have digitized on the glass of the "copier," and the image is scanned in and sent to the computer.

Printer, Plotter, and Film Recorder

The *printer* is a cousin of the text CRT; anything you can show on a text CRT can be typed out on paper by the printer. Because the printer puts its output on paper, you can carry the printer's output around with you after the printer has been turned off, something you obviously cannot do with a CRT. To emphasize these differences, output on paper is called *hardcopy*; the images on any CRT are called *softcopy*.

The *plotter* is the hardcopy cousin of the calligraphic CRT. It can make line drawings on paper, often in color.

The *film recorder* (or sometimes a *video recorder*) is the hardcopy cousin of the color CRT. It takes a color, shaded image and records it onto one or more frames of film or videotape.

Data Tablet, Puck, and Mouse

A *data tablet* is a large, flat piece of plastic. It usually comes with a *stylus* (or pen). This pen has two special features: a long wire coming out of the pen connecting it to the computer and a small switch in the tip of the pen. You can hold the pen and draw with it on the tablet as though it were a regular ballpoint pen, but it does not leave ink behind. Instead, the computer can electronically determine just where the pen is (as long as the pen is on or near the plastic surface of the tablet); that is, the computer can *track*, or follow, the pen.

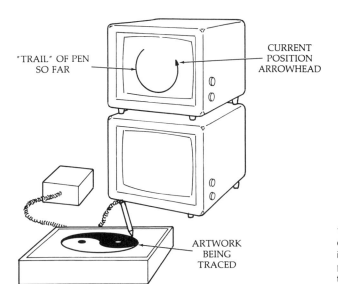

"TRAIL" OF PEN
SO FAR

CURRENT
POSITION
ARROWHEAD

ARTWORK
BEING
TRACED

1-6. A data tablet can be used for drawing freehand pictures. A cursor is displayed on one of the CRTs to provide feedback in the form of a tracking display.

The computer will usually let you know that it is monitoring the stylus by displaying your movements on one of the CRTs. Fig. 1-6 shows a typical tracking display. The computer has drawn a small arrowhead called a *cursor* on one of the CRTs. The upper-right corner of the tablet corresponds to the upper-right corner of the CRT, and the other corners match as well. You can point to any position on the screen by moving the pen to the corresponding place on the tablet. As you move the pen, the arrowhead on the screen moves with you.

There is a small switch in the tip of the pen that closes when you press the tip of the pen onto the surface. Picking the pen up off the surface opens the switch. One use of this tip switch is for line drawing. To draw a line, you move the pen to the beginning of the line, click down on the switch, and then (still pressing with the pen to hold the switch down), move the pen to the other end of the line, where you pick up the pen and open the switch.

One variation on this theme is for the tablet to be *pressure sensitive*, so it can respond to how hard you press down with the stylus. Another variation is for the stylus to be *tilt sensitive*, so the computer can detect at what angle you hold the pen. These enhancements can make using the computer a more intuitive kind of experience when the computer is running programs that look for this information and uses it to help you.

In addition to a stylus with just one button (in the tip), you may sometimes use a *puck*, illustrated in Fig. 1-7A. A puck is a small box having a small see-through crosshair at the top with several buttons below it. The computer can read the position of the puck just as for the stylus and can respond to the pressing of different buttons as commands.

A similar device is called a *mouse*, shown in Fig. 1-7B. A mouse is a small, hand-held box with one or more buttons on top of it. Generally, a mouse does not need a special tablet to run around on; a mouse includes special mechanical or optical parts that keep track of how far it has moved since the last time the computer asked it where it was. This fact raises an interesting feature of the mouse not found in the tablet devices: *relative positioning*.

The puck and stylus are used with a tablet. When the computer asks for the position of the puck or stylus, it receives an *absolute position*. That is, the answer might be "3 centimeters from the left side of the tablet and 6.5 centimeters from the bottom." But the mouse only knows how far it has moved relative to the last time you asked; a typical mouse position would be "2.5 centimeters to the left and 1 centimeter below where I was before." It only knows this because the sensors on the bottom of the mouse (usually a ball or a small light source) are keeping track

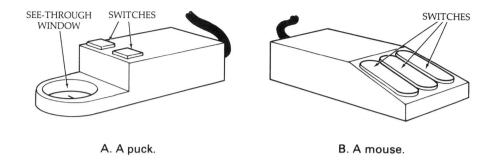

SEE-THROUGH
WINDOW   SWITCHES   SWITCHES

A. A puck.   B. A mouse.

1-7. A puck (A) moves about on the surface of a tablet and provides absolute
position. A mouse (B) can move on any surface and provides relative position.
Both devices can be equipped with buttons.

of how the mouse is moving on its surface. If you pick the mouse up and move it through the air before setting it down again, the movement will not be registered. But if you pick up the stylus, move it through the air, and set it down again, it can tell just where it is with respect to the surface of the tablet.

The tablet, then, is an *absolute positioning device*, while the mouse is a *relative positioning device*. Both techniques can be useful in different circumstances, and some equipment will switch between the two techniques depending on the situation.

Joysticks and Trackballs

Joysticks are shafts that freely rotate and swing from left to right and top to bottom, pivoting from the bottom of the shaft. Sometimes you can rotate the handle as well (Fig. 1-8). The computer can determine the current position of the joystick and react to it in the same way that a television set can determine the position of the channel selector and respond to it by tuning into the correct channel.

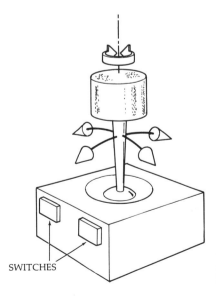

SWITCHES

1-8. A joystick can be swung in any
direction and can also be twisted at
the top.

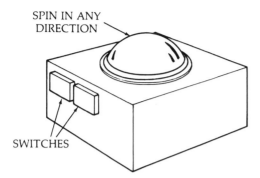

1-9. A trackball can be freely rotated in any direction.

A *trackball* is usually a hard plastic ball that you can spin in any direction with the force of your hand (Fig. 1-9). The computer responds to the trackball in one of two ways. The first is to monitor how long the ball is spinning, and as long as it spins to the right (for example), a cursor on the CRT will track the movement and go right at a constant speed no matter how fast the trackball is being moved. The other way is for the arrow to move with a speed relative to the speed of rotation of the trackball. For example, spinning the trackball to the right very fast would cause the cursor to move to the right very fast. Spinning the trackball slowly to the left would move the cursor slowly to the left. Since the interpretation of the motion is up to the computer, you can find systems that switch between the two techniques depending on the situation.

Space Tracker

A *space tracker* is a three-dimensional version of the data tablet. It consists of two parts: a *source* and a *sensor*. The source is a small box (about the size of a rolled-up sock) that you set down somewhere near where you will be working. The sensor is a small unit (about the size of a pea-nut) with a wire coming out of it going back to the computer. The source sends out a special radio signal that is picked up by the sensor. With that information, the sensor can determine not only where it is in space, but also its orientation.

One good way to see the power of a space tracker is to imagine being on a bow-and-arrow range. On the far wall is a target, and to make your shot you pretend that there is an arrow attached to the tracker. When you move the tracker around, you are moving the arrow; when you twist and turn the tracker, you are pointing the arrow. You could mount a button on the side of the tracker, so that when you press the switch, the computer would read the position of the tracker and figure out where your arrow would land.

You can use a space tracker to accurately pick up and move imaginary objects in space; it is particularly useful when setting up an animation. When you use a space tracker you will usually get some kind of visual feedback from the computer to help you figure out where you are and what objects you are interacting with.

The sensor usually gives the computer six pieces of information, three each to describe its position and orientation. For this reason space trackers are sometimes called *six-axis positioning devices*.

Hand Tracker

A *hand tracker* is a glove that fits on your hand just like a regular glove. But within the fabric of the hand tracker are special devices that can determine just how much each knuckle is bent.

One popular use of hand trackers is as a *gesture interface* to the computer. Almost every culture contains meaningful hand gestures; for example, in ancient Rome (and in many of today's cultures) a closed fist with a thumb pointing up meant approval, while thumb down meant disapproval. When you are far away from a keyboard and a computer needs a ''yes'' or ''no'' from you for something, you might make one of these gestures as an answer. If you are wearing a hand tracker then your gesture can be recognized by the computer and it will proceed appropriately.

If you attach a space tracker to your wrist, just above the glove, then the computer can also determine where your hand is in space. (The next section shows how useful that combination can be.)

Head-Mounted Display

A *head-mounted display* (or *HMD*) is usually a color raster display that travels with you, rather than sitting on a table. In a simple HMD, two lightweight, small displays are mounted on a band on your forehead; small mirrors reflect the images into your eyes (the displays are especially chosen for low power and safety). Two displays are normally used so that each eye can be shown a different image, which provides stereo vision. The mirrors are only *half-silvered*; this means that their silver coating covers only about half of their surface. So half of the image you see is coming from the displays, while the other half is the world in front of you, passing through the clear parts of the mirrors. The HMD also includes a space tracker mounted on top, so the computer can determine where your head is located and, implicitly, where you are looking. Most HMD systems assume you are always looking straight ahead, so to look to your side you must turn your head.

The idea behind head-mounted displays is to imagine that, instead of sitting in front of a CRT looking at a world, you are walking around *within* the world generated by the computer.

The HMD system is typically used with hand trackers. The whole system involves a hand tracker on each hand (to tell the computer what your hands are doing), a space tracker on each wrist (to tell the computer where your hands are), and an HMD with space tracker on your head (to tell the computer where your head is and where you are looking).

As you walk around your room, the computer is constantly checking where your head is and in what direction it is pointed. The computer figures out what you would see if you were at that location and looking straight ahead within the imaginary world, and draws those pictures on the displays in the HMD. In effect, you are walking around and seeing a *virtual* (or *imaginary*) world—you can walk around objects, look under them, and in general act as though they were really there.

In addition to just looking at this world, you can interact with it. Suppose you had a three-dimensional character sitting in a chair and you wanted the character to stand up. You could reach out with your hands and grab the character. The computer would know what you are doing, since it knows just where your hands are, and, of course, it also knows where everything is in the imaginary world it is showing you. As you raise your hand the computer will update the world that you see, so that the character will really appear to be standing up!

There are some drawbacks to this system. All of the computer-generated objects are semitransparent because you can always see the real world behind them. And you can walk through things if you please! More seriously, your hands don't actually feel the things you touch and move. These drawbacks hinder the reality of the virtual world, but they do not really diminish its utility. A person wearing such an HMD cannot be fooled into thinking that he or she is in another world, but the HMD is still very useful for practical work, such as posing characters.

Another form of head-mounted display encloses your head in a helmet, so that the only things you see are the computer-generated images. The advantage is a potentially improved illusion in that since you only see what the computer draws, the world can be as realistic as the computer can make it (and there's no real world to compare to). The drawback is in not seeing anything but the imaginary world. If the computer world includes all of the furniture in the room and you were careful, you could avoid the real objects. Unfortunately, if a cat slips into room while you are wearing the helmet, neither the computer nor you would be aware of it. You might reach out to pick up an imaginary telephone and grab a real cat's tail instead!

SUMMARY

This chapter presents the distinction between a scale model, which is a copy of some object (created from surfaces), and a mathematical model, which is a collection of ideas and concepts linked through mathematical relationships.

To create a scale model you may work with a prepared modeling system, where you describe a model that you have already created on paper. Alternatively, you may use an interactive modeling system that allows you to create your model interactively with the computer.

One technique for describing your model is called subtractive modeling, which involves removing bits of surface to create a model. You may instead put pieces together to form a model, using additive modeling, also called solid modeling and constructive modeling.

When the computer draws your objects for you, it may use only lines, which results in a line drawing, or it may try to simulate three-dimensional shapes, resulting in a shaded drawing. Shaded drawings usually look better than line drawings, but they can take much longer to generate.

The pictures are drawn for you by a program called the renderer. The renderer may create a static image, which is intended to be stored or photographed (or later used as part of an animation). Other renderers create dynamic images that, when created fast enough, appear to move as you watch and you perceive motion in real time.

When you create your model, it may be defined with no possibility for alteration when animated, that is, as a static model. If you explicitly include the capability for the model to change within itself, then it is called a dynamic model.

The computer is made up of physical equipment, or hardware, and the programs that it executes, or software.

A computer's text CRT and keyboard are essentially analogous to a standard typewriter. Usually the display is monochrome, meaning black-and-white. A color raster CRT (or color CRT or color monitor) is a device capable of showing you a colored image, such as a synthetic three-dimensional scene. A calligraphic (or vector) CRT specializes in drawing only lines, although they are usually drawn more quickly than on a color CRT.

An image digitizer can take a physical picture and turn it into a form acceptable for the computer. This function is called digitizing.

When an image is on a screen, it disappears when the screen is turned off. It is, therefore, a softcopy image. You can create hardcopy by sending the image to a printer, which can print text, a plotter, which can make line drawings, or a film recorder (or video recorder), which accumulates successive images so that they may be played back in succession as an animation.

A data tablet enables you to interact with the computer using a stylus or puck, which are small devices that can roam across the surface of the tablet. These are absolute positioning devices, so they know just where they are at all times. A similar device is the mouse, which is a relative positioning device; it can report how far it has moved relative to the last time the computer asked. Enhancements to these devices are the addition of buttons on the puck and mouse and a small switch on the tip of the stylus. A stylus may also be pressure-sensitive or tilt-sensitive. Feedback is offered to you through the location of a cursor on one of the screens.

A joystick is a shaft that pivots at the base, allowing you to rotate it in any direction. A trackball is a sphere mounted in a special box that can follow the movement of the ball and report it to the computer.

A space tracker, or six-axis positioning device, consists of a source and a sensor. The sensor can determine just where in space it is located relative to the source and can also determine its orientation in space. A hand tracker is a glove that can report to the computer the amount of bend at each knuckle on your hand. This makes possible a gesture interface with the computer, where it takes its input from your hand positions.

A head-mounted display is a device that allows you to physically walk and move within a computer-generated virtual world. In an open display, the image is usually provided in stereo through the use of two small displays and a set of half-silvered mirrors. In a closed display, you are shown the images from within a helmet that surrounds you. A head-mounted display may be coupled with hand trackers on each hand and several space trackers to provide a rich, body-oriented means of communicating with the computer.

2 GEOMETRY AND COLOR

Many of the techniques for producing computer graphics are drawn from three fields: physics (for an understanding of light), computers (for the actual programming involved), and geometry (for building models and then manipulating them).

This chapter focuses on geometry, but not the descriptive geometry often taught in high school, where one might prove that two triangles are the same. Instead, the discussion centers on applied geometry, which is used to measure sizes and angles, locate points in space, and manipulate objects. This chapter also introduces several different ways to describe colors in a computer graphics system.

DIMENSION

Throughout this book, the word *dimension* is often considered as synonymous with the intuitive notion of direction. For example, a piston has one dimension of travel available to it; up/down (Fig. 2-1). A ball on a pool table may travel in two dimensions: left/right and forward/backward (Fig. 2-2). It is an important fact that the total motion of the ball on the table, whatever its direction and speed, may be represented by its individual speeds along each dimension. For example, Fig. 2-3 shows a pool ball heading down a pool table. The motion of this ball can be described by one component down the length of the table, and by another component across the width of the table. These two motions taken together cause the ball to move at an angle and head in a diagonal toward the pocket.

Each of these two independent motions is referred to as a component; the complete name is a *vector component* (vectors are covered later in this chapter). "Component" is used as a synonym for "part," so the vector components of the ball's motion are the different parts of the total motion. Describing the speed of the ball in each dimension completely describes the motion of the ball. Fig. 2-4 shows a few examples of how different components make up a single vector.

A kite can fly in any direction within three dimensions (Fig. 2-5). Using the same idea as applied to the pool ball, the kite's motion in three dimensions (forward/backwards, up/down, right/left) can be described by its motion in each one of the three dimensions listed separately but taken together (Fig. 2-6). These three separate motions, which taken as a group represent the total motion of the kite, are the three vector components of the kite's motion.

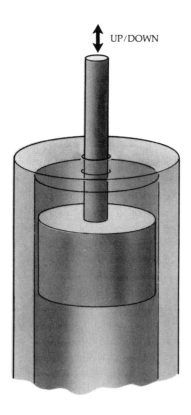

UP/DOWN

2-1.   A piston can move only in one direction: up/down.

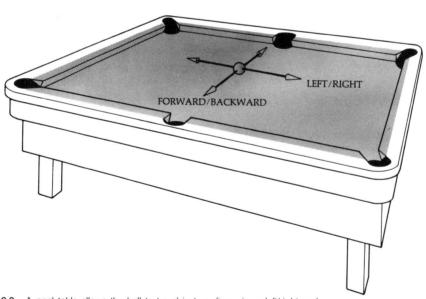

LEFT/RIGHT

FORWARD/BACKWARD

2-2.   A pool table allows the ball to travel in two dimensions: left/right and backward/forward.

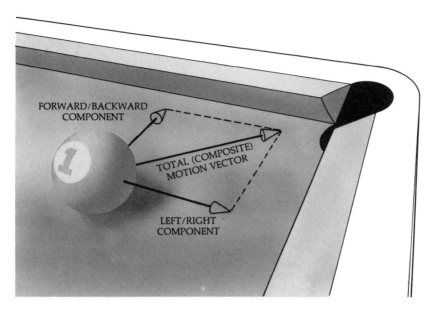

2-3. When a pool ball moves towards a pocket, its complete motion can be described in terms of its component motion in each direction.

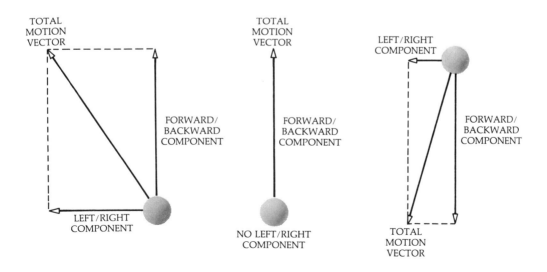

2-4. How different components make up a single vector.

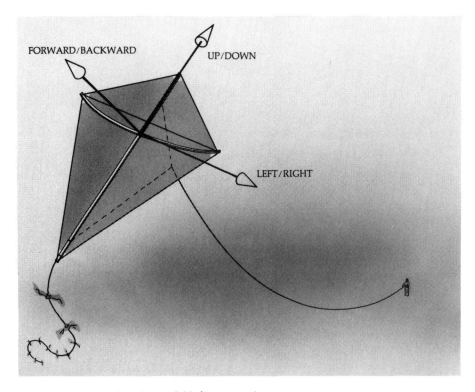

2-5. A kite has three dimensions available for movement.

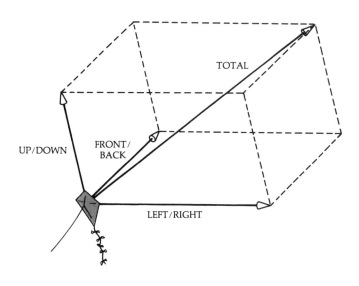

2-6. A three-dimensional vector and its components.

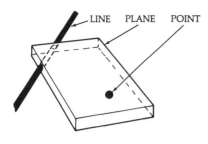
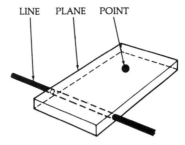

2-7. A plane is defined by a line and a point.

POINT, LINE, PLANE, AND SPACE

A *point* is a single location in space that can be located precisely. A point is not really a thing; rather, it is a place where a thing can be.

Imagine two points. They can be anywhere at all and still be connected by a *straight line*. Basically, a line is the simplest way to connect two points. A more common definition is that a line describes the shortest distance between two points.

Now imagine a line joining two points and a third point not on the line. A *plane* is defined as the flat surface that passes through both the line and the third point. Fig. 2-7 shows two line/point combinations and a section of the planes that unit them.

Lastly, envision a fourth point not on the plane or the line. All four points are in space, which is the three-dimensional world in which we normally live.

So space is three dimensional, a plane (like the surface of a pool table) is two dimensional, a line (like the motion of a piston) is one dimensional, and a point is zero dimensional.

COORDINATE SYSTEM, ORIGIN, AND AXIS

Imagine flying the kite shown in Fig. 2-5. As already stated, you can describe its motion in three dimensions by specifying its speed in each direction separately, and then taking the three values as a group. This idea may not seem particularly useful right now, but it becomes important in the discussion of how to animate three-dimensional objects.

Describing the motion of the kite does not describe the kite completely. You know how it is moving, but where is it? To tell someone else how to locate your kite from a swarm of theirs, you have to describe its position relative to a reference point. For example, in Fig. 2-8, you might say "My kite is the one immediately to the left of the dragon kite." In this case, the dragon kite is the reference point. This use of another kite is a poor choice for a reference point, though, because the reference kite is moving. Another problem with this reference point is that everyone has to stand where you are standing for "left" to mean the same thing for them. A better reference point is independent of all objects being measured—a big rock on the ground might do in this case.

Precise measurements can be made from such a nonmoving reference point, commonly called an *origin*. You might find, for example, that the kite is 20 feet south, 15 feet west, and 25 feet above a white rock. This description of the kite's position is better than the previous one because it is true for all observers: They do not have to be standing where you are for your west to be their west, as they would if their left were to match yours.

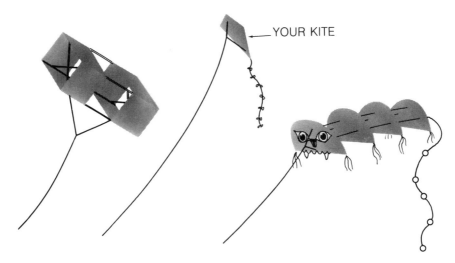

2-8. Identifying "your kite" in relation to another kite.

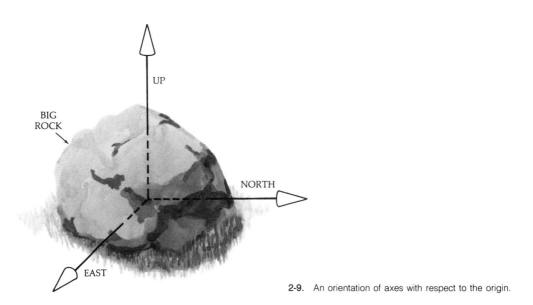

2-9. An orientation of axes with respect to the origin.

So, the kite is located by stating its distance from the origin in three dimensions. The directions are north/south, east/west, and up/down, and each direction has a distance associated with it. When measuring along a line (for example the line of north/south) that line is called an *axis* (plural axes). If you measure something with a yardstick, then you are measuring *along the axis* of the yardstick, or, the yardstick is the *axis of measurement*.

Not just any three distances will serve to specify the kite's location. The distances have to be chosen along axes that give the most amount of information. The way these axes were aligned is shown in Fig. 2-9. A combination of axes such as shown is called a *coordinate system*. Most of the coordinate systems used in this book have either two or three axes.

Remember that the discussion of the pool ball and kite included a description of the motion of these objects using only the vector components of their motion. These vector components must be chosen in a particular way to really describe the complete motion of the object. The coordinate system I am using, commonly called the *Cartesian coordinate system*, has proven to be a useful and complete system for describing the motion of an object as a certain amount along each axis. This system is not the only one that works, but it is the one used most often in computer graphics.

For the rest of this book, when I mention a coordinate system, assume that there is also an origin. (A set of axes and an origin is sometimes called a *frame*, but I prefer coordinate system.)

Mathematicians are fond of using abstract names for things. Coordinate systems are used so often that it has become inconvenient to label the axes north/south, east/west, and so on. Instead, the axes are labeled with completely arbitrary letters. These letters have evolved by convention to be *X*, *Y*, and *Z*. Fig. 2-10 shows a coordinate system with the axes labeled with these letters. The units on these axes are also completely arbitrary, usually marked off as distances of one, two, three, and so on, without any mention of feet, yards, inches, or whatever. Distances are also marked off in the other direction (on the other side of the origin), referred to as negative one, negative two, negative three, and so on, thereby establishing the *positive* and *negative* axes, one each along *X*, *Y*, and *Z*.

The coordinate system allows the precise location of a point within it. Fig. 2-11 shows a point called R (an arbitrary name). You can find this point by going three units along the *X* axis, four units along the *Y* axis, and then two units along the *Z* axis. We usually represent this point in shorthand by naming the distances that must be traveled between parentheses and separated by commas, and always in the order (X,Y,Z) For example, R is at (3,4,2). Note that it does not matter where you are standing when you measure to find point R; it is in the same place for everyone.

In this book, an uppercase letter (X) is used for the name of an axis, and a lowercase letter (x) is used for a value on that axis. Thus, some arbitrary point might be said to have coordinates (x,y,z), so you can refer to its coordinate along the *X* axis as *x*.

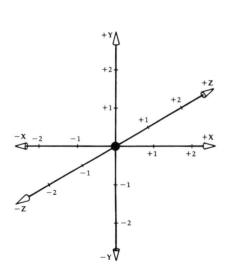

2-10. Marking the three-dimensional axes with distances from the origin.

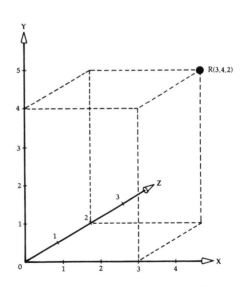

2-11. Finding the three-dimensional point R at (3,4,2).

ORIENTATION OF COORDINATE SYSTEMS

Recall that in the previous section I stated that it was important for everyone to agree on the coordinate system being used and where the origin is located. It is equally important to agree on the names of the axes. The naming of the three axes can be done in two different ways.

Imagine holding up your left hand, fingers pointing straight up, thumb pointing right. If you compare your hand to Fig. 2-12A, you will see that your thumb lines up with the (positive) X axis, your fingers point in the (positive) Y axis, and coming out of your palm is the (positive) Z axis. If you push your hand forward, you are traveling in the positive Z direction. This is called the *left-handed coordinate system*.

If you now try the same experiment with your right hand, you will see that you can line up your thumb with the X axis, fingers with the Y axis, but to get the Z axis coming out of your palm, you need to reverse the direction of the Z axis. Fig. 2-12B shows the new system, called a *right-handed coordinate system*. Every coordinate system commonly used in computer graphics is one of these two; you need only test both hands to find out which it is. The technique is always the same: thumb = X, fingers = Y, palm = Z. Only one hand will work, and that will tell you which coordinate system you are using.

Some computer graphics packages use a left-handed coordinate system for some operations and a right-handed coordinate system for other operations; other packages use only one coordinate system for everything. It is important to know which system is being used at all time so that objects go where you want them to go.

You also need to know about rotating things around the various axes. For example, a child in a swing is rotating about the axis of the top bar in the swing set (Fig. 2-13). It is obvious that the swing is going around the axis, but you need to define the direction of its motion and the

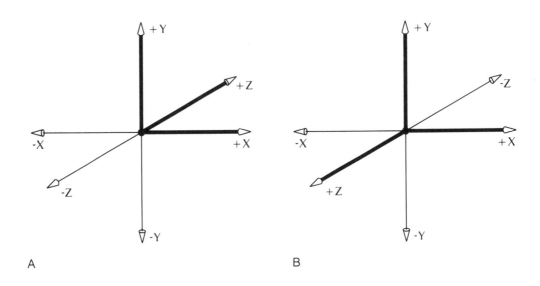

A   B

2-12.   A left-handed (*A*) and a right-handed (*B*) coordinate system.

amount of rotation. Rotation in one direction is called positive, and rotation in the other direction, negative. You need a scheme that allows you to uniquely define positive and negative directions of rotation for any axis.

That scheme is the *handed rotation rule*. Fig. 2-14 gives an example for a right-handed coordinate system. To find the direction of positive rotation, point your right thumb along the axis away from the origin. Curl your fingers around the axis, and they point in the direction of positive rotation. An angle measured in this direction is a positive angle; an angle in the other direction is negative. Fig. 2-15 shows some examples. Note that the direction of positive rotation in the figures is given by the right-hand rule in a right-handed system. Use your left hand in a left-handed system.

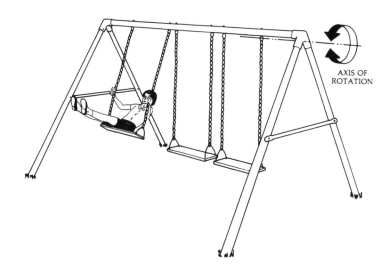

2-13. The top bar of the swing set is the axis of rotation.

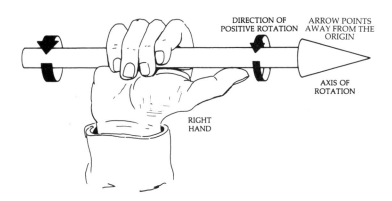

2-14. The right-handed rotation rule.

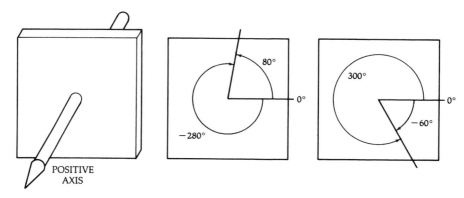

POSITIVE
AXIS

2-15.   Measuring angles in a right-handed system.

ANGLES, RADIANS, AND DEGREES

The only things that seem to separate two lines from each other (besides their length) are their relative directions. Fig. 2-16 shows several lines. Those lines can be described as almost horizontal, almost vertical, and between horizontal or vertical, but they have no assigned numerical value for the amount to which they line up.

If you examine the point of intersection between two lines, you can measure the amount to which they line up by measuring the *angle* between them. The most common system of measuring angles is to cut up a circle into 360 pieces, or *degrees*, as shown in Fig. 2-17. If you measure the two intersecting lines in Fig. 2-18, you can find that they meet at an angle of about 26 degrees (angles are usually measured with a device called a *protractor*, which is sort of a round ruler). The smaller the angle between the two lines, the more they *converge*, or line up. As the angle gets larger, the lines increasingly *diverge*, or fail to line up. At 90 degrees, the two lines have diverged as much as they can. A 90-degree angle is called a *right angle*.

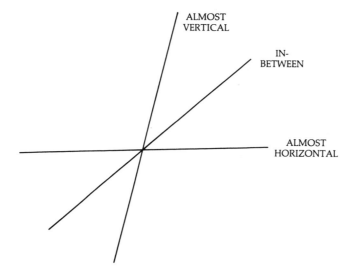

ALMOST
VERTICAL

IN-
BETWEEN

ALMOST
HORIZONTAL

2-16.   Some lines at different angles.

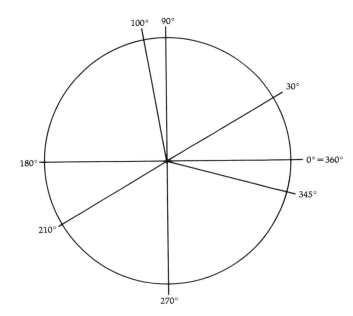

2-17. A circle can be divided into 360 degrees, usually counted counterclockwise with 0 at the right.

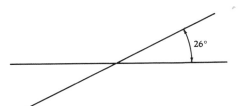

2-18. Two lines meeting at an angle of 26 degrees.

When measuring angles, *radians* can be used instead of degrees. There are π radians (or 3.14 of them) in 180 degrees, because π (a Greek letter pronounced "pie") works out to about 3.14 (the ratio of the circumference of a circle to its diameter). Therefore, a right angle (90 degrees) is equivalent to π/2 radians.

Where did the numbers 360 and π come from? The following discussion explains why 360 degrees and π radians are useful values.

Actually, the number 360 was chosen for dividing up a circle for the same reason there are sixty minutes in an hour and sixty seconds in a minute. Those numbers are easily broken up into many smaller, equal pieces that are easy to work with because they are whole numbers. Fig. 2-19 shows a circle with various divisions marked off. For example, 360 degrees can be divided into two pieces (180 degrees each), three pieces (120 degrees each), four pieces (90 degrees each), five pieces (72 degrees each), and so on. Note that each of these pieces of the divided circle is a whole number of degrees. No fractions are needed, even to describe a fifth of a circle, which is very convenient. The number 360 is one of the smallest that is easily divisible by so many small numbers (1,2,3,4,5, etc.) without using fractions.

The ratio of a circle's circumference (the length of the circle if you straightened it out) to its diameter is called π. It turns out that every circle, no matter how large or small, has exactly the same ratio of circumference to diameter. But why say there are two times π (2π) radians in a circle? Fig. 2-20 may help show why. Suppose a circle has a radius of 1 (the units are arbitrary; you may imagine the word "meter" or "inch" after every number if you like). Its diameter is two times the radius, or 2. Since π is equal to circumference over diameter, then circumference is equal to diameter times π, which in this case is 2π. If an angle is $\pi/2$ radians, and there are 2π radians in the whole circumference, the length of the circle that the angle isolates is equal to $\pi/2$. In general, the length of circle enclosed by an angle is equal to the angle itself. It turns out that this is a very handy connection when you are working with circles.

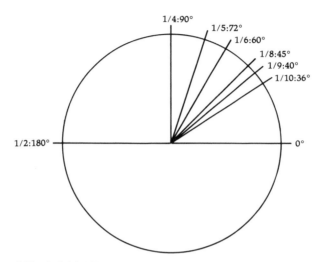

2-19. A circle's 360 degrees can be divided by many small numbers without using fractions.

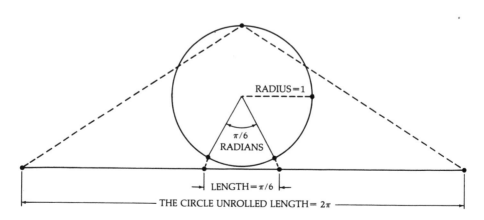

2-20. Using radians and a circle of radius 1, the measure of an angle is equal to the length of the circle it encloses.

DERIVATIVES AND TANGENCY

The discussion so far has focused on straight lines, but in practice curved lines are used as often as straight lines (if not more) to describe information to the computer.

Fig. 2-21 shows several curvy lines. You want to know how the line is curving at different points along its length. A person could tell by looking at it, but the computer needs some kind of formal concept for "how the line curves." One very useful technique is to draw a straight line that just grazes the point you are interested in. It does not matter if this line intersects the curve in other places, but you do not want it to actually cross the line at your point of interest. The key idea here is that the straight line is drawn so that it just touches the curve at the place where you want to determine the line's curviness. You can then measure the *direction* (or *slope*), of the straight line and that tells you in what direction the curve is curving at that point. Fig. 2-22 shows how this technique can describe the orientation of the line at different points. The advantage of this technique is that it is relatively easy for the computer to find the straight line that just grazes a curve at a particular point.

These straight lines are called *tangents*, and they meet the curve at the *point of tangency;* that is, the straight line is tangent to the curve. The slope of the line is called the *derivative* of the curve at that point. It tells how much (and in what direction) the curve is curving at the point being inspected.

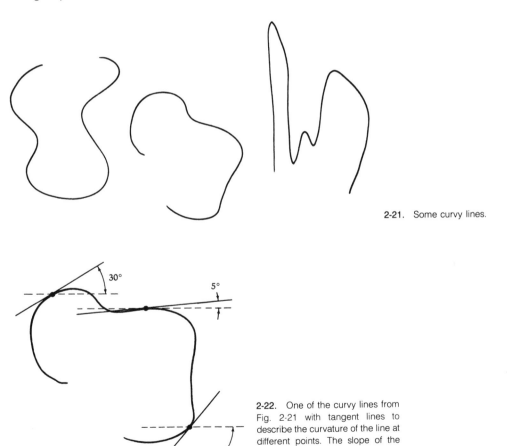

2-21. Some curvy lines.

2-22. One of the curvy lines from Fig. 2-21 with tangent lines to describe the curvature of the line at different points. The slope of the tangent is the slope of the line at that point.

Surfaces also have derivatives. At a given point, find the plane that just grazes the surface, analogous to the line that grazes the curve in the previous discussion. Fig. 2-23 shows such a surface and associated plane. The plane, called a *tangent plane*, is also said to be tangent to the surface. Every point on a surface, just as every point on a line, has its own derivative (or slope of the tangent) and, thus, its own tangent (plane or line).

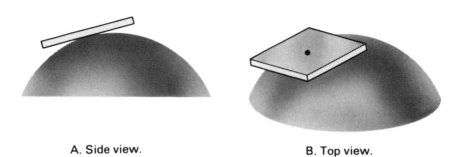

A. Side view.   **B. Top view.**

2-23.   The tangent plane grazes a surface at a single point.

TRANSFORMATIONS: TRANSLATION, ROTATION, SCALING, AND SKEWING

In computer graphics points are used as placeholders in space. For example, to describe the flight of a baseball, the three-dimensional location of its center at various moments as the ball flies can be given.

This kind of approach is convenient, because it enables the manipulation of entire objects by manipulating only a single point. This procedure is aided by giving every object its own private coordinate system. If an object is modeled in this coordinate system and the point that is the origin of this system is moved, then the whole object moves relative to the original position of the coordinate system.

One way to transform an object is to imagine that object sitting within a shoebox. All of the points on the surface of that object are then given with respect to one corner of the shoebox. If you pick up the entire shoebox and move it around the room, the coordinates of the object—with respect to the shoebox—do not change: The coordinates of the shoebox with respect to the room are changing. (Of course, the coordinates of the object with respect to the room are changing too, but that can get complicated.) Focus on the two different descriptions: the object with respect to the shoebox (the object's own coordinate system), and the shoebox with respect to the world (the position of the object's coordinate system with respect to the *global* coordinate system). This separation of issues is very useful when modeling and setting up animations (as covered in later chapters).

The advantage of manipulating the coordinate system instead of the object is that complex operations can be performed while keeping descriptions of both the objects and the manipulations simple. An analogy can be made with an overhead transparency projector. A transparency about the size of a piece of notebook paper might appear huge on the screen when projected. The transparency is your object, and the projector is enlarging the object so that it appears huge to your viewers. They would think that to modify the picture you would have to climb up on a ladder and draw enormous lines. But the truth is much simpler, since your object is still defined simply; it just looks different after going through the projector. So you can change your object easily, since you still have the original description; it just looks different to the outside world.

Consider a three-dimensional example. Suppose you want to stretch a coffee mug so that it becomes very tall. Using this approach, you would leave alone the description of the mug (in its own coordinate system), but you would tell the computer to stretch that coordinate system. So when it is time to draw the mug, the computer will get the (unchanged) points of the original mug, but then stretch them out before drawing the mug. If you ever want to change the handle, it will be easy, because you still have the original mug; any changes will automatically appear stretched. Using this technique is a lot easier than trying to figure out how to make changes in objects that have been transformed, especially since some transformations can get complicated. So it is possible to deform the appearance of the shape of the model without changing its description at all!

These following four manipulations of a coordinate system are called *transformations*. It is important to note that the order of applying these transformations makes a great deal of difference in the final orientation and location of the object. Let us now explicitly change our point of view and think of transformations as changing the local coordinate system of an object, rather than the object itself. All subsequent transformations take place with respect to this modified coordinate system. For example, rotation followed by scaling produces a very different result from scaling followed by rotation, as shown in Fig. 2-24. Not all pairs of operations have this distinction, but enough do that you should plan your order of transformations carefully.

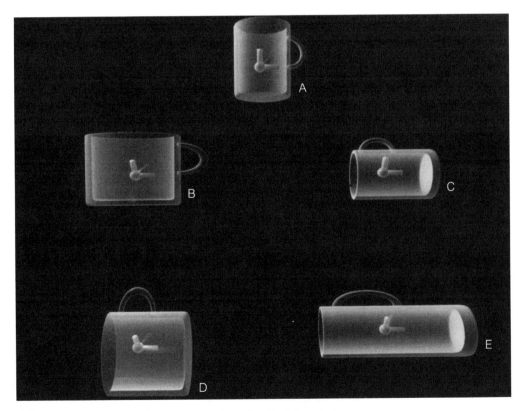

2-24. The order in which transformations are performed is critically important, because each transformation takes place in the coordinate system resulting from previous transformations. The original object is shown in A. It may be first scaled horizontally (B) and then rotated in the plane (D). Alternatively, the object in A may be first rotated (C) and then scaled (E) Notice that D and E are very different. (Image courtesy of Digital Arts.)

To show the effect of each transformation I will apply it to a coffee mug. Fig. 2-25A shows the mug centered around its origin. The other mugs are independent results of applying just one transformation to this original mug.

Moving an object along any straight line is called *translating* that object. You might translate the coffee mug of Fig. 2-25A five units along the *X* axis and three units along the *Y* axis, for example, with the result of Fig. 2-25B. The simplest means of translation is to ignore the object's private coordinate system and just move the object. But a much more powerful technique is to leave the object fixed in its own system and move the system.

Another common manipulation of an object is *rotation*. Given an axis (or line) in space (perhaps even one of the coordinate system axes) and an angle, you can spin an object around that axis by the given amount and produce a new copy of it at the new location. Fig. 2-25C illustrates this concept. If you are in a right-handed system, the right-handed rule tells you which way to rotate for positive rotation; in a left-handed system, use the left-hand rule.

Another useful manipulation is called *scaling*. To scale an object is to stretch it or compress it by different amounts along different axes. The effect of scaling by a number greater than one is to make it larger, by pushing every point away from the origin. Scaling by an amount less than one shrinks the object, pulling every point in toward the origin. Fig. 2-25D shows the effect of scaling along only one axis, commonly called *differential scaling*. Fig. 2-25E shows scaling along all axes simultaneously, called *uniform scaling*.

Although scaling is a useful concept, it is really only a special case of another idea called *skew* (or *shear*). When you skew an object, it is as if you were sliding it over by a changing amount. The skew operation is defined by two coordinates and an amount. For example, if you skew along *X* relative to *Y*, all vertical lines become tilted. They remain parallel, but slanted, as in Fig. 2-25F. The horizontal lines (those parallel to the *X* axis) are unaffected. Notice that in a single skewing nothing is ever rotated; it only slides over.

That scaling is a special case of skewing is a result of the mathematics involved. But, in general, scale means a simple stretching along one of the axes, and skew means a sliding operation.

2-25. The effects of transformation on a simple shape. The original object, a coffee mug, is shown in A. The mug may be translated (B), rotated (C), scaled along one axis only (D), scaled along all axes (E), or skewed (F). (Image courtesy of Digital Arts.)

VECTORS

Points are suitable for describing the location of something in space, but they are best for things that are sitting still. A point can tell you where a leaf in a river is at a particular time, but not in which direction it is headed, or how fast it is moving.

Location, direction of movement, and speed of movement are three common pieces of information that are often used together. A symbol has been invented to represent all three of them at once: a *vector*.

A vector may be symbolized by an arrow. An arrow begins at some point (location), points in some direction (direction of movement), and has some length (speed of movement). The beginning of the vector is its *base* (or *tail*), and the point at its tip is its *head*. A long arrow denotes a large speed, a short arrow means a small speed. Some vectors are shown in Fig. 2-26. Note that the velocity is tangent to the track in the roller coaster in Fig. 2-26C.

Vectors find applications throughout computer graphics. Although vectors are often used to represent the direction and speed of movement at their base, they can represent other features of that point as well. In fact, a vector can be used to represent any three pieces of information. For example, a vector could represent a tiger. The base of the vector is the position of the tiger, the length of the vector indicates how hungry the tiger is, and the direction of the vector indicates where the tiger is looking at the time of measurement. Many vectors could represent a group of tigers on a field, describing where they are, where they are looking, and how hungry they are, all at once.

COLOR

Color is discussed throughout this book: the colors of light sources, the colors of reflective objects, the colors of transparent objects, and so on. There are many popular ways to describe a color in a computer graphics system. I briefly cover four of these color models (a model in the mathematical sense, since a color model is a description of color, not an actual surface or object).

The first color model, the spectral *energy curve*, is also the most detailed. First you need to know that your eyes are sensitive to a wide range of signals. In fact, the light energy that your eyes detect is exactly the same as the energy that a radio detects or the energy that runs through

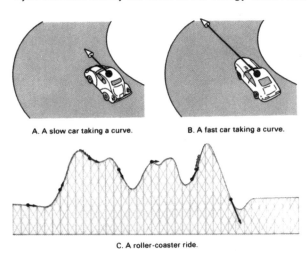

A. A slow car taking a curve.   B. A fast car taking a curve.

C. A roller-coaster ride.

2-26. Vectors can be symbolized by an arrow, which gives a point, a direction, and an amount.

your walls in electric wires. The only difference between all these kinds of electromagnetic energy is the frequency at which a particular signal is vibrating. Your eyes are sensitive to those frequencies that lie within the visible spectrum.

Fig. 2-27 shows approximately where the eye's sensitivity lies in the world of radiated energy. Any energy that is vibrating at about the right frequency and enters the eye will give the brain some impression of color. If the frequency is a little lower than the middle of the range, red is perceived; if it is a little higher than middle, blue is perceived. (I am concentrating here on one location in the eye; of course, you usually see many different colors from many different objects in your field of view.)

If many different light signals come into the same point of the eye at once, the visual system will merge them and you perceive some single color. So you might be looking at a red chair, but what actually enters the eye is some red energy, along with some blue, green, and orange as well.

One way to describe the information for a particular color is to draw a diagram showing how much energy is entering the eye throughout the visible spectrum. Fig. 2-28 shows the spectral energy curve for a yellow gladiolus petal. The plot indicates how much energy is in the signal at each visible frequency. If the eye receives light that has a distribution like Fig. 2-28, you perceive a shade of yellow.

Drawing spectral energy curves is an accurate way to describe a color, but it can be difficult. You may often want just a particular shade of red, and not really be interested in what the spectral energy curve for that shade of red looks like.

To avoid becoming entangled in energy curves, various schemes have been proposed to help select a color quickly and intuitively. One popular system, another color model, is called the *Hue, Lightness, Saturation* system (HLS). The HLS color system is based on two cones, joined at their bases as shown in Fig. C-5A. The bottom tip of the lower cone is black; the top tip of the upper cone is white. The central column contains all the grays; this is called the *lightness* column. If you take a slice through the middle of the joined cones you get a picture like Fig. C-5B. Notice that the color runs around the outside of the disk in a cyclic order. In the middle of the disk is fifty percent gray. As you move outwards, the colors become deeper and richer. Traveling outward is called increasing the *saturation*. Traveling around the disk selects different *hues*. To find a particular color you move around and within these paired cones. It can become a fairly intuitive way to find most colors; for example, you quickly find that pastels are located near the top of the upper cone. The mechanics for moving around this HLS color system will depend on your particular system.

When you select a color using HLS, the computer will internally convert it into an equivalent combination of red, green, and blue (*RGB*). The RGB system, a third color model, is often used within the computer because those are the three colors that the machine can directly display on the face of a picture tube; other colors are combinations of red, green, and blue (since they can serve as primary colors for light). The RGB color model is a cube (often called the color cube or the RGB cube), shown in Fig. C-6. Black is located at one corner; white, at the opposite

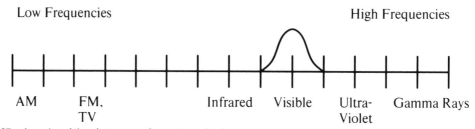

2-27. A portion of the electromagnetic spectrum showing where the visible frequencies lie.

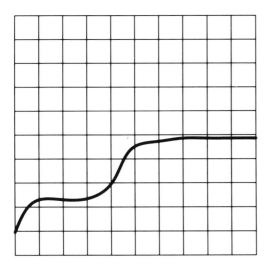

2-28. The spectral energy plot of a yellow gladiolus petal. For each visible frequency (along the horizontal axis), the intensity of the radiated light (on the vertical axis) is plotted.

diagonal. The three edges of the cube that share the black corner are labeled Red, Green, and Blue. To pick a color you select a point in the cube, then get a mixture of the three primaries. Although RGB is useful for the computer, most people find that it is not a very intuitive way to pick colors.

The last color model considered here is a strictly textual model. You type in the color you want according to a carefully controlled scheme. For example, you may specify "light vivid blue" or "dark reddish green." (The exact words vary a bit from model to model.) If your system supports a textual color model, you may find that the particular colors you get are not exactly what you want; you may then specify commands such as "slightly redder or "much darker" to adjust the color.

Figure 2-29 shows one color selection program that provides several color models simultaneously. In this program, you are free at any time to change any value in any of the models; the other models are then adjusted automatically so that they indicate the same color. The shaded area in the center shows the color you have selected.

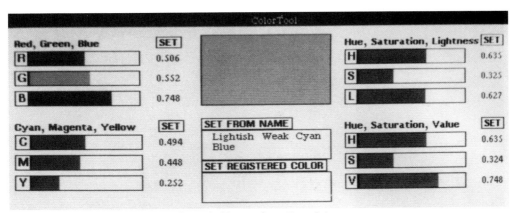

2-29. An interactive color selection tool. (Image by Maureen Stone, Xerox Palo Alto Research Center)

SUMMARY

Each direction in which an object is free to move is called a dimension. The motion of an object may be described by its motion in each direction listed separately but taken together; each piece of the motion in such a description is called a component or vector component.

A point is a single location in space; it is a zero-dimensional object because it has no freedom to move. A straight line joins any two points; it is a one-dimensional object because the line may be slid along its length. A line and a point not on that line determine a plane, which is the flat sheet that contains both the line and point. A plane is two-dimensional because it may be slid around within its own flat sheet. A plane and a point not on the plane determine space, which is three-dimensional.

Space is measured using a coordinate system that is built from a reference point at the origin, and the axes radiating from it. If the axes are at right angles to each other, the system is a Cartesian coordinate system, or a frame. Axes are labeled $X, Y,$ and Z in a three-dimensional Cartesian system, and a point's coordinates are written in the same order (X, Y, Z), with values (x, y, z). The half of an axis labeled with positive values is called the positive axis; the other half is the negative axis.

There are two possible orientations of the axes in three dimensions; they are called the left-handed coordinate system and the right-handed coordinate system. Positive rotation about the axes is determined with the appropriately handed rotation rule for that system.

To measure the relationship between two lines, measure the angle between them, in either degrees or radians (there are 360 degrees, or 2π radians, in one circle).

To measure the slope of a curvy line at a point, draw a tangent line at that point; the slope of the tangent is the slope of the line at that point. The tangent meets the curve at the point of tangency. The slope is also called the derivative of the curvy line at that point. In three dimensions, the tangent plane can be found at a point.

Transformations of an object can take place either with respect to the points of the object themselves or as a modification of the coordinate system in which they live. Originally, all coordinates are expressed with relation to the global coordinate system.

Moving an object along one of the axes is called translation. You can also rotate an object about some axis. If you stretch or compress the object by the same amount along all three axes simultaneously, it is a uniform scaling of the object; otherwise it is a differential scaling. Lastly, you can skew the object along one axis with respect to another axis, which is useful to make objects with a fixed base appear to slide.

A vector is a convenient way to encapsulate three pieces of information. The tail of the vector identifies a point in space; the head identifies another point. An arrow is drawn from the tail to the head. The location of the tail, the length of the arrow, and the direction in which the arrow is pointed are all represented by the vector.

When you specify a color, you describe the color with respect to a color model. The most detailed model describes color as it is measured physically, by specifying its spectral energy curve, which shows the amount of energy in a particular color at each visible frequency. It is not always easy to determine the curve for a particular color, or the color that a particular curve will generate. The Hue, Lightness, Saturation (HLS) model identifies a color by its position in a double-cone color space. The Red, Green, Blue (RGB) model identifies a color by its proportions of these three primaries; the physical model is a cube. A textual color model allows you to specify a color with a short list of adjectives and color names.

3 COMPUTER GRAPHICS HARDWARE

The devices covered in Chapter 1 are primarily for communication with the computer: keyboards and other devices for giving commands and screens for viewing the results. This chapter focuses on what is happening inside the computer hardware.

Understanding some of the internal workings of the machine will help you make sense of some of the limitations and problems encountered when actually making images. That understanding will also help you make better images because you will better know how to control the machine and direct it to make the sorts of images you want to see.

NUMBERS AS ATTRIBUTES

Most programmers try to make communication between people and computers as easy and natural as possible. But natural languages are usually not sufficient for specifying actual values for the computer to process; the computer works with numbers, and often the user must supply input to the computer as numbers.

For instance, you might be interested in telling the computer how bright a light source ought to be, or how red you would like a table to be. In such cases, you are concerned less with the *qualitative*, or verbal, description ("it is very red"), and more with the *quantitative*, or numerical description (for example, "it is position six on the color wheel"). It is said that such numbers are *characteristics* of the models to which they are applied. *Attribute, argument, coefficient* and *parameter* are all common synonyms for characteristic in this context.

As an example you could describe how bright a light should be by using a scale from 0 to 10, with 0 as dark and 10 as bright. Then instead of saying "fairly bright," which is a qualitative description the computer cannot work with, you can say "3.4" or "7.1," quantitative answers that may be understood directly by the computer.

BITS, BYTES, AND WORDS

A computer typically has three main components: the *input/output devices*, the *processor*, and the *memory*. In Chapter 1, many of the most popular and common input/output (or I/O) devices in a computer graphics station were introduced. The processor is the part of the computer that actually executes programs. You need not be concerned much with the processor, since as long as it has been well programmed, and functions correctly, you will not have to deal with it directly. However, it will be useful to understand something about a computer's memory system, because a good understanding of how the memory works can help you use the computer efficiently.

A computer memory is made up of a great many small locations, each of which can hold only a small amount of information. Imagine the stockroom of the world's biggest shoe store. A small wall of shelves is shown in Fig. 3-1. Every pair of shoes that is, or may be, in stock has its own storage place on the wall. You are taking inventory and all you are interested in is whether or not there is a box of shoes in a given place. You are not concerned about style, color, or anything else; only if there is a box in each place on the wall.

As you look at every possible place for a box of shoes to be, you ask, "Are there shoes here?" You might write down Y for "yes" and N for "no" (many computer systems use the words *true* and *false* as synonyms for "yes" and "no"). You might also write down a 1 for "yes" (or true) and a 0 for "no" (or false). In this way you can represent the entire wall as a sequence of zeros and ones, which would tell you exactly where there are shoes and where there are not.

Fig. 3-1B resembles how a computer's memory looks—simply a big list of ones and zeros, and nothing more! It is a very simple scheme that might appear impractical or even useless for storing information on a routine basis, but it is exactly what comprises a computer memory. With this simple structure, you can store everything from checkbook-balancing programs, to the data those programs use, to pictures and even animations.

These ones and zeros are stored in different ways for different uses. Some are stored internally in the computer as immediate information; for example, any program the computer is actually running sits in the computer's internal memory. Sometimes this data is stored on magnetic tapes or disks where it can be safely kept for long periods of time.

You need to know exactly what is meant by *memory storage location* because that term can either mean the location where the memory itself is stored (like the plastic box where you keep floppy disks), or a spot inside a memory itself where information may be placed. Usually, which definition is meant will be clear from the context in which the phrase appears. Each storage location in memory (where you can store exactly one zero or one) is called a *bit*. A group of eight bits taken together is called a *byte*. Groups of bytes then make up *words*. The number of bytes in a word varies from computer to computer, but it is usually a multiple of two.

These terms are used so that you can compare the size of different computer memories, find out how much room a computer has left to store new information, and otherwise discuss memory sizes.

Often the single unit of a bit is inconvenient. Computer memories usually contain hundreds of thousands of bits, and the numbers describing the size of the memory become unwieldy. It is more common to talk about bytes. But even bytes are too small, and are often referred to as thousands of bytes (*kilobytes*) and millions of bytes (*megabytes*), as in "This is a twenty-megabyte

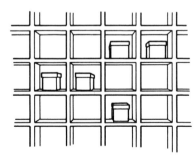

A. Stockroom wall.

B. Inventory sheet.

3-1. Shelves from a shoe store stockroom wall (A) and the corresponding inventory sheet (B).

memory," meaning it has twenty million bytes of storage. To get an idea of what this means, you can usually consider a single byte as just the right amount of room to store one character of text (a letter, number, or punctuation mark). For example, this book (without captions on the illustrations) contains about half a million characters, so 500 kilobytes (or one-half megabyte) of memory is enough to hold the text of this book. Sometimes kilobyte is abbreviated to K; for example, a disk big enough to hold 300 kilobytes is usually called a 300K disk.

MEMORY TYPES

There are many different technologies for memory storage. The subject can quickly become very complex, but one important distinction about types of memories can be made without arousing concern over the technological details of how they are manufactured and used: We will divide memories into the categories *long-term* and *short-term*.

We can approach this distinction with an analogy. When close friends tell you of their birthdays, you generally think of filing that away as information to be remembered over a long span of time; you do not want to forget it right away. Psychologists say this kind of information is stored in *long-term memory*. On the other hand, when driving down a freeway and you see the sign for your exit, you want to remember for the next minute or so that your exit is coming up, but you don't want to retain this information any longer. After you take the turnoff, the memory "My exit is coming up" is useless and need never be remembered again. This kind of information is stored in *short-term memory*.

Computers also have long- and short-term memories. A short-term memory is used by the computer for storing programs, pictures, and any temporary data it may need. When the power is shut off, all information in the short-term memory is lost. Early short-term memories were physically constructed out of small rings of magnetic material called cores. For this reason, a computer's short-term memory is sometimes called *core memory*, even though almost no one uses real cores anymore.

On the other hand, long-term memory is usually external to the computer and is mediated by human users. This memory will not lose its information when the power is shut off. Such memories consist of magnetic tapes, magnetic cards, floppy disks, optical disks, and so forth.

FRAME BUFFERS

So far I have covered computer memories in a general sense. But there is one particular kind of memory that is of great importance to users. It is a piece of memory arranged into a grid of memory locations and then enhanced with special hardware. This special memory is called a *frame buffer*. Its name gives a clue to its function: It stores (or buffers) one frame of video. To really understand how this important piece of hardware works, I need to make a slight digression into the mechanics of how a television picture is produced.

How CRTs Draw Pictures

Assume that a CRT monitor is receiving a signal that describes the picture you want to draw. This signal could come from an antenna (as in a TV) or through a cable (as from a VCR or a computer). Basically, the signal contains a small amount of information for each dot on the screen; for example, "this dot is bright green, now this one is light green, now this one is dark blue," and so on.

The hardware inside the CRT consists of three electron guns, special devices that can shoot a tight beam of electrons from the back of the tube to the front, where they hit the screen. The inside of the screen is covered with a dense coating of phosphors of three different colors. A phosphor is a chemical that glows for a short time when struck by an electron beam. Fig 3-2 shows the inside of a picture tube. In essence, each individual spot on the screen contains its own little triplet of phosphors, one each of red, green, and blue that together make a set of primary colors for light. Just as any pigment can be made from the three primary colors of pigment, so any color can be made from these three primary colors of light.

To make the composite dot (sometimes called a triplet) appear a particular color, each little bit of phosphor at that dot is hit with just the right amount of electrons—the more electrons, the brighter the glow. So you can create a reddish yellow by making the red phosphor glow brightly, the green phosphor glow slightly less brightly, and leaving the blue one dark.

Rather than have one beam of electrons race around from phosphor dot to phosphor dot within a triplet, most CRTs contain three electron guns that work together. When it is time to draw a spot on the screen, each gun is aimed at one of the three phosphors in that spot's triplet, and all three phosphors are illuminated at once, each with the proper brightness as given by the input signal. So it is sometimes said that a CRT has a red gun, a green gun, and a blue gun, which taken together are called the color guns. These names refer to the color of phosphor that is consistently illuminated by that gun; the guns themselves only emit streams of (uncolored!) electrons.

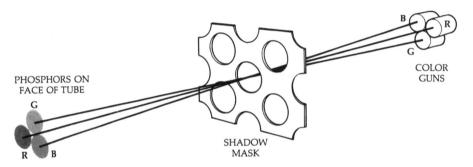

A. Arrangement of electron guns and shadow mask in color crt.

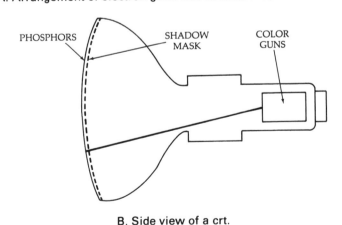

B. Side view of a crt.

3-2. The interior face of a picture tube is made up of clusters of three phosphors. One of the electron beams consistently hits the same color of phosphor in each triplet.

The monitor also contains electronics that control at which triplet the electron guns are pointed and what intensities they have at each spot. The internal circuits of the monitor cause the electron beams to sweep the entire surface of the tube once every thirtieth of a second. Each sweep is made from the upper-left corner to the lower-right corner, much in the way an English book is read. The picture is created by building up many *scan lines*, which are the individual horizontal paths of the electron beams. Fig. 3-3 illustrates this process.

In most CRTs, there are two *fields*, or sets of scan lines, which are *interlaced*, or alternated in drawing (Fig. 3-4). Suppose the CRT is about to start drawing a new picture. The beams start at the upper-left corner and sweep out all the odd-numbered scan lines, which taken together are called the *odd field*. The beams then return to the upper left and sweep out the even-numbered scan lines, or the *even field*. Each field takes a sixtieth of a second to complete, so it takes a thirtieth of a second to complete the entire picture, or one *frame*. When the monitor draws alternate fields like this it is called *interlaced scanning*. You can also buy monitors that just sweep from the top down, hitting every scan line one after the other on every sweep. These are called *noninterlaced monitors,* but they are far more rare than interlaced monitors.

After completing a frame (that is, drawing the odd field and then the even field), the beam goes back to the upper-left corner and starts drawing the next frame, beginning with its odd field.

Whatever colors (if any) the beams cause to appear as they travel are controlled by the signal arriving from the video source, usually an antenna or cable. For each dot on the screen, the

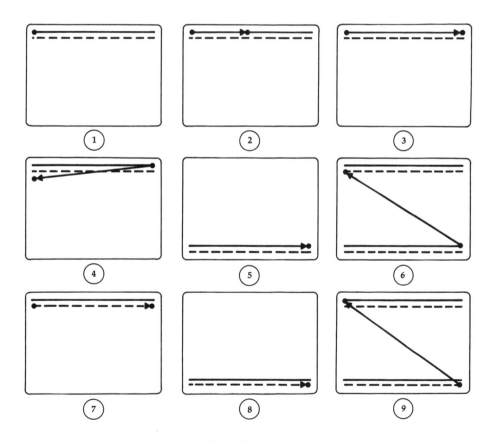

3-3. The travel of an electron beam—top-down, left-to-right.

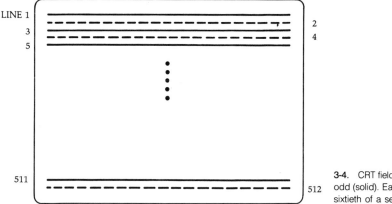

LINE 1
3
5

511
512

3-4. CRT fields: even (dashed) and odd (solid). Each field is drawn in a sixtieth of a second.

signal describes the color and the brightness of the color at that point. The circuits of the monitor then control the strength of the beams to make the correct phosphors glow the correct amount to get that color to appear. The signal arrives in the correct order for the monitor to scan the picture tube as was just described: upper left to lower right, in alternating fields.

Frame Storage

If you could make a videotape recording of the input signal and replay it thirty times a second into the monitor's input, you would get the same picture over and over. But instead of receiving it from the air, you would have your own copy of the instructions to the monitor and you could modify it at will. For example, you could change the colors at certain points by changing the videotape in a careful way.

A large piece of computer memory can be used as tape and tape recorder in one, and it contains information for every spot on the screen. Such a piece of memory is called a frame buffer, as previously mentioned. "Frame" comes from the single complete frame that is stored and "buffer" is computer slang for memory. So, with a large piece of memory set up, controlled by the computer, and connected to a monitor's signal input, a CRT can be made to draw a picture under control of the computer.

Another way to think about frame buffers is to consider the TV tube as a giant grid of small squares, as illustrated in Fig. 3-5. Each square (or dot) on the screen has a corresponding place

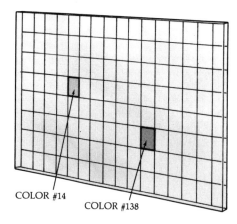

COLOR #14

COLOR #138

3-5. The face of a TV screen. Each spot on the screen has an associated number that indicates which color number should be used to paint that spot.

in the computer's memory. When the monitor is ready to fill in that square with the desired color, the computer supplies the correct intensities of red, green, and blue for that triplet, causing that color to appear at that spot on the screen.

A particular spot on the screen is sometimes called a *pixel* (or *pel*), both contractions of "picture-element."

Color Maps

The question now arises: How is the color stored in the frame buffer? The answer to this question opens the doors for an explanation of many cinematic special effects and tricks.

The frame buffer can be thought of as having a number stored for every pixel on the screen. The number is like the numbers used in a paint-by-numbers set: The value in the frame buffer does not describe the color itself, it simply identifies which color it is from a given set of numbered colors. Fig. 3-6 shows this "color-by-numbers" idea.

For the following discussions, assume that every pixel in the image is represented by eight bits in the frame buffer. Those eight bits give the number of the color that should be used for that pixel.

With eight bits, 256 different numbers can be represented; the range from 0 to 255 is often used. So if a certain shade of red is assigned to color number 0, a shade of yellow to color number 1, a shade of orange to color number 2, and so on, you can have a total of 256 different colors on the screen from a single eight-bit frame buffer. But so far I have only shown how to select which color to display, not where those colors come from.

A small piece of memory is usually set aside within the frame buffer hardware (but off the screen) to hold the information about the actual color content of the 256 different colors; this is called the *color map* or *color table*. Each entry in the color map represents one color, and consists of three numbers: the amount of red, green, and blue light that make it up. Typically eight bits are also used to encode the brightness of each primary for a given color, so the intensity of each primary is represented by a number from 0 (off) to 255 (fully on). As a result, the color black would be no color at all and would be represented as (0,0,0), where the color intensities are given in the order (R,G,B). Pure red would be (255,0,0); a mixture of red and blue might be (124,0,44), and so on. White would be (255,255,255).

You may have noticed a coincidence here, and it should be pointed out that it is only a coincidence. The frame buffer holds eight bits per pixel, so each pixel could specify one of 256 colors. When I discussed the color map, I said that each entry contained three eight-bit quantities describing the intensities of the phosphors for that pixel. Often both the frame buffer and the color table have eight-bit entries, but that is just a coincidence based on convenient use of hardware. You can find frame buffers with more or fewer bits per pixel, and color tables with

Frame Buffer   Color Map Color CRT Image

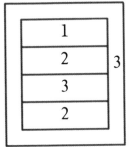

3-6. Each point on the screen contains the number of the color to be placed there.

41

more or fewer bits per primary. More bits in the frame buffer give you more colors to choose from; more bits in the color table give you finer control over the brightness of each phosphor.

The color map has one entry for each color on the screen, so if you are using an eight-bit frame buffer that can choose among 256 colors, then there will be 256 entries in the color map.

Here is an overview of how a picture is built up. Since the computer is generating the signals for the monitor, it knows which dot is the next one to be drawn. It first looks up that dot's location in the frame buffer and finds a color number. It then looks into that entry in the color map for the intensities of the primary colors needed to make that color. Figure 3-7 shows this process graphically.

Different color maps can give rise to significantly different images even with the same data in the frame buffer. An example of the same image with different color maps is shown in Fig. C-7 (that is, the contents of the frame buffer are unchanged; only the colors to which they refer are changed). Remember that you are always looking at a picture that is heavily dependent on the particular color map in effect at the moment; a different color map can make the picture look very different, without any alteration to the frame buffer contents.

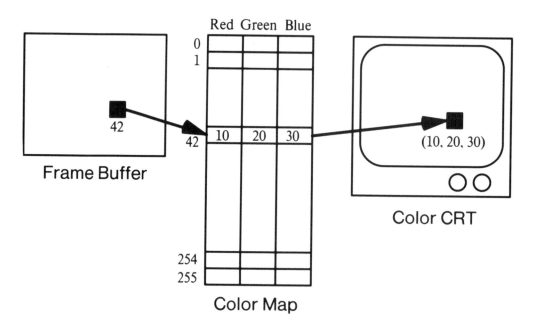

3-7. The frame buffer holds the value 42 at a given pixel. The color map holds the color (10,20,30) for color number 42, so that is that color of that pixel on the screen.

Frame Buffers with More Than Eight Bits

With one eight-bit frame buffer, there are 256 different colors available. These colors can be any color the user desires by manipulating the color map, but only 256 different colors can be on the screen at once.

However, the situation changes if many more bits are available at every pixel. Take, for example, three eight-bit frame buffers used at the same time to provide twenty-four bits per pixel. Figure 3-8 shows how this looks. With this kind of storage available, a color map is not even necessary. Each pixel has three sets of eight bits for a total of twenty-four bits per pixel. It is easy to tell the hardware to treat the first eight bits of every pixel as the red intensity for that pixel, the next eight bits as the blue intensity for that pixel, and the last eight bits as the green intensity. Consequently, every pixel in the frame buffer, instead of representing which color is to be selected from a table, now directly holds the red, green, and blue components of that color itself.

The result of storing the color directly in the frame buffer is that every dot on the screen may be a different color. If you use a frame buffer that is 512 pixels wide and 512 pixels tall, then there are 512 times 512, or over a quarter million, different colors possible on the screen at once! The drawback is money: A twenty-four-bit frame buffer will cost about three times what an eight-bit frame buffer costs. But the advantage is a wider selection of colors.

Typically, the number of bits in a frame buffer is called its *depth*; thus I have been discussing frame buffers that are twenty-four bits deep.

You should also note that even a twenty-four-bit frame buffer will usually contain a special form of color maps. These are three separate maps, one for each color. In other words, there is one table that accepts a red intensity as input and gives a new red intensity as output, another for green, and another for blue. It is the output of the color maps that goes to the monitor. One common use of these maps is to make them effectively useless or transparent: Entry 0 is set to have the value 0, entry 1 to have the value 1, and so on, for each of the three colors. That way the numbers you get out of the frame buffer are unchanged when they pass through the color map on their way to the monitor.

GAMMA CORRECTION

The most common reason to have color maps at all in a twenty-four-bit deep frame buffer is to allow different colors in the picture to be scaled up or down in brightness. It turns out that if you draw two large gray squares side by side, the left one showing (50,50,50) and the right one showing

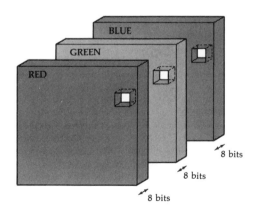

A. Three 8-bit frame buffers.

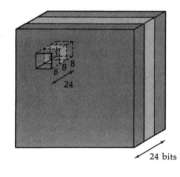

B. A 24-bit pixel.

3-8. RGB values can be stored directly in the frame buffer if it is deep enough.

(100,100,100), the one on the right usually will not appear to you to be twice as bright as the one on the left! There are two reasons for this, both caused by an effect called *nonlinearity*. Something is nonlinear if its output is not a simple, constant proportion of its input. The intensity of a phosphor on the screen is a nonlinear response to the intensity of the beam striking it. And your perceived brightness of that spot is a nonlinear response to the intensity with which the spot glows.

You can correct for the nonlinearity of the monitor by creating a special color map, which boosts the intensity of some colors and drops the intensities of others. The shape of this color map is dependent on measurements made on your particular monitor. Those measurements are used as input to a mathematical equation, which results in a value for a parameter called *gamma*. From the value of gamma for your monitor you can create a new color map called the gamma-correction map, or sometimes just the gamma map.

Loading a gamma map into the color map is called *gamma-correcting* or *linearizing* the monitor. Typically most systems have a built-in program that you run to apply gamma correction to a picture by adjusting the color maps. Figure 3-9 shows a black and white ramp, both before and after gamma correction. Typical values of gamma are usually around 2.0. Using a value of gamma that is too large will make your image very bright, and tend to reduce contrast. A value of gamma that is too small will usually result in a dark image. Many artists find it convenient to slightly adjust the value of gamma on an image-by-image basis, which provides a little bit of control over the overall brightness and contrast, though strictly speaking there should only be one gamma curve for all images.

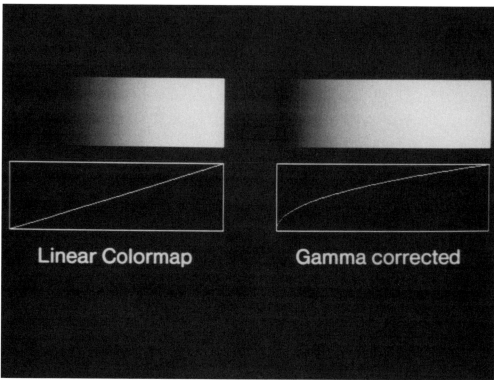

Linear Colormap **Gamma corrected**

3-9. The ramp on the left is shown as viewed through a linear color map. The ramp on the right is shown as viewed through a color map that has been gamma corrected. The plots beneath show the intensity displayed to the viewer.

INTERPOLATION

One of the advantages of using a computer for animation is that the computer can do a lot of the mechanical tasks that would otherwise have to be done by people. One such task is called *interpolation*, the job of starting with some known information and using it to estimate some other, unknown information. To set up an interpolation, you give the computer two or more *extremes*, or *endpoints*, and ask it to fill in the in-between spots with new values.

For example, look at Fig. 3-10. On May 1 it was 30 degrees outside, and on May 10 it was 60 degrees. These are the endpoints, and now you may ask what the temperature was on May 5.

You find the temperature at any point in the given range by interpolating between the two extremes. If you connect the two extremes with a straight line (Fig. 3-11), then this is called *linear interpolation*. Thus linear interpolation tells you that on May 5 (halfway between May 1 and May 10) the temperature was 45 degrees.

You might, however, choose to perform a *nonlinear interpolation*, which literally means interpolating with anything other than a straight line. This curve may be created in many ways. Fig. 3-12 shows some nonlinear interpolation curves and how they affect the value of the graph you are interested in. Nonlinear interpolations are often used in computer-assisted animation to make movement look smoother.

A special type of nonlinear interpolation is to fit a smooth curve to the available data. There are many ways of fitting a smooth curve to available points. One of the most popular methods is called *spline interpolation*. In general, a *spline* is just a curved line that satisfies some particular properties. One kind of spline is a curved line that goes through all the data points offered; this is called an *interpolating spline*. Other kinds of splines just pass near the points; these are called *approximating splines*. There is a large body of theory on the different kinds of splines and how they work, but they are really all used for the same purpose: to somehow get a curvy line to interpolate some data points in a reasonable way.

Historically, each of the points given to a spline for interpolation is called a *knot*. Fig. 3-13 shows how one set of knots might be joined by an interpolating spline and an approximating spline. The best way to understand the splines that are implemented at your computer graphics site is to play with different arrangements of knots and see what happens. Another common way of saying "draw a spline to connect these data," is to say, "*fit* a spline to these data."

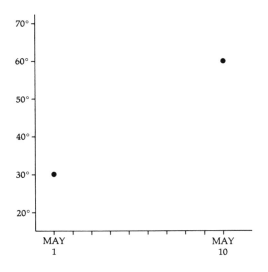

3-10. Two recorded temperatures on different days.

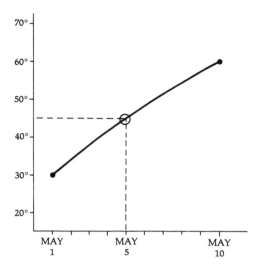

3-11. To linearly interpolate the temperatures, a straight line is drawn between them and values on that line are in-between values.

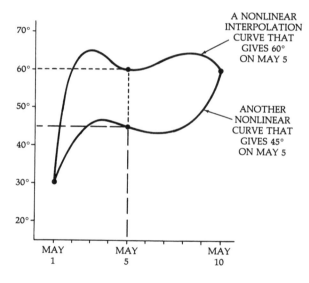

A NONLINEAR INTERPOLATION CURVE THAT GIVES 60° ON MAY 5

ANOTHER NONLINEAR CURVE THAT GIVES 45° ON MAY 5

3-12. Nonlinear interpolation joins the two data points with anything but a straight line.

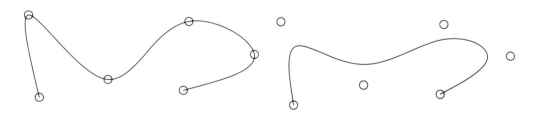

3-13. One set of knots shown joined both by an interpolating spline (left) and an approximating spline (right).

RANDOM NUMBERS

Often when simulating some natural phenomenon, you want the results to have some kind of randomness in them. For example, you might want the computer to simulate the rolling of a pair of dice in a backgammon program, so, of course, you want the dice to be as unpredictable, or random, as possible. Randomness appears everywhere in the kind of objects you want to model with computer graphics: the texture on a tree's bark, the location of goose bumps on cold skin, the placement of leaves on a tree, and so on. Rather than explicitly locating every goose bump on someone's arm, it is preferable to be able to say to the computer, ''put down a bunch of random goose bumps on this arm.''

It is not possible for the computer to make truly random numbers, but there are some good techniques for faking them. The different techniques generate random numbers in different ways. Usually, there are some very large-scale patterns to the kinds of numbers that come out of a *random-number generator*. Sometimes numbers seem to group around a particular average value instead of being spread across a wide range smoothly. To help discuss these effects, it is said that different random-number generators produce numbers with different *distributions*. When modeling some natural phenomena like the ones just discussed, using different distributions will usually yield different pictures. Fig. 3-14 shows some possible distributions. In particular, the distribution in Fig. 3-14A is called a *bell curve* or a *Gaussian* (pronounced Gow'-see-in) distribution. The Gaussian distribution is closely related to the so-called student curve used by many teachers when determining a final grade for a course or test. Fig. 3-14B gives a different distribution showing the probability of rolling the numbers 2 through 12 with a pair of dice.

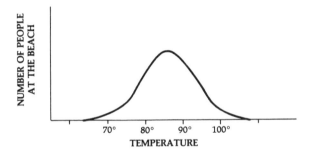

A. Number of people at the beach represented with a bell curve, also called *Gaussian distribution.*

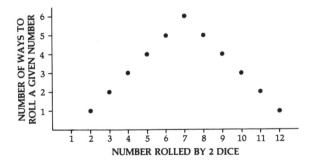

B. Number of ways to roll a given number represented with a linear graph.

3-14. Plot showing how often each number created by a random number generator comes up in a distribution graph.

SUMMARY

Numbers are quantitative measures of something, as opposed to the qualitative descriptions used in natural language. These numbers may be used as parameters (or attribute or characteristic) to a mathematical model.

A computer's memory system is composed of bits, which are the fundamental unit of information: Each bit may represent a 1 (true) or a 0 (false). Groups of eight bits taken together are called a byte: bytes are grouped into words. The unit kilobyte refers to one thousand bytes, while megabyte refers to one million bytes.

Memories are classified as short-term (or core memory) or long-term. Short-term memory is used to hold information immediately useful to the computer. Floppy disks, tapes, and other storage devices are used for long-term memory.

A monitor draws a color image by using a set of three electron guns to send beams of electrons towards the face of the CRT; there they strike a triplet (or one screen dot), composed of three differently colored phosphors, whose brightness is proportional to the intensity of the electron beams that hit them. Since each electron gun is trained on one set of phosphors throughout the screen, the beams are sometimes referred to as color guns: a red gun, a green gun, and a blue gun, although they all fire beams of equivalent electrons.

The triplets on the screen are arranged in scan lines, which are horizontal rows. The even-numbered scan lines are called the even field, while odd-numbered scan lines make up the odd field. Together, they form one frame. Typical monitors draw just the even field and then just the odd field, each one taking one sixtieth of a second; this process is called interlaced scanning. Monitors that hit all scan lines one after the other use noninterlaced scanning.

A frame buffer is a large collection of short-term memory. Each triplet on the screen has a corresponding entry in the frame buffer; both the triplet and the entry are commonly called a pixel (or pel).

Typical frame buffers contain some off-screen memory devoted to storing a color map (or color table). Each entry in the color table contains three values; one each for the red, green, and blue components of the color represented by that entry. Each pixel in the frame buffer holds a number that tells which color number from the color map is associated with that pixel.

The number of bits in a frame buffer is called its depth. If there is sufficient depth in a frame buffer, each pixel can store the red, green, and blue intensities directly for each triplet so that a color map is not strictly necessary.

But almost all frame buffers have a color map, whatever their depth. This map is used to compensate for nonlinear properties of the monitor. This correction is based on a factor called gamma, leading to the term gamma correction.

Another important function offered by the computer is the general technique of interpolation. This process starts with two or more extremes, or endpoints, and creates new values between them that satisfy some criteria. If, when plotted, all of the values lie on a straight line, then the process is called linear interpolation; anything else is called nonlinear interpolation. One of the most useful techniques for interpolating is to use a spline, which is a curve whose shape is based on the knots, or data. If a spline passes through the data, it is called an interpolating spline; if it only passes near the data, then it is an approximating spline.

Computers are also useful for creating random numbers, even though they cannot do a perfect job. A program called a random-number generator produces numbers with some distribution, which tells how often each number is created. A very popular distribution is the Gaussian distribution (also known as a bell curve); this distribution closely approximates many distributions found in nature.

4 SURFACES AND MATERIALS

The first step in creating a three-dimensional scene is to build the models that inhabit that scene. These models are typically constructed out of simpler surfaces that are combined to make more complex objects. The optical properties of these surfaces are very important because they strongly influence how that object looks when illuminated. It is not enough merely to assign a color to an object. There are numerous material properties that must be specified to make an object look just the way you want.

This chapter covers some important concepts shared by all surfaces. It then discusses a particular way of defining a material based on eleven important properties that describe the appearance of that material.

SURFACES

When you use a computer to render objects in a scene, models of the objects must first be built. These models are usually collections of simpler surfaces, such as polygons, spheres, and cylinders. All these shapes are called *surfaces*. In the present discussion, the word surface will describe only the geometry of an object.

It is helpful to make a broad distinction between two types of surfaces. Fig. 4-1 shows some surfaces that have edges, and such surfaces are referred to as having a top and bottom (or front and back, left and right, and so on). This kind of surface is called an *open surface*.

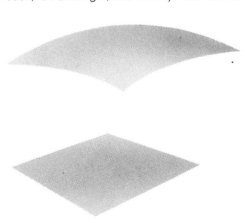

4-1.   Open surfaces with a top and bottom.

Now consider Fig. 4-2. The surfaces here can only be considered overall as having an inside and outside, and are called *closed surfaces*. Any closed surface may be built using a collection of smaller open surfaces, correctly shaped and placed. For example, an inner tube is a closed surface. When the tube is punctured, it can be patched with a small flat piece of rubber, which is itself an open surface. If an inner tube has been patched many times, then you might find that nothing remained of the original rubber. In that case, the closed surface of the inner tube is made up of nothing but many smaller, open surfaces (the patches).

The idea of combining surfaces to make a more complicated one is a central concept in computer model making. The fundamental simple surfaces that any system provides are called the *primitive surfaces* (or just *primitives*), and any new objects made from them are called *complex* (or *aggregate*) *surfaces*. Different computer modeling systems will offer you different sets of primitives. A typical collection of primitive surfaces is shown in Fig. 4-3.

Some other kinds of objects do not naturally fall into either of the open or closed classifications; for example, what kind of surface is a cloud? Or a waterfall?

Surfaces, which are thin sheets or shells of particular shapes, have no thickness. They are suitable if you are only interested in the outside of something that is opaque.

But suppose you want to model a hollow crystal ball. The ball itself is a thick shell of glass with air on the inside. One approach is to think of somehow making "thick" surfaces, but that is a difficult technique to control and apply.

A better approach is to use several closed surfaces, one within the other. You can make use of a popular convention: When an object is a closed surface, all points inside the object are assumed to be made of the same material as the surface itself. So you begin to build your hollow crystal ball with a large sphere by telling the computer the ball is made of glass. Thus everything inside the sphere is glass as well. Then make a smaller sphere, made of air, and place the air-filled sphere within the glass-filled sphere. Most systems assume that when a small object sits within a larger object, the smaller objects have priority for the description of their interior. The general rule is that the properties of a point are those of the smallest closed surface surrounding it.

Thus, in your overall model you have a large sphere with glass on the inside until a certain point, where the inside becomes air. The effect is like having a single, thick surface. You can use this trick to make any number of nested surfaces and to build surfaces of any kind of thickness. For example, you can put a cube of air within the glass sphere, if you wish.

With this convention you can refer to the inside of objects without having to explicitly describe the insides; they are made up of the same material as the surface that surrounds them.

4-2. Closed surfaces with an inside and outside.

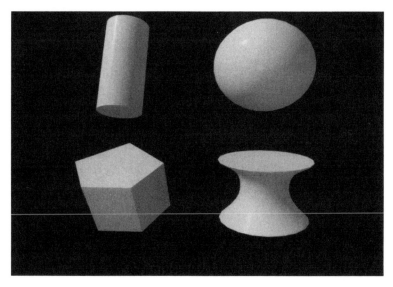

4-3. Some primitive shapes. (Image courtesy of Digital Arts.)

Visible and Hidden Surfaces

Whenever several opaque surfaces are within the same scene, some may appear to be in front of other surfaces. Given a scene and a point of view, the surfaces that are blocked from view are called *hidden surfaces*. The surfaces that can be seen are called *visible surfaces*. The distinction between hidden and visible surfaces can easily change if the surfaces move, or even if the viewpoint moves a bit. Some surfaces might be only partially hidden; they are included in the visible surface category.

It is very important to the overall realism of a picture that hidden surfaces are not visible. Imagine a scene with a car parked in front of a house. You cannot see the house through the car doors, although you can see it through the car windows. If your computer-generated picture somehow had the house drawn in front of the car it would look wrong. Figuring out which surfaces are visible and which are not is called the *hidden-surface problem*.

It is not always immediately obvious which surfaces are visible and which are hidden. For example, consider Fig. 4-4. This is a line drawing of a cube, but it is difficult to tell the orientation of the cube. With the hidden surfaces (or lines) removed (Fig. 4-5), the ambiguity is resolved.

One simple solution to this problem is to draw everything in the scene, starting from the farthest object to the nearest. Nearer objects are simply drawn on top of farther objects, just as if you were laying successive layers of paints on a canvas. So for the car-and-house scene, the entire house would be drawn first, then the far parts of the car, and then the nearest parts of the car. When finished, the near objects cover the far objects. Of course, much care must be taken when handling special cases, such as transparent windows. In general, this *painter's algorithm*, though quick and simple, is not a good solution to the whole rendering problem (for one thing, as presented it is very inefficient because you spend a lot of time drawing things that you then cover up). Better hidden-surface techniques are described in later chapters.

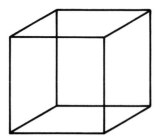

4-4. Ambiguous orientation of the faces of a cube. It is hard to tell which face of the cube is closer to you.

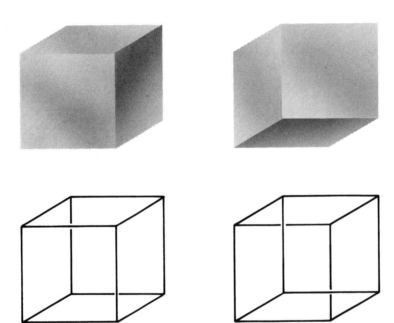

4-5. With hidden lines broken where they pass behind, it becomes easy to tell how the cube is oriented.

Surface Normals

Once the computer has decided that a particular surface is visible, it needs to consider each point on the surface and determine what color an observer would see looking at that point. This determination is not always easy. Even a simple red rubber ball can look very different under different lighting conditions. And if the ball is shiny and has highlights and reflections, things can quickly become complicated. The job of determining the apparent color of a surface is a common task in graphics and has been given the name *shading*. So, computing shading for a surface means finding out the color of the light leaving the surface towards a viewer.

When the computer has a surface ready to be shaded, there are several pieces of information it must have. Some of this information consists of the orientation of the light sources, and how bright they are, and the texture of the surface. Another important attribute of a surface, called the *surface normal*, is usually not defined by the modeler directly but is automatically derived by the computer. However, because it plays an important role in understanding shading, you should have some grasp of the concept. The word *normal* is key to the meaning of the name: A normal is usually a line perpendicular to a plane. Fig. 4-6 shows some examples of surface normals. Even when dealing with a curved surface, you can find the normal at (almost) any point by finding the normal to the plane tangent to the surface at that point.

The surface normal is a vector. It has a length and a direction. When drawing the normal for a particular point on an object, you usually put the tail of the arrow right on that point to emphasize the connection. As shown in Fig. 4-6, surface normals are usually drawn just like other vectors, as a line with an arrowhead. You will see later that the direction of the surface normal controls the shading at that point. The length of the surface normal is usually unimportant. What is important is the direction in which it is pointing.

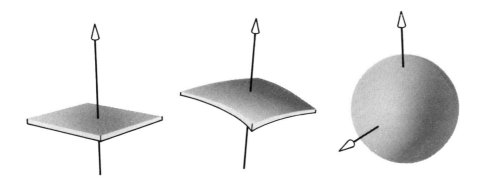

4-6. A surface normal is a vector perpendicular to the tangent plane.

MATERIALS AND THEIR PROPERTIES

Once you have defined the shape of a surface, you need to specify how it looks. The appearance of an object depends greatly on the material from which it was made (or with which it was covered). This section covers various properties that determine how a material appears visually. For convenience, a collection of *material properties* is simply referred to as a *material*.

The most important material properties are those that describe how an object responds to light arriving at its surface. In general, that light may either be *reflected* (if it bounces off of the surface), *transmitted* (if it passes through the surface), or *absorbed* by the surface itself.

In the following sections eleven material properties are discussed. You create a material by specifying the values for these properties: two properties are colors, and the other nine are single values. The properties are organized into two groups: those describing how a material reflects light, and those describing how a transparent material alters light passing through it.

Reflection

Perhaps the single most important aspect of how an object looks is its color. Color is a tricky subject to discuss, because the apparent color of an object is due to a combination of its material color and the color of the incident light. This chapter concentrates on the material properties that determine color; Chapter 5 covers lighting and how it affects the appearance of a surface. Here it is assumed that all objects are illuminated with white light.

Suppose that you are looking at the cover of a notebook, and it looks dull red. This is because the illuminating white light is striking the surface of the notebook, and some of that light is being absorbed. The frequencies of light that are not absorbed are reflected, and when that reflected light reaches your eye you perceive red. A blue notebook appears blue because it absorbs all but the blue-colored light. Any light not reflected by these notebooks is absorbed and turned into heat. (You have experienced light turning into heat if you have ever walked barefoot across a parking lot on a hot summer day, trying to stay on the cool white lines painted over the hot black tar. Black objects heat up because they absorb almost all the incident light, while white objects stay cool, because they reflect almost all the incident light.)

The material at an object's surface determines what light it reflects and what light it absorbs. This color of this material is called the *surface color* of the object.

Most opaque objects have a finish that is either matte (or dull), shiny, or somewhere in between. This difference in appearance is directly connected to the physics of what happens to light at the surfaces of objects. Light that is not absorbed may be reflected in one of two different ways: *specular* and *diffuse*.

Specular Reflection

Specular reflection is the kind of reflection that occurs at the surface of objects with very smooth and shiny finishes, like a mirror or a polished dinner plate. The direction of this specularly reflected light is easy to determine with the help of a basketball analogy. If you are standing on a hard, smooth floor, and you want to bounce a basketball to a friend standing some distance away, you can throw the ball towards the ground at a point exactly between the two of you. You know that the ball will travel towards your friend, but towards the ground as well, until it hits the ground, when it will start traveling upwards, but still towards your friend. You can imagine the whole path of the ball as lying within a vertical plane; when the ball hits the court it stays in the plane but starts traveling up instead of down. Specular reflection is based on the same principle: light strikes a surface and bounces off, staying in the same plane.

A front-surface mirror (one with the reflective coating in front of the glass, rather than behind) is an excellent example of specular reflection; light bounces right off the mirror's surface.

If you are not standing directly in the path of specularly reflected light, then you will not see it. This is why two people can be looking at the same object, but only one person sees a highlight: only that one person is in the path of the light specularly reflecting at that point. (Think of the basketball court again; a bounced ball travels only to one person.) Two people can even see different highlights in different places, if there are several light sources (*e.g.,* you can shine a light off a mirror into someone's eyes, while someone else is combing his hair in the same mirror).

On some kinds of materials, such as plastics, specularly reflected light bounces right off the surface with hardly any change in color. If you look at a shiny piece of plastic, you will notice that the color of a highlight is usually the color of the light source, independent of the color of the plastic. A colored pool ball shows this very well. Some other kinds of surfaces do color their incident light before it is reflected. When light specularly reflects off of a metal surface, the light actually interacts with the metallic material; how much interaction occurs depends on the type of surface and the angle at which the light arrives. At a shallow or glancing angle, the color of the light is hardly changed, and the color of the reflection is still the color of the light source. But at a sharper angle, the light actually mingles with the surface material a bit before it is reflected, and some of the light is absorbed. If you shine a white light on a smooth piece of copper at a steep angle (that is, the light is arriving almost perpendicularly to the surface), you will see that the color of the reflected light is copper-colored, not white. This change in color of specularly reflected light due to the properties of the material is called *color-shifting*.

Many systems automatically take care of this color-shifting for you, but you may need to specify how much of it should occur. For a plastic, there should be no color-shifting. For a metal, there should be maximum color-shifting (white light arriving head-on to the surface should leave with the color of the surface). Other materials are in between these extremes. Because plastic and metal are at the extremes of this scale, sometimes the amount of color-shifting due to a material is called its *metallic coefficient*. Plastic would have a metallic coefficient of 0, while a pure metal would have a metallic coefficient of 1.

Another surface property that affects appearance is *roughness*. Any surface can have roughness simultaneously on several different scales. For example, an automobile tire has deep grooves, so it appears rough from a distance, but the rubber walls of the grooves appear very smooth to the naked eye. Closer examination of the rubber with a microscope reveals it to be very rough as well, though on a smaller scale. The effect of such small-scale roughness may be most easily seen in the size and sharpness of a highlight. If the surface is very smooth, the highlight will be very small and crisp. If the surface is slightly rough, any highlight will be more spread-out, and it will have a fuzzier edge. Fig. 4-7 shows six spheres with different degrees of surface roughness.

Historically the term for describing roughness has come to be called the *highlight factor*, because of its effect on a highlight, or sometimes the *highlight exponent*, because of its mathematical implementation. Some systems call it a *roughness coefficient*, which is a better name.

Diffuse Reflection

Diffuse reflection occurs at the surface of objects with rough finishes at a very fine level of detail (this surface coarseness is of a much smaller scale than the roughness that spreads out a highlight in a specular reflection). This fine-grain coarseness makes the surface appear matte, or dull. On a very small scale, the roughness of these surfaces causes the light to bounce off in unpredictable directions.

As an analogy, think again of a basketball court, but this time replace the smooth, hard floor with a very bumpy and choppy surface, like a rocky field. When the ball hits this rough surface, it will bounce off whatever rock or chunk of ground it happens to hit, and go off in an unpredictable direction. If you throw the basketball towards the ground over and over, you would probably hit a slightly different spot each time, and that would cause the ball to bounce away in a different direction each time.

Diffuse reflection takes this kind of reflection to its limit: when light strikes a slightly rough surface, you never know in which direction it will be reflected. In fact, it turns out that all directions

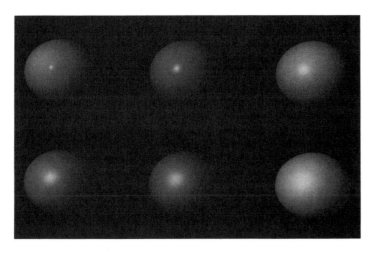

4-7. One sphere shown with several different highlight factors. (Image courtesy of Digital Arts.)

55

have equal probability. So light is constantly arriving at different points on the surface, and bouncing off in all directions at once. This is the essence of diffuse reflection: incoming light is reflected equally in all directions.

Look, for example, at a piece of rough cardboard. The intensity of the reflected light that you see does not depend on where you stand; since light is reflected in all directions equally, any point you look from is receiving the same reflected light.

The color of diffusely reflected light is a simpler matter than that of light reflected specularly. Diffusely reflected light is the same color in all directions, regardless of the direction of the incoming light. When the light arrives at the surface, some is absorbed. Whatever light is not absorbed is diffusely reflected equally in all directions, with the same color and intensity.

Both specular and diffuse reflections are idealizations; in the real world, nothing is a perfect specular or diffuse reflector, but a combination of both. If something reflects in a predominantly diffuse way we call it a matte surface; if predominantly a specular reflector, we call it shiny.

Part of the description of a material in computer graphics are two values that indicate how much a surface reflects diffusely, and how much specularly. These values are called the *diffuse* and *specular reflection coefficients* of a material.

Fig. 4-8 shows two views of a table and lamp in a lighted room. The table has a rough wooden surface, but the surface is waxed, so the table reflects light both specularly and diffusely. In Fig. 4-8A the lamp is off, so the surface of the table is seen only by diffusely reflected sunlight (any specularly reflected sunlight is going off in some other direction than this point of view). In Fig. 4-8B the light has been turned on, and the specular reflection of the lamp can be seen as a highlight on the surface.

Transmission (Transparency)

When light arrives at a transparent surface, some of the light actually passes through the surface. If the surface is also shiny, some of the light may be reflected too: this is why you can see highlights on a glass cup.

Imagine a thick piece of red glass, with a beam of light arriving at one side, passing through, and then exiting from the other side. As the light passes through the glass, it interacts with the glass itself, and is gradually absorbed and diminished. When the light finally reaches the far side and exits from the glass, it is less bright than when it entered. And if the light entered the glass with a white color, it exits with a red color. The light is absorbed within the glass in just the same way as it is absorbed at the surface of an object; some light frequencies are converted into heat, and others pass freely. In this case, only those frequencies that, taken together, give the sensation of red exit from the far side. If the glass were twice as thick, then even more of the light would be absorbed.

This absorption of the light is dependent on three factors: the *body color* of the object, the *density* of the material, and the distance traveled by the light within the object.

Body color is the internal color of the material, as opposed to its surface color. For example, imagine a crystal ball of blue glass, covered with a layer of transparent red plastic. The body color of the ball is blue, though its surface color is red.

The density of a material controls how much light is absorbed as it passes through a piece of the material. Imagine two sheets of glass with the same red color, one much denser than the other. Light passing through the denser material will be absorbed—and therefore colored and darkened—more than light passing through the less dense material.

Some systems assume all objects in the world have a uniform density, so you have no control over this effect. Other systems expect you to know that a higher density means that the light is absorbed more, and expect that you will choose a darker color for a denser material to simulate this effect (even if you think two otherwise equal materials have the same color when you ignore density). Some systems allow you explicit control over material density.

A

B

4-8. Examples of diffuse and specular reflection. In *A*, all the light is reflected diffusely, and no highlight is visible. In *B*, a highlight can be seen. (Images courtesy of Digital Arts.)

The distance traveled by light through an object is automatically calculated by the computer when making an image. This distance is used to determine how much the light is darkened by its passage through the material, as controlled by the material's density.

A common name for describing the light that passes through a transparent surface is *transmitted light.* So we say that a sheet of glass both reflects and transmits some of its incident light. Transmitted light interacts with the object material in both specular and diffuse modes, just like reflected light.

Specular transmission occurs when light passes through a material with a very regular internal structure, like a piece of window glass. In the ideal case, the light simply passes through without any scattering or spreading. The color of the light is always changed by the material, though, and as a result exits with a different color than it had when it entered (unless the material is perfectly clear).

If the material has some large-scale irregularities within its structure, then specularly reflected light may spread out a little during its passage, just like light specularly reflecting off of a surface. As with specular reflection, the effect of these irregularities is easily seen on a highlight. Thus you may also specify the *transparency highlight factor* or *transparency highlight exponent,* though a better name is *internal roughness.*

Besides coloring, another effect distinguishes specular transmission from specular reflection: light *refracts* (or bends) when it passes from one material to another. Refraction has been thoroughly studied by physicists, who have come to understand it very well.

Experimenters have studied the amount by which light bends when it passes from air (or vacuum) into a variety of materials. For each material they have measured the *index of refraction,* which is a material property related to the density of the material and the color of the incoming light. To determine how much the light of a particular color bends when passing from one material to another, one must compare the indexes of refraction of the two materials. Though the index of refraction is technically different at different wavelengths, many systems use just a single value and bend all light by the same amount. For many applications this is a fine approximation, but this simplification means that if you shine a white light into a prism the entire beam will bend, and emerge as a redirected beam of white light. If you allow each wavelength of light to have a unique index of refraction, different colors will bend by different amounts, and a white light shining on a prism will break up into a spectrum.

Fig. 4-9 shows a ruler in a jar of water. It appears to be bent because the light is traveling between water, glass, and air, and at each transition the light bends some more. Of course the ruler is not actually bent, but that is how it appears, due to refraction.

Sometimes the physics of this situation works out in such a way that the light bends so much that it appears to reflect back into the material rather than pass through the surface to the other side. This phenomenon is called *total internal reflection* (or TIR), and it can be very useful in practical situations. In fact, this is one principle behind the optic fibers that carry telephone conversations: the fibers are transparent so that light can pass along them, but they are designed so that whenever light strikes the wall of the fiber, it is reflected back into the fiber itself rather than passing

4-9. When light passes from one medium to another, it is reflected by an amount dependent on the indexes of refraction of the two media.

out into the air. The fiber is coated with a thin shell of another material; when light strikes the boundary between, it is reflected back into the core. You can see the result of total internal reflection with a ruler and a glass of water. Look very carefully, edge-on, at the surface of the water. You will notice that the ruler seems to disappear right under the surface! This is because the light coming from those points of the ruler just under the surface is striking the surface at such an angle that the light is reflected back into the water, rather than out into the air.

All of the effects of refraction, including total internal reflection, are handled automatically by the computer. You do need to supply the index of refraction for your material, though.

Just as with reflection, diffuse transmission is a simpler subject than its specular counterpart. Diffuse transmission occurs when light passes through a material that has a very disorganized internal structure, such as piece of frosted glass. Looking through such a piece of glass it is hard to tell what is on the other side; you can make out rough forms sometimes, but the light is very diffused and scattered. When light exits from a diffuse material, it travels away from the surface in all directions equally, just like diffuse reflection.

Just as with reflection, you specify the amount of transmission with *specular* and *diffuse transmission coefficients*.

SUMMARY

The basic piece of any geometric model is the surface. If the surface has a top and bottom, then it is called an open surface. If the surface has only an inside and outside, then it is called a closed surface.

Surfaces may be combined to make more complex objects. The surfaces directly provided by any modeling system are called the primitive surfaces for that system. The objects built from those primitives are called complex surfaces.

A point in space inherits its material properties from the smallest closed surface that encloses it. Thus, all the points within a glass sphere are glass as well, though only the spherical surface is directly modeled.

From a given point of view, those surfaces that are completely unseen are called hidden surfaces. All others are called visible surfaces, even if only a piece of the surface is actually visible. Hidden surfaces often need not be drawn by the computer, which means that a picture can be drawn more quickly if the hidden surfaces are removed. Determining which surfaces are hidden is called the hidden-surface problem. One solution to this problem, called the painter's algorithm, is to draw all surfaces in order, from the farthest away to the nearest. Those surfaces that are not at all visible at the end of the process are hidden.

An important property of almost all surfaces is the surface normal. This is a vector that is perpendicular to the surface at a given point. It provides information about the orientation of that surface at each point.

The optical appearance of a surface is determined by the material from which it was made. In computer graphics, each surface must be accompanied by a material description, which is a collection of individual material properties. Eleven properties together form a very general description of a material. Not all systems offer you control over all of these particular properties; some offer more, some fewer.

A material's appearance may be divided into two general categories: reflection and transparency (or transmission).

The most important property involved in reflection is surface color, which determines which frequencies of light are reflected by the surface, which in turn determines what color is perceived by a viewer looking at the surface. Light that is not reflected is absorbed, and turned into heat.

Light that is not absorbed may be reflected in two different ways: specular and diffuse.

Specular reflection is typical of shiny objects: it is the process whereby light bounces perfectly off a surface. The color of specularly reflected light is dependent on the color of the incident light, the color of the object, the type of material the object is made of, and the angle of incidence of the incoming light.

Some materials, such as most plastics, do not color specularly reflected light at all, so the color of a highlight is the color of the light source. Other materials, such as metals, on the other hand, usually do modify the color of the incoming light. When the light arrives at a shallow angle (almost parallel to the surface), the color of the light is unchanged. But as the angle becomes steeper and more head-on to the surface, a metal surface affects the color in a process called color-shifting. How much color-shifting should occur is described with a parameter called the metallic coefficient.

Another aspect of specularly reflected light is typically noted in the shape of highlights. If a surface is perfectly smooth, then highlights are small and have sharp, crisp edges. If the surface is rough at a very small scale, then the highlight tends to spread out a little and have softer edges. The amount of roughness is described by a value called the highlight factor, highlight exponent, or roughness coefficient.

Diffuse reflection is typical of matte objects, such as a piece of rough cardboard. Such materials scatter the incoming light in all directions uniformly. The color of the incident light is always modified by the color of the object, but the direction of view and the angle of incidence are irrelevant.

A material description typically includes two values indicating the amount of diffuse and specular reflection occurring at that surface; these are the diffuse and specular reflection coefficients.

Transmitted light is light that has passed through a transparent material. Such light is always affected by the body color of the object. The density of a material determines how much the light is absorbed as it passes through an object made of that material. The total amount of light absorbed by traveling through a transparent medium is due to a combination of the body color, the density, and the distance traveled by the light.

Specular transmission is the passage of light through a material with a very regular internal structure. As with specular reflection, you may specify a specular highlight factor or specular highlight exponent, though a better name is internal roughness.

When light passes between two materials of different densities it bends, by an amount determined by the index of refraction of each material. Real objects bend different frequencies of light by different amounts, so the index of refraction depends not only on the materials, but also on the frequency of the light under consideration. Many systems use a single index of refraction for an entire material and bend all light by the same amount.

The light may bend so much that it actually appears to be reflected; this phenomenon is called total internal reflection, or TIR. It is a very useful property in real applications, though sometimes unexpected in computer images.

Diffuse transmission occurs when light passes through a material with a rough internal structure; upon exiting from the material the light is scattered in all directions with equal color and intensity.

As with reflection, the description of a transparent material includes diffuse and specular transmission coefficients, which tell how much light is passed through the material in these two different ways.

The eleven material properties in this chapter are summarized in the following list:

Reflection
(1) surface color
(2) specular coefficient
    (3) surface roughness coefficient
    (4) metallic coefficient
(5) diffuse coefficient

Transmission
(6) body color
(7) body density
(8) specular coefficient
    (9) internal roughness coefficient
    (10) index of refraction
(11) diffuse coefficient

5 LIGHTING AND SHADING

Any three-dimensional scene must be illuminated. This is true whether the scene is a real model for traditional filmmaking, or a computer graphics model for rendering by a machine.

In computer graphics, each *light source* is described by a collection of *light source properties* that together make up a *lighting model*, similarly to the way a material is described by a collection of material properties. The first part of this chapter describes the most popular characteristics used in computer graphics lighting models.

The second part of this chapter discusses *shading*. In computer graphics the term "shading" refers to determining the color of the light reflected or transmitted by a particular point on a surface. Shading is determined by combining a material description with a lighting description. The way this information is used to create a color is called a *shading model*.

In this chapter and throughout the rest of the book, the term "color" is used to represent a complete description of a color sensation (usually excluding intensity); this is the common usage in computer graphics. For example, a color may be described by three values specifying its hue, lightness, and saturation (using the HLS color model in Chapter 2). When I wish to speak only of hue, or any other particular aspect of a color, I will do so explicitly.

The term shading also has a special meaning in the field of computer graphics, where it refers precisely to the job of determining the color and intensity of light leaving a point on a surface. It is unfortunate that this word has a rather different meaning in the field of art, but the word is too well entrenched in both fields to change it in either one.

LIGHTING MODELS

To render a scene a computer must have a description of the light sources: where they are, what color they are, how intense they are, where they are pointed, and so on. This information is supplied by a lighting model.

Here the word model refers to a mathematical system that mimics a real system, because typical lighting models use imaginary light sources, not real ones. So the computer pretends that light is being radiated from a point (or region) in space, even though there is no physical model present. If the light source itself is outside of the scene, or very far away, then you can usually avoid really building a geometric model for the light. But if, for example, you are rendering a living room scene with a desk lamp, then you will want to build your physical model so that your modeled light bulb contains the point from which the light is supposed to radiate. Otherwise you will have light (and maybe shadows) originating from some vacant point in space!

Light Specifications

The most complete description of a light source would contain all the information you need to describe a real light source. These various specifications are *intensity, color, position*, and *direction* of the light source.

One way to describe how a light source radiates light is by using a *goniometric intensity diagram* (the word goniometric refers to the particular form of this type of diagram). In a goniometric intensity diagram, you take a cross section through the light and plot how much light is radiated in all directions. A line sticking out of the plot shows the "front" of the light. Fig. 5-1 shows four goniometric intensity diagrams.

You can think of a goniometric intensity diagram as telling you how much light is being radiated in each direction. As you walk around the light source, you measure how much illumination is coming your way. Then you mark the diagram with a dot; the location of the dot indicates how much light is being emitted in that direction. For example, a dot near the center means not much light, while a dot farther out means more light. Figure 5-1A shows a light source that resembles a desk lamp: most of the light is going forward, but some is coming out from the sides. No light is coming out of the back of the lamp. Figure 5-1B shows a similar lamp, but this one is directing more of its light forward and rather little to the sides.

Typically, not only does the intensity of the light vary around the surface of the bulb, but so does the color. In this case, you could also use a *goniometric color diagram*, in which the color at each point indicates the color coming out of the bulb in that direction.

Although implicitly this discussion has been about common light bulbs, these techniques apply equally well to anything that radiates light, from a fluorescent tube to a candle flame. In the case of a flame, the goniometric and color diagrams would need to change over time, but the concept is the same.

Building up goniometric diagrams requires a lot of work. If you are simulating a real light source, you have to get the measurements for the light or measure them yourself. Then you have to enter them into the computer. The advantage is that if you do so, you will have a very accurate description of a real light source, and you may see the improvement in your pictures. If the rest of your image is also very realistic, this form of light description might contribute to the believability of the image. The disadvantage is that building the light description diagrams and then entering them into the computer can be difficult. A good compromise is to build up a library of diagrams and then use the appropriate ones when you need them.

The realism that comes from using goniometric diagrams is not free. Using such a description of a light source will usually slow down the computer. This work can be greatly reduced by replacing each plot with a single value. The simplification means that a light source has a single intensity and a single color, uniformly radiated in all directions. Figure 5-1C shows the goniometric diagram for this kind of light. Note that you need only specify the radius of the circle to completely describe the light. It is surprising how well this simplification can often work: the scheme is so useful that it is the only technique offered by some systems for designing light sources.

Another common simplification is to assume that the light is radiating only in a single direction; such a light source is then "pointing" its light directly forward.

In addition to the goniometric diagrams, the third, and last, piece of information needed to describe a light source is its position (including orientation) in space. Remember that the lighting model is a mathematical model; the computer is not using this information to build surfaces, but rather to determine illumination. If your light source is far away and not directly visible in the scene, then you need not bother with any physical surfaces for it. But if the light source is within the scene, you will want to build some kind of physical model around it (for example, a light bulb or a lamp) to justify its presence.

Sometimes you want your light sources to be quite controlled in their illumination. For example, theater lighting designers use a number of mechanical devices to "clip" the light. *Barn doors*

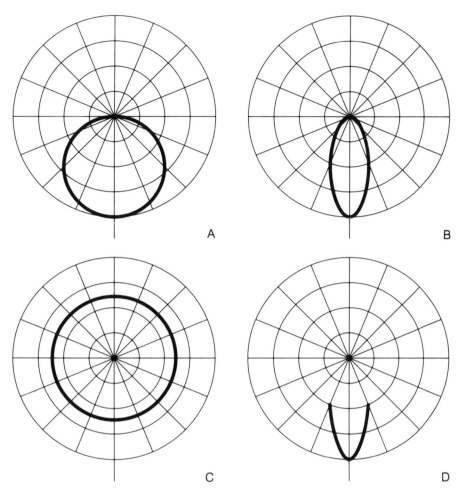

5-1. Four goniometric plots of light sources. A and B are directed lamps, C is a uniformly radiating point light source, and D is a directed lamp with shutters applied. The projecting line at the bottom indicates the ''front'' of the light.

are sheets of metal that create a sort of square tunnel for the light so it does not spill over onto the sides of the stage. *Spotlights* cast a long beam of light in a particular direction, rather than shining out in all directions.

You can usually include these sorts of effects in your lighting of a computer-generated scene, but different systems require different approaches.

If you can specify goniometric and color diagrams for your lights, then you can build these light directors right into the plot. No light is radiated outside of a narrow beam in Fig. 5-1D.

Alternatively, if your system supports shadows, then you can surround your (uniformly radiating) local lights with shutters that you model directly into the scene. In effect you are directly simulating what the physical shutters do; they stop the light from passing through, so light can only travel in directions not blocked by the shutters.

Another method is to use direct lighting control. Some systems allow you to specify shutters directly as part of the light description, and you need not worry about how they are made to work. If you use a programmable light source (a feature of shading languages, discussed in Chapter 13), you can, in effect, make the shutters built-in to the description of the light source.

LOCAL VERSUS INFINITE LIGHT SOURCES

Suppose that you want to make pictures as quickly as possible, so you use a light source description of a single color and a single intensity. You can achieve still more speed if you make yet another simplification. If you describe where a light source is located by giving its position and orientation, then you call that light a *local light source*, meaning that its description is local to the scene (or at least within the scene's world, and at least potentially in the scene if you move and point the camera the right way). Or you can leave out the position of the light altogether, and then you will have an *infinite* or *remote light source*.

A local light source, because it is part of a scene, can influence different objects in different ways. Objects closer to the light are brighter; those farther away receives less light. Fig. 5-2 shows four balls lit by a single, local light source somewhere roughly between and above them. Notice that the illumination of each ball is different, because each ball is in a different location. Fig. 5-3 shows the effect of a local light on a single polygon.

On the other hand, an infinite light source is thought of as infinitely far away. A good example is the sun as seen from the earth at some particular moment. Sunlit objects on the earth all appear the same way (unless they are in shadow). Fig. 5-4 shows the same four balls as Fig. 5-2, but this time they are lit by an infinite light source. To describe an infinite light source, you ignore its position in space and specify only its direction of illumination. You assume that the light is so far away (in the mathematical limit, infinitely far away) that everything in the scene can look in the same direction to see the light source. This condition is not true for local lights; if you and I are standing on opposite sides of a lamp, then we cannot both look in the same direction and simultaneously see the lamp. But for all practical purposes, we can stand outside and see the sun simultaneously, both looking in the same direction.

You can approximate an infinite light source with a local light source placed very, very far away.

So why bother with infinite light sources at all? Because they're faster. Many of the shading calculations that must be done for individual infinite light sources can be automatically combined before rendering begins into a single, special form of infinite light. Then the computer can simply illuminate the world with this single, new light, and thus eliminate the time required to process each light individually. Not all the shading can be reduced this way, but a substantial amount of it can. The result is that if you double the number of infinite light sources in your scene, you do not double the amount of rendering time, though it will increase a bit. Local light sources

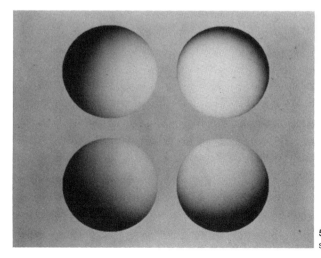

5-2. Four spheres lit by a local light source.

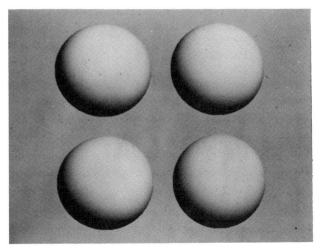

5-3. Shading on a single polygon from a local light source. (Image courtesy of Digital Arts.)

5-4. The same spheres shown in Fig. 5-2, shaded by an infinite light source.

cannot be combined in this way, so they must still be handled one by one. If you double the number of local lights in a scene, your shading time will roughly double as well.

Most scene designers will try to use as many infinite light sources as they can, and then use a few local light sources for particular effects.

Ambient Light

Ambient (or indirect) light is sort of a sticky issue in computer graphics these days. Indirect light refers to light that is "all around" in a scene; it describes the light that does not come directly from a light source, but rather arrives at a surface by bouncing around in the scene. When you are in a living room lit by one or two lamps, everything not directly lit by the lamps is receiving such light. It leaves the lamps, bounces off the walls, the floor, the ceiling, and all around, until it reaches almost everywhere in the room. This effect is one reason why ceilings are painted white or another light color: to bounce light back down into the room.

For a long time, indirect light looked like a difficult problem to computer graphics programmers. How do you handle light that arrives at an object through some complicated series of bounces around the room? There were no really good, practical answers, so an artificial construction was invented.

The problem was approached this way: If you cannot directly track the light bouncing around in a scene, assume it happens anyway, and just add some constant amount and color of light to every object in the scene to simulate the indirect light. So in most lighting models, in addition to a description of each light source, there is also an ambient or global light value that is simply added to every object every time you need to find its illumination. In computer graphics, the term "ambient light" is usually used to refer to this particular technique of adding some constant illumination to every object.

Researchers have recently begun to find good ways to correctly model indirect light, so ambient light as defined here is beginning to fall out of favor (radiosity, discussed in Chapter 12, is one approach). If you use such a technique to really calculate the indirect illumination on an object, your scenes may look better, but they also take longer to create. That is why in everyday, practical systems, many people still use an ambient light description in their lighting models.

So, ambient light is a useful trick, but use it with care. If you use too much ambient light, everything in the scene will automatically be given a lot of incoming light, and your picture will look washed out. Too little ambient light will typically make some objects appear black where they are not receiving direct light; almost always these objects should receive some light, so you can still see them. A little ambient light is useful, but too much or too little looks wrong. The right amount varies from system to system, but with practice you will get a feel for how much ambient light you like in your scenes.

Darklights

One interesting effect that you cannot achieve in real life is the specification of objects that I call *darklights*. A darklight is just like a regular light source except that it has negative color; that is, instead of adding light to a scene, it removes light. If you think of a regular light source as projecting a beam of light, a darklight can be thought of as projecting a beam of shadow.

Most rendering systems support darklights automatically, since they simply add in the contributed color of each light source. If the color of a light is negative, then some of the incident light falling at a point is removed. Darklights are just as useful as regular lights for emphasizing detail and structure in an image. If you want a shadow to fall in a certain place, but you do not want to move your lights, point a narrow darklight at the place where the shadow should be. You can set up the general lighting for a scene, and then add touch-up darklights and spotlights to emphasize contrasts and direct the viewer's attention.

SHADING

Suppose that you have created a model that you want to render. Also suppose you have specified the material properties for each surface, and you have provided a set of light sources. For the computer to draw a picture of your model on the screen, it must mathematically project the lights onto the surfaces and see how they are illuminated. Once the computer knows how much light is falling on a particular point on a surface, it can simulate the reflection and transmission of that light off of and through the surface, to determine the color of light leaving the surface and arriving at the screen. (Remember that by "color" we mean a complete description of the light.)

The process of determining the color of light leaving a surface is called *shading*. The shading process uses the geometry and material properties of the surface, determines the incident light, and from that information finds the light leaving the surface. In general, one point at a time is shaded. In shading, the point for which you want to compute shade is called the *shading point*.

Shading is an area in which there are many options and approaches. Only the most popular and conceptually straightforward techniques are presented here. As with anything that tries to simulate reality, the more realism you want, the more work you must do. Once you understand lighting and shading, you can move on to more complex techniques if you want or need to. Some of these techniques are discussed in Chapter 12.

For the purposes of this discussion, consider each point on each surface in the scene individually. This approach is not the most efficient, because it is often helpful to use information from nearby points to save time. But even when speedup techniques are used, the basic ideas are the same as for working with individual points.

There is a fundamental simplification common to almost all computer graphics systems that will help make things easier for you: No modeled objects emit light on their own. All surfaces are either reflective, transparent, or both. Light is only created by light sources given in the lighting model. Of course, you can surround a light with a transparent bulb, but it is not the bulb itself that is glowing, it is the light source placed within the bulb.

The advantage of using a lighting model is that when you want to find the color and intensity of the light falling on an object, you can divide that incoming light into two parts: the light coming directly from light sources, and the light coming from other objects (for example, the walls or ceiling in a room scene). In many shading systems the light coming from other objects is ignored, and only the light coming directly from light sources is considered.

Although shadows are actually part of shading, they are usually handled with a separate process, and so are covered in the discussion of other rendering techniques in Chapter 11.

Recall that materials are discussed in terms of how they reflect and transmit light. Since shading is concerned with how light interacts with a surface, the mechanisms of reflection and transmission are important to shading. Most shading systems also distinguish between specular and diffuse effects for both reflection and transmission, making a total of four effects that must be examined to find the total light leaving a surface at a point.

The following discussion emphasizes reflection, and how the diffuse and specular components are handled. Transmission is not discussed explicitly, but with minor changes you can substitute the word "transmission" for "reflection" in the following text and the statements are still valid.

Diffuse Shading

Fig. 5-5 shows several flat surfaces in different orientations relative to a light source. You can capture the essence of diffuse shading from a few observations about how much of a surface is directed towards the light source.

Fig. 5-6 shows some flat surfaces with their normals, and a light-source vector. The first observation you can make is that when a surface is directly edge-on to a light source, no light is actually falling onto the surface. The second observation is that when the surface is directly facing the light source, it is receiving as much light as it can. In terms of normals, the more the normal points towards the light source, the more light will reach the surface.

The computer needs an exact method for determining how much a surface "points towards" a light source (assume a local light source for this discussion). The method requires two vectors. The first is the surface normal at the point you want to shade. Place the tail of the normal right at the point on the surface you are trying to shade. The second vector is drawn from the point being shaded to the light source. Notice that both vectors begin at the same point. Then you find the angle between the two vectors. Generally speaking, the smaller the angle, the more light is arriving at the surface.

If you use an infinite light source, you can still use the same setup. But instead of drawing a vector to the light source, simply place a vector pointing opposite to the direction you specified

5-5. Polygons appear brighter as they present more of their face to the light source. Here the light source is from the upper left.

5-6. Polygons (with normals) at different orientations to an infinite light source. The amount of light a polygon receives depends on how much its surface normal aligns with the direction vector of the light. (Image courtesy of Digital Arts.)

when you described the light. That vector points back to the "infinitely far away" point from which the light is coming. Then you find the angle between the two vectors, as before.

This comparison of the surface normal at a given point with a vector to the light source is at the heart of all shading techniques.

Now you know how much light is arriving at the surface, which is all you need to know for diffuse reflection. This is because diffusely reflected light is scattered in all directions evenly. Consequently, the more a normal lines up with the vector pointing back to the light source, the more light the surface receives, and thus, the more light it reflects.

Specular Shading

Specular shading is used to account for specular reflections, or highlights, which can be tricky, because they appear different depending on where you are standing and in what direction you are looking.

For example, suppose you are in a bathroom with a mirror mounted in front of you and a light off to one side on the wall behind you. If you stand in the right place, you can see the light reflected in the mirror. But if you move, and then look right at that same place in the mirror, you will not see the light at all! So the same point on a surface can sometimes show you a specular reflection, and sometimes not. It depends on where the objects are and where you are looking from.

In shading, it is not difficult to find out how much specular light will leave a surface towards your eye. What happens is that the light from the light source strikes the surface and then bounces off, just like the basketball bounced off the surface of the smooth, hard court described in Chapter 4. If your eye happens to be near where the light is bouncing towards, you will see the light; otherwise you will not. This reflection does not have to be very crisp; if the reflecting surface is slightly rough, the bounce will not always be exact, and the highlight will spread out some. The amount of spreading is controlled by the surface roughness material coefficient discussed in Chapter 4.

Thus, to find the amount of specularly reflected light that you can see from a given point of view, you find the incoming light and bounce it off of the surface. If it bounces into (or near) your eye, you will see the reflection (or highlight, which is just a reflection of the light source Itself).

SUMMARY

Just as in the real world, objects in a computer-generated scene must be illuminated to be visible. The illumination on an object is combined with the material specification to determine shading,which is the job of finding the color and intensity of light leaving a point on a surface.

Specification of the lights illuminating a scene is accomplished with a lighting model. This is a description of the lights that shine on the scene. Any geometrical objects that should be associated with the lighting model (light bulbs, filaments, lamps, and so forth) must be explicitly created and entered into the scene description as geometric models.

The radiation of a light source may be described with a kind of plot called a goniometric diagram. You may build a goniometric intensity diagram, which specifies the intensity of the light in various directions away from the source. Further specification of the light includes a goniometric color diagram, which describes the color of the light in various directions.

Either of these plots may be modified to simulate the effects of traditional, mechanical lighting tools such as barn doors and shutters. Either or both plots may be replaced with a single value, representing either a constant intensity or color of light in all directions.

Light sources that are near enough to a scene so that their placement is important are called local light sources. If only direction is important, then you may use an infinite light source, which is considered to be a light source infinitely far away from the scene. Because of the mathematics of shading, the calculations for many infinite light sources can be combined into one operation, so that adding an infinite light source to a scene does not slow down the picture creation as much as adding a local light source.

Ambient (or indirect) light can usually be found in real scenes; this is the light that bounces around the scene so that every object receives some light. The correct simulation of indirect light can add realism to an image, but it can also be very time-consuming. An alternative is to use the ambient-light technique, which involves adding a small amount of constant light to every point on every surface. Unless you simulate indirect light accurately in your scene, you will need to add some ambient light to make your images look good. The amount of ambient light used must be carefully controlled, however; too little and the image will be dark, too much and the image will be washed out.

Darklights may be used to remove light from particular places in a scene. These are exactly the same as regular lights, except that their light intensity is negative, which causes them to remove light from a region, rather than adding. Darklights are useful for making subtle changes to a scene's illumination and casting fake shadows.

To determine the color of light leaving a point on a surface, the illuminating light and the material description are combined in a process called shading. The result is a color and intensity for the light leaving that point. This light is a combination of diffuse reflection, specular reflection, diffuse transmission, and specular transmission.

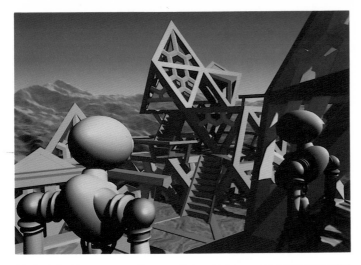

C-1. *Condo Mondo* is a scene composed from many objects, each built from a prepared model. (Image by Ned Greene, copyright © New York Institute of Technology.)

C-2. *The Ant's Picnic* was created on an interactive modeling system. (Image by Eric Bier, Xerox Palo Alto Research Center.)

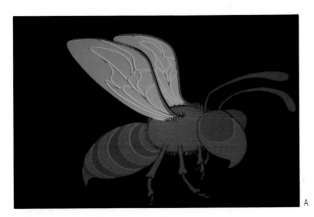

A   B

C

C-3A, B, C. Texture mapping with a material map. *A* shows the material map, and *B* the final result; *C* shows the original box. Displacement mapping was also used to round the corners and pull in the sides just under the lid. (Image by Rob Cook, Pixar.)

C-4. *Inside A Quark* uses bump mapping on the bark of the vines and picture mapping on the leaves. The petals are color-interpolated by Gouraud shading. (Image by Ned Greene, copyright © New York Institute of Technology.)

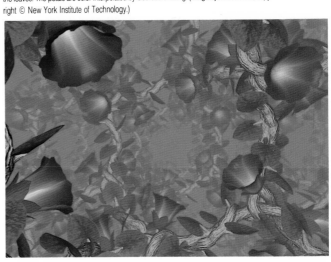

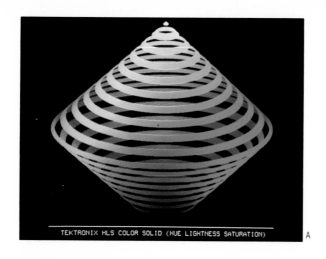

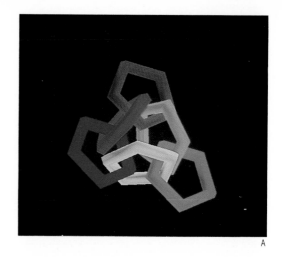

A

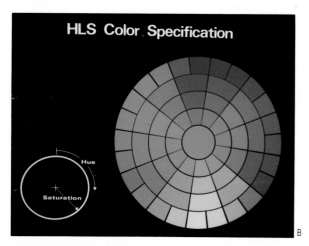

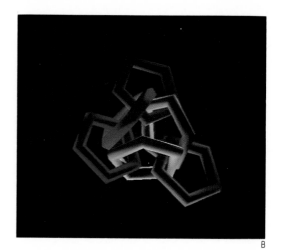

B

C-5A, B. The Hue, Lightness, Saturation (HLS) color model. (Image *A* courtesy of Tektronix, Inc. Image *B* by Paul Sholtz, used by permission of IBM Corp.)

C

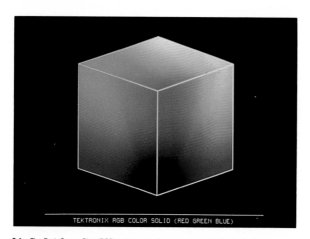

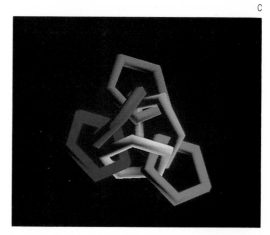

C-6. The Red, Green, Blue (RGB) color model. (Image courtesy of Tektronix, Inc.)

C-7A, B, C. One image, viewed with three different color maps. (Images by Andrew Glassner.)

A

B

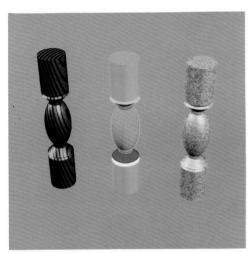

C

C-8A, B, C. Decal textures and space textures. *A* shows a block and a sphere textured with a single wood-grain image applied to the surface. *B* shows the same objects textured with a space texture. *C* shows that the space textures flow smoothly from object to object. (Images copyright © 1985 by Darwyn Peachey, University of Saskatchewan.)

C-9. A vase sitting in a marble space texture. (Marble Vase copyright © 1985 Ken Perlin.)

C-10. A teapot textured with a wood-burl space texture. (Image by Frank Crow, Xerox Palo Alto Research Center.)

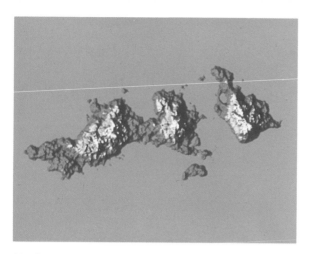

C-11. Fractal islands. The islands have been colored by height above sea level. (Image copyright © 1982 by Benoit B. Mandelbrot. Programming by Richard Voss. Used by permission.)

C-12. *Fractal Planetrise* shows several different uses of fractals. (Image copyright © 1982 by Benoit B. Mandelbrot. Programming by Richard Voss. Used by permission.)

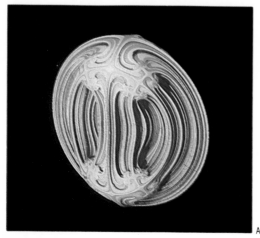

A

B

C-13A, B. Abstract three-dimensional fractals. (Images by Alan Norton. Used by permission of IBM Corp.)

C-14. *1984*. Motion blur on the balls and soft penumbras on the shadows are visible. The shadows and reflections are also motion-blurred. (Image by Tom Porter, Pixar.)

C-15. In this frame from the animation *Dino's Lunch* the motion blur of the fast ball as it flies into Dino's mouth is visible. (Image copyright © 1988 by Andrew Glassner, Computer Graphics Laboratory, University of North Carolina at Chapel Hill.)

C-16. A waterfall created with particles. (Image by Eric Grant, Computer Graphics Laboratory, University of North Carolina at Chapel Hill.)

C-17. Both the grass and the leaves in this forest were created with particle systems. (Image courtesy of Pixar.)

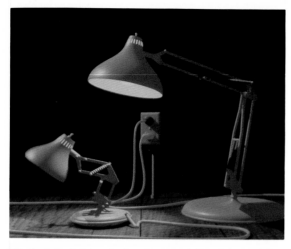

C-18. The shadows in this frame from *Luxo, Jr.* were created with the shadow maps in figure 11-8. (Image courtesy of Pixar.)

C-19. *Simulated Steel Mill* was created using radiosity techniques. Notice the smooth gradations of light throughout the scene. (Image by Stuart Feldman and John Wallace, Program of Computer Graphics, Cornell University.)

C-20. A ray-traced abstract image, showing reflections. (Image copyright © 1988 by Eric Haines, 3D/Eye Inc.)

C-21. Radiosity was used to create *Constructivist Museum.* Notice the subtle shading due to the louvers in the ceiling. (Image by Shenchang Eric Chen, Stuart I. Feldman, and Julie M. O'Brien, Program of Computer Graphics, Cornell University.)

C-22. A ray-traced realistic image, showing the use of many textures to add visual richness to the scene. (Image copyright © 1988 by Eric Haines, Program of Computer Graphics, Cornell University.)

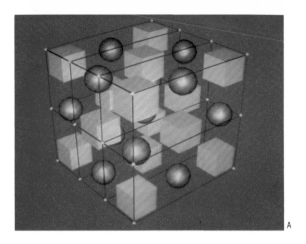

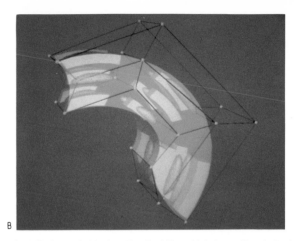

C-23A, B.   An example of free-form deformation. *A*: The model of spheres and boxes is placed into a flexible gel. The small spheres and sticks represent handles for manipulating the gel and the objects within. *B*: The model after the handles have been moved a bit. (Images courtesy of Tom Sederberg, Brigham Young University.)

C-24.   *Acer Graphics*, a maple tree. (Image by Jules Bloomenthal, copyright © New York Institute of Technology.)

C-25.   A model of ocean waves. (Image by Alain Fournier and Bill Reeves, courtesy of Pixar.)

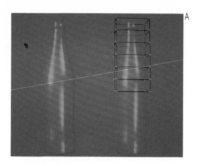

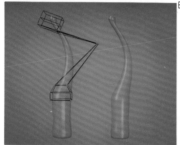

C-27. A dragon's head created with free-form modeling techniques. The eye was created with a spatial texture, and the flames were created with particle systems. (Image copyright © 1988 by David Forsey and the Computer Graphics Laboratory of the University of Waterloo.)

C-26A, B. An example of free-form deformation. *A*: a bottle is created, and placed into a flexible gel. *B*: The handles are moved into position, and the resulting bottle is rendered. (Images courtesy of Tom Sederberg, Brigham Young University.)

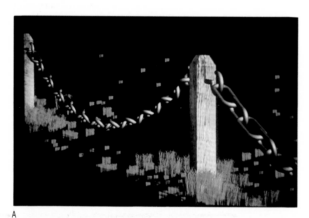

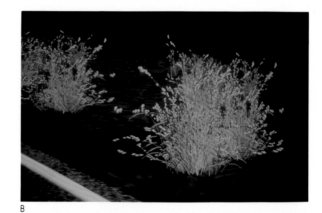

A

B

C

D

C-28A, B, C, D. A matting sequence. *A, B,* and *C* show the result of compositing twelve different individually rendered images. *D* is the result of *A* over *B* over *C*. (Images courtesy of Pixar.)

6 POLYGONS AND POLYGONAL MODELS

One of the most versatile modeling primitives is the *polygon*. Basically cut-out pieces of flat material, polygons can be combined to build (or approximate) almost any surface. They are simple to use and manipulate, and are capable of great modeling power. This chapter introduces polygons and provides some basic tools for working with them to make models.

This chapter also covers a variety of shading techniques primarily intended for polygonal models. These methods help you to make a flat, polygonal model appear to be a smooth surface, by carefully estimating the shape of that smooth surface from the underlying polygons.

POLYGONS

A polygon is like a cut-out piece of cardboard. More formally, a polygon is defined as a set of noncrossing straight lines joining coplanar points that enclose some single, convex area. This definition is really useful only once you already know what it means, so I will examine it piece by piece.

Drawing a polygon is like playing a connect-the-dots game. The idea is to draw straight lines from one dot to another in a specified sequence. Most connect-the-dots games are played on a sheet of paper. Perhaps it is obvious that all the points must then lie "flat" on the sheet of paper. Points that all lie in the same plane are said to be *coplanar* (or simply *planar*). The part of the definition about enclosing some single area is best shown by example, as in Fig. 6-1. Lines that make up a polygon are not allowed to cross each other.

Fig. 6-1 shows that a set of fewer than three points cannot enclose an area, so you need at least three points to make a polygon. This rule holds true for all polygons discussed in this chapter: A polygon must have three or more points. Each line in a polygon is called an *edge*. Each corner is called a *vertex* (plural *vertices*).

How To Model A Polygon

Suppose you have drawn a polygon on a sheet of paper and measured all the points, so you know the coordinates of each vertex. How do you describe this polygon to the computer so that you can use it in pictures? The answer is to type in the coordinates of the points in exactly the order you want them joined to produce the polygon. Listing the points in the correct order is very important: Fig. 6-2 shows that from a given set of points, an incorrect numbering can violate the definition of a polygon and lead to trouble, not to mention the wrong shape. It is necessary

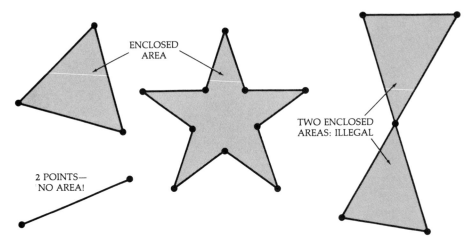

6-1. Some polygons and nonpolygons.

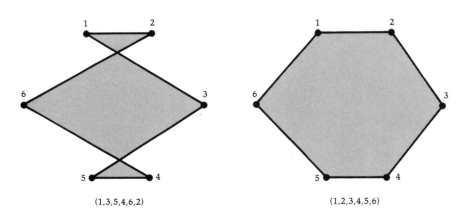

(1,3,5,4,6,2)

(1,2,3,4,5,6)

A. This numbering encloses three areas and makes an illegal polygon.

B. This is a legal numbering, or listing of the vertices.

6-2. The order in which the vertexes are specified determines the shape of the polygon.

to adhere to the definition given, because computers will always assume you mean what you type, and unless you and the computer agree about what you mean, then the results will not be what you wanted.

A polygon has two *faces*, which are often referred to as *front* and *back*. If you curl the fingers of your right hand in the direction of successive points in your point list (as in Fig. 6-3), your thumb will point out away from the front face of the polygon (some systems use the left-handed variation of this rule). The heel of your hand points to the back face. The definition of which face is the front and which is the back depends completely on the order in which you name the points, and on your system. When the polygons are drawn on the screen, you might see a mixture of front and back faces among the polygons there. I mention the distinction between the two faces because some polygon rendering systems treat *back-facing* polygons (those whose back is seen

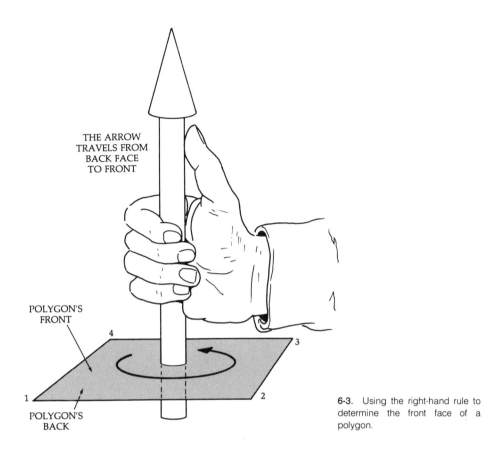

THE ARROW
TRAVELS FROM
BACK FACE
TO FRONT

POLYGON'S
FRONT

4

3

1

2

POLYGON'S
BACK

6-3. Using the right-hand rule to determine the front face of a polygon.

from a given point of view) in a special way to speed up the rendering of an image. In fact, in some situations back-facing polygons are not drawn at all!

The phrase in the definition about "a single, convex area" refers to the piece of the plane that lies within the polygon. A single area means that you can always put your pencil down in any point in the polygon and reach any other point in the polygon, never lifting your pencil from the paper and always staying inside the polygon (for the given definition, vertices and edges are not inside the polygon).

The "convex" requirement is also important for most systems. One formal meaning of *convex* is that given any two points within the polygon, you must be able to draw the straight line connecting those points and never go outside the polygon. If a polygon is not convex, then it is *concave* (in Fig. 6-7, the keyhole is a concave shape). An easy way to check if a particular polygon is convex or not is to imagine that all the vertices are nails in a wooden board. Stretch a rubber band around the polygon, and then let go. If the final shape of the rubber band is the same shape as the polygon, then it is convex; if there are any vertices not touched by the rubber band, then the polygon is concave.

When you compute the surface normal for a polygon, it is defined to point so that the normal comes out from the front face. This formalism helps in shading polygons, as you will see.

Almost all polygon rendering systems will accept and correctly render polygons that meet the working definition given. Some pieces of the definition may be relaxed for different systems and the polygons will still be drawn correctly. The next sections present a brief review of some nonstandard kinds of polygons.

Nonplanar Polygons

Part of the definition of a polygon stated earlier was that the points must all lie in the same plane. If that requirement is eliminated, then polygons may be *nonplanar*. Fig. 6-4A shows a planar polygon, and Fig. 6-4B shows that polygon being lifted out of the plane in which it was defined. Sometimes a computer will correctly render a nonplanar polygon, and sometimes it will not; it all depends on the particular program. It is worth experimenting with on your system, but the results will not be universal, or even consistent, unless the program was specifically designed to handle such a variant. The reason is that the mathematics most programs use to shade a polygon assume that it is planar. A program must be written with special mathematics to handle nonplanar polygons, or the results of shading a nonplanar polygon may be unpredictable.

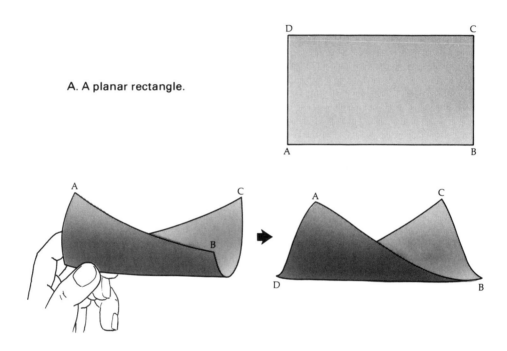

A. A planar rectangle.

B. A nonplanar bow tie.

C. Four points that cannot make a single planar polygon.

6-4. All polygons must normally be planar.

Self-Intersecting Polygons

Now suppose that the polygon encloses more than one area, which is the same as letting lines cross. Such a polygon is called *self-intersecting*.

Self-intersecting polygons can always be considered as a collection of polygons that fit the original definition, as Fig. 6-5 suggests. Any self-intersecting polygon can be remade out of nonintersecting polygons, but you may need to define a few new points. Self-intersecting polygons are primarily useful for saving computer time and storage, but at the expense of making things a bit more difficult for the modeler. So, although you may encounter self-intersecting polygons, the time you need to work them out properly usually exceeds the worth of the computer resources saved. They are also much less versatile when you decide to change your model and move some of the polygons about, so they are probably best avoided.

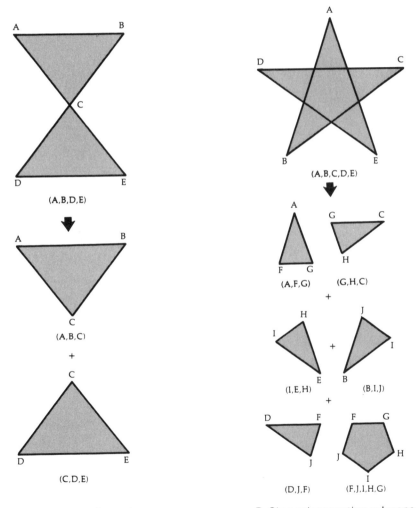

A. Two nonintersecting polygons.

B. Six nonintersecting polygons.

6-5. Self-intersecting polygons can be built out of nonintersecting polygons.

Concave Polygons

Some systems handle concave polygons with no problem. But even if your system does not, you can still manage. You can always turn a concave polygon into a collection of smaller, convex polygons. This transformation can sometimes be hard to do and often turns into quite a mess. Some of the convex-only systems provide an automatic program that will test all of your polygons to see if they are concave, and, if so, divide them up into many smaller triangles. This process is called *triangulation*. It might either return those triangles for you to use in your model, or it might insert them into your model for you, so you do not have to think about it.

Polygons with Holes

Some systems allow you to define a polygon within a polygon. In this case the inner polygon is defined to be a "cut-out" of the outer polygon, effectively creating a hole in the outer polygon. Fig. 6-6A shows an example of a window frame, which may be built in two different ways. Fig. 6-6B shows how to assemble the window by simply putting together pieces around the holes. Fig. 6-6C shows that in this case it is easier to build a single large polygon and cut four small holes within it with additional polygons. Usually this act of cutting holes must be explicitly indicated to the computer with a special command.

Not all polygon-rendering systems are sophisticated enough to deal with holes. Fig. 6-7 shows that although it can be a nuisance, a hole can always be improvised by building up an appropriate collection of pieces around the hole.

Some systems allow many holes in a single polygon, as in Fig. 6-6C. And, of course, once a hole has been cut out, objects behind the polygon may be seen. Also, other polygons may be placed inside the hole, which is often helpful for detail work and special effects. (Chapter 7 describes transparency mapping as an alternative to building explicit holes into your polygon.)

POLYGONAL SURFACES

Polygons are not really very useful by themselves. The real power of polygons comes when they are combined to make a more complex model.

There are two general kinds of models that can be built with polygons, and the difference between the two arises from how the results are to appear. Technically, a closed surface built out of polygons is called a *polyhedron* (plural *polyhedra*). Therefore everything built out of polygons is a polyhedron, but two classes can still be distinguished: flat objects and curved objects. (These terms refer to how you want the objects to look to the eye, not how they are built, because all polyhedra have flat faces.)

Flat objects are relatively easy to model with polygons. A typical flat object is a box or simple desk. All the parts of the object are flat sheets, and you can simply put many polygons in space in the right places to make one of these shapes.

But suppose you have only polygons at your disposal for modeling, and you want to make a model of a simple guitar case, as in Fig. 6-8 (forget about subtleties such as hinges and stitching, and concentrate on the shape of the case). The problem lies in making the case sides appear smoothly curved, using only polygons that are flat by definition. For a simpler approach, assume that you can use concave polygons. Then you can use a single polygon (although with many edges) for the bottom of the case, and another just like it for the top.

Now you can approximate the sides with many small polygons. How many will be enough? This is an important question. If you are modeling something flat, like a box or simple desk, then you want all of the surfaces to appear flat. But if you want to model something curved, like the

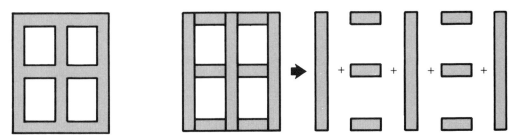

A. We want to model this window frame.

B. For a system without holes.

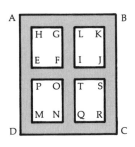

START POLYGON #1 ABCD
HOLE HGFE
HOLE LKJI
HOLE PONM
HOLE TSRQ
END POLYGON #1

C. For a system with holes.

6-6. Polygons with holes can be built out of polygons without holes.

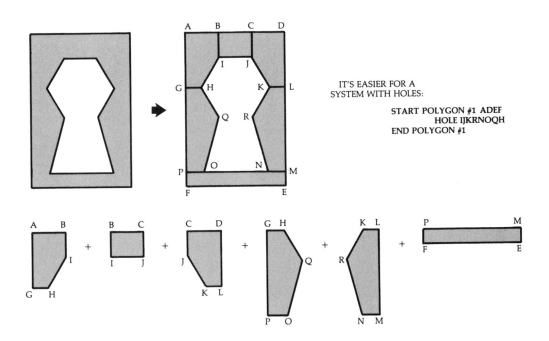

IT'S EASIER FOR A
SYSTEM WITH HOLES:

START POLYGON #1 ADEF
HOLE IJKRNOQH
END POLYGON #1

6-7. Even a concave hole can be created as long as all the polygons are convex.

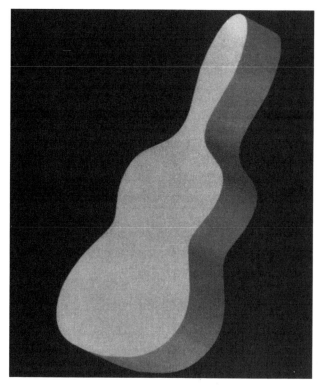

6-8. Picture of a simple guitar case.
(Image courtesy of Digital Arts.)

side of the guitar case, then you want the composite surface to appear curved. Ideally, you would not be able to see the individual polygons at all.

The most straightforward way to approach this problem is to use lots of polygons. But this solution can be cumbersome: the bigger the model, the longer it takes to draw. And you may find out that you still have not used enough polygons for some close-up scenes.

There is a special technique for taking a collection of polygons and drawing them as though they made up a curved surface. It is basically a trick, but it works. The polygons will still be in the model, and will be rendered as polygons, but the shading will be computed so that it looks as though the surface is curved. This technique is described in detail later in this chapter; here I will show how to prepare your model so that the smoothing trick will work.

You only need to add one more piece of information to your model to make smoothing work: *vertex normals*. The surface normals described in Chapter 4 are perpendicular to the face of each polygon, and are properly called *face normals*. Where two or more faces share a vertex, the computer can automatically compute a vertex normal, which is simply the average of the normals of all the polygons that share that vertex. The normal of each polygon counts equally in this average. Fig. 6-9 shows an example of computing a vertex normal.

When you want to render a polygon as though it were part of a smooth surface, give the computer the polygon itself plus the vertex normal for each vertex of the polygon. Of course, any other polygons that share one of those vertices will pass in the same vertex normal when they get rendered. The surface will appear smooth, even when it is not, because the vertex normals match where polygons touch.

Note how vertex normals get calculated. A good intuition is that the vertex normal usually (although not always) would be the normal to the surface at that vertex, assuming all the flat polygons in that neighborhood got "smoothed out" into a single smooth surface.

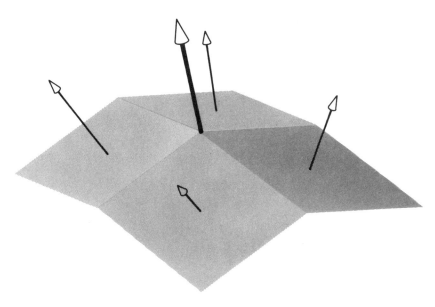

6-9. A vertex normal is created by averaging together the surface normals of all polygons that share that vertex.

POLYGON SHADING

A variety of shading models are appropriate for use with polygons. Two steps occur in each of these models: a preparation step and a shading step. The preparation step is usually unique to polygons, and it handles the special smooth-shading trick I mentioned earlier in this chapter. The second step, which actually calculates the shading, is more generic and may be applied to any kind of surface.

Generally, each of the different polygon shading models has two names. One name is descriptive of the process and usually has something to do with the mathematics of the shading. The other name honors a person who had ideas fundamental to that shading process (this is standard practice in many fields; consider the volt—Count Alessandro Volta—and Pavlovian reactions—Ivan Petrovich Pavlov).

Lambert (Faceted) Shading

One technique used with polygonal models is often called *Lambert* (or *faceted*) shading; objects shaded according to this scheme usually appear to be made up out of many little tiles, or facets. Of course, this appearance is what you would expect from a flat polygonal model, and sometimes it is exactly what you want.

Remember that in order to find out how much light is arriving at a point on a surface, you need to find the surface normal at that point. Lambert shading uses the face surface normal for all points on the polygon. This approach makes sense, because a polygon is flat. Using the same normal for every point on the polygon means that every point on the polygon is shaded just like every other point. Thus, the entire polygon has the same shade. (Fig. 5-5 shows an example of a model shaded with Lambert shading.)

Lambert shading is the quickest and (from the computer's point of view) the easiest of the shading techniques in popular use in computer graphics. It is commonly used when a modeler or animator wants to check the shape or movement of a model but does not need a lot of realism and wants quick results. For final production, a more sophisticated shading model is usually used.

Recall that the surface normal of a polygon is defined to point away from the front face. It is often useful to shade only those polygons whose front or back face points towards the light source, leaving the opposite face black, transparent, or unshaded.

Most programs that use Lambert shading do not do a very good job of handling highlights (see Fig. 6-13A, in which a very sharp highlight is located right on one of the vertices of a sphere). The problem is that no polygon ever "sees" the highlight directly. The four polygons that share the vertex that picks up the highlight each receive a small, equal amount of shading, but the bright spot that indicates a highlight is missing.

Smooth-Shading Techniques

The next two shading techniques under discussion try to remove the faceted appearance of Lambert-shaded objects by proceeding as if the polygonal model being shaded were just an approximation of a smoother object. For example, a sphere can be approximated polygonally, as illustrated in Fig. 6-10. The polygonal appearance can be reduced in this case by adding more polygons, but the problem is only diminished at the cost of a larger model and slower rendering, and not really resolved. Furthermore, in many models it is very difficult to arbitrarily add more polygons where the model does not look quite right.

Smooth-shading techniques try to eliminate the faceted appearance by smoothing the surface of the object. It would be difficult for the computer to create a new, smoother model, so instead the computer attempts to shade the existing model as if it were smoother.

Lambert-shaded objects look faceted because each entire polygon is shaded with the surface normal. When you use smooth-shading techniques, you pretend that the polygonal model is really curved. In a curved model, the normal would change as you moved about on the surface. So smooth-shading techniques change the normal as they shade different points on the same polygon. Fig. 6-11 shows the results: in both parts the objects share exactly the same surface description. Note the straight edges where the cones meet in Fig. 6-11B. The surfaces are still flat polygons; they just look smooth.

The different smoothing techniques produce pictures with varying amounts of realism, based on the amount of work the computer must do, and, consequently, on the time the user must wait to receive a completed picture.

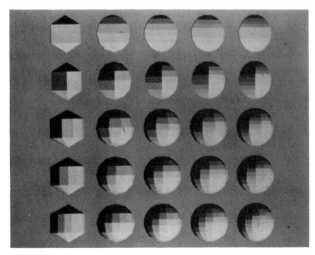

6-10. Using different numbers of polygons to approximate a sphere.

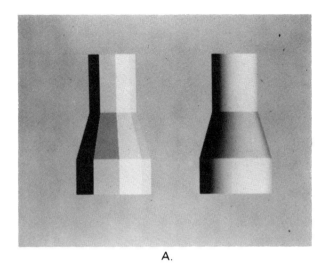

A.

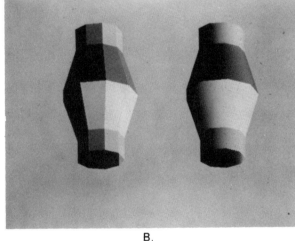

B.

6-11. Smooth shading can help make objects appear rounder. On the left of each image the object is Lambert shaded; on the right, the same model is shaded with Gouraud shading. Notice that the silhouette in B still gives away the polygonal model.

Gouraud (Smooth) Shading

Gouraud (pronounced Guh-roe'), or *shade-interpolating*, shading is one technique for making a polygonal model appear smooth. The basic idea behind Gouraud shading is that shading is computed at every vertex instead of at every polygon. The shades at the vertices of a polygon are smoothed and blended across its surface, which effectively smoothes the polygonal model. Fig. 6-12 shows conceptually what Gouraud shading does to shade a polygon.

It is strange that this new shading of polygons causes the entire model to look smoothed. Note that the surface itself is not changed in any way. It is still composed of polygons. But by blending the shading across the surface of each polygon, Gouraud shading creates the illusion of a smooth object.

How does Gouraud shading compute the shade at a vertex? Remember that the normal at a vertex is the average of all the normals that share that vertex. So Gouraud shading simply

6-12. The Gouraud technique shades a polygon by interpolating the shade at the vertexes across the face.

computes the shade for the vertex using the "average" normal that is already there.

Gouraud shading relieves most of the crisp borders around polygons that are so evident in Lambert-shaded pictures. Because it may be efficiently programmed, it is not much more difficult from the computer's standpoint, so it is relatively fast.

Gouraud shading is an improvement over Lambert shading, but it still has its problems. You often still can see where polygons touch each other, although it is usually less noticeable. The effect is particularly visible when the model has a high degree of curvature, such as the end of a fishhook.

Another disadvantage of Gouraud shading is that highlights can look peculiar. Consider Fig. 6-13, where a light source has been placed so that the center of a very sharp highlight is located right on one of the vertices of a sphere. If you compute the intensity of light at each vertex and then blend as Gouraud shading instructs, you get the shading shown in Fig. 6-13B, which looks odd if the objects are spheres. The problem arises from blending the light intensity across the face of the polygon. As a result, the shape of the polygon influences how the shading appears, which gives away the underlying polygonal model that you are trying to hide.

Gouraud shading can only give highlights when they happen to fall on a vertex. Even then, highlights often come out blurred or distorted. Another problem of Gouraud shading is that it does not work very well with local light sources.

Phong (Normal Interpolating) Shading

Another shading technique that can handle local light sources and highlights in a more convincing manner is called *Phong* (pronounced Fong), or *normal interpolating*, shading. In contrast to Gouraud shading, which finds the surface normal at each vertex, shades that vertex, and then blends the shades across the polygon, Phong shading finds the surface normal at each vertex, and then blends the surface normal over the face of the polygon, comparing it to the light vector and computing a new shade for every point on the screen, as shown in Fig. 6-14. This increased complexity makes Phong shading a much slower process, but results in superior-looking pictures.

Fig. C-13C shows how well Phong shading works. For every point on the polygon the surface normal is found by interpolating all the vertices in the polygon. Then diffuse and specular shading

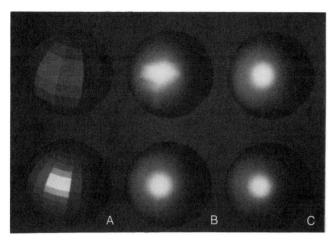

6-13. A comparison of shading techniques. The left column shows Lambert shading, the middle column shows Gouraud shading, and the right column shows Phong shading. Each row of spheres was built from exactly the same model and light source. Note the poor highlights on the Gouraud spheres, and the Mach bands in the upper row.

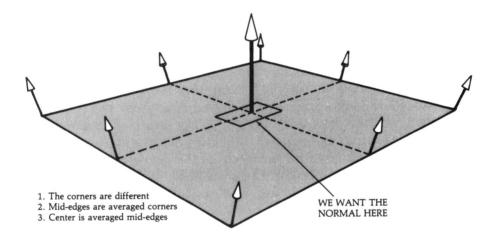

1. The corners are different
2. Mid-edges are averaged corners
3. Center is averaged mid-edges

WE WANT THE
NORMAL HERE

6-14. Phong shading interpolates the normal from the vertex normals on a point-by-point basis before shading.

components are computed for that normal. Although it is the slowest method discussed so far, Phong shading is often the standard shading model employed in realistic three-dimensional rendering systems today.

Problems with Smoothing Polygonal Models

Polygonal models are an excellent technique for three-dimensional modeling. They allow exact surface descriptions (of polygonal objects), they are easy to define and manipulate, they are easy to change, and they offer a high level of realism when an appropriate shading technique is used. But they do present some problems. Some of these problems come from the shading techniques, others from the fact that polygons are by definition bounded by straight lines, and some are a result of the mechanisms of the human eye.

Consider the outside edges, or silhouette, of an object rendered with Phong shading. It may look quite smooth and acceptable at first glance, but there is a problem at the outside edges (see Fig. 6-13C). The edges are not really round. Objects in high contrast or in extreme close-up will exhibit this effect, which can ruin the illusion of reality. The only way to alleviate this problem is to add more polygons to the object description before rendering.

Another problem is a result of the averaging of surface normals of polygons to compute a vertex normal as in Phong and Gouraud shading. Fig. 6-15 shows several polygons that clearly point in different directions. The surface normal at each polygon is indicated. Also indicated are the surface normals at each vertex. Note that all the vertices have the same averaged surface normal. Thus, Gouraud shading would assign the same shade to each vertex, causing the whole object to be one shade. Phong shading does no better. Since all the surface normals at the vertices are the same, interpolating between two equal surface normals always give the same surface normal, and the shade assigned to that point will also always be the same.

This problem can be corrected as shown in Fig. 6-16, by adding some smaller polygons at the edges where the big polygons meet.

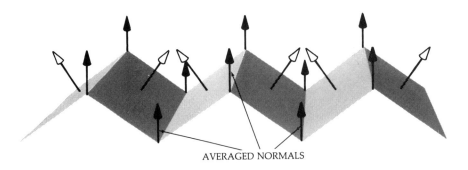

AVERAGED NORMALS

6-15. All the averaged normals point in the same direction, so shading them would result in the whole object having the same shade.

6-16. Inserting more polygons into the model from Fig. 6-15 can help make the shading more accurate.

Mach Bands

The last problem that needs to be discussed here, although it is common to all computer-generated images, is usually most visible in images built from polygonal models. The human eye is particularly sensitive to contrast. Given a scene of smoothly changing colors, the eye will easily pick up any region of rapid brightness change. This sensitivity gives rise to an effect called *Mach bands*, illustrated in Fig. 6-17.

The figure shows two gray-scale wedges; next to each wedge is a plot of the intensity of each line, which is constant across the line. Look at the gray scales where the rate of change suddenly increases or decreases (that is, where the plot suddenly changes direction). You will perceive a lighter or darker region right at the transition point. This change in color is an artifact of human perception. (Some people hypothesize that we see Mach bands because it is helpful to be able to see edges very quickly in a complex environment. Consider a leafy jungle—one would want to see any approaching animals very quickly and clearly!) Mach bands are not caused by a fault in the process of modeling with polygons; they occur in the real world as well. For instance, note how easy it is to find places in a rainbow where the colors appear to change quickly, even though you know they change smoothly across the spectrum.

Although Mach bands are most noticeable in Gouraud-shaded objects, they are also perceptible in some Phong-shaded images. Mach bands give away the edges of the polygons in a smooth-shaded model. You can try to suppress Mach bands by using more polygons where your model changes curvature. Remember, it is not the amount of curvature that causes Mach bands, but sudden, radical changes in curvature. Also remember that Mach bands are strictly a visual phenomenon; if you change the background of your picture, or view it in different circumstances, Mach bands may appear, disappear, or change in intensity.

6-17. Mach bands occur where the rate of change of brightness suddenly changes. Next to each wedge is an intensity plot. Notice the artifacts in the wedges where the plot has a sudden change.

SUMMARY

Perhaps the easiest surface for building models is the polygon. A polygon is a set of noncrossing straight lines joining coplanar points that enclose some single, convex area.

To create a polygon you merely list the points that form the vertices, in the order in which they are to be joined. Successive pairs of points form edges. Once defined, the polygon will have a front face and a back face. The orientation of the faces is found by curling the fingers of your right hand in the direction of successive points; your thumb points away from the front face.

To determine if a polygon is convex, imagine a nail at every vertex. Then stretch a rubber band around the nails and let go; if there are any nails not touched by the rubber band then the polygon is concave.

Some systems allow variations in the strict definition of polygon given above; such systems allow a polygon to be nonplanar, self-intersecting, concave, or to enclose holes. Any polygon that can be built from from one of these alternative definitions can always be exactly duplicated with one or more standard polygons.

When several polygons are combined to form an object, that object is called a polyhedon. Polyhedra are typically used for modeling surfaces with flat sides, such as a box or desk. But because polygons are so powerful and easy to use, techniques have been developed to draw a polyhedral model as though it was really a smooth, curvy model. These techniques are applied when shading is computed for the model.

Every planar polygon has a single normal, perpendicular to its surface (usually the normal points away from the front face). This is called the face normal. When multiple polygons share a single vertex, the face normals for all the polygons may be averaged together, to form a vertex normal at that vertex. Often this vertex normal is the normal at that point to the surface that would be formed by smoothing the underlying polygonal model.

Lambert (or faceted) shading uses only the face normals. Since every point on a polygon has the same face normal, each point receives almost the same shading. This causes the model to appear to be made of flat surfaces. Though the fastest technique in this chapter, faceted shading usually misses highlights.

Gouraud (or shade-interpolating) shading attempts to smooth the appearance of a polygonal model by blending shades across the polygon. When a polygon is to be drawn, each vertex is shaded using the lighting model and the vertex normal. The colors computed at each vertex are blended over the face of the polygon. Gouraud shading will only include highlights if they happen to fall on a vertex; even then, the highlight will usually have a shape that gives away the shapes of the polygons in the model.

Phong (or normal-interpolating) shading attempts to make a polygonal model appear smoother by interpolating the vertex normals across the face of the polygon. When a point needs to be shaded, a new surface normal is built at that point from a combination of the vertex normals. Then that point is shaded with the newly-built normal. Phong shading is far slower than either Lambert or Gouraud shading, but it is much more realistic. Phong shading handles highlights much better than the other two models, and does a better (though still imperfect) job at hiding the underlying polygonal model.

All three shading techniques share the problem that the silhouette of a polygonal surface is not smoothed, and this can give away the underlying polygonal model if the polygons are big enough to be noticeable.

The human eye is very sensitive to changes in the rate of change of shading. The eye picks out these places and perceives Mach bands, regions of light or dark at the boundaries between polygons, where the rate of change of shading changes. One way to suppress Mach bands is to add more polygons to an image where sudden changes of curvature occur.

7 TEXTURES

There are two important visual effects missing from the discussion so far: textures and shadows. Textures give visual interest to shapes—the stitched thread on a baseball, the grain in a piece of wood, the lines on a ruled sheet of paper. Shadows on the other hand tell you where things are—from the shape of a shadow you can tell how near something is to a light, and from the shadows themselves you can learn which objects are in front of which others. This chapter discusses textures; shadows are covered in Chapter 11.

Much more than just paint on surfaces, textures are a powerful modeling technique. For example, a texture can indicate transparency at every point on a surface, or it can specify which of several materials were used to build a surface. A texture is a description of a surface that can tell everything about it except its basic shape.

In the real world most objects are textured. In computer graphics a texture is something that modifies the appearance of an object, or even (on a small scale) alters its shape. For example, an orange can be considered a sphere with a bumpy texture on it. A relief globe of the earth is marked with color to indicate political boundaries, and has a bumpy texture to indicate mountains.

It would be difficult to directly model these kinds of detail onto a surface. Rather than model detail explicitly, you create a texture and apply it to the surface.

PICTURE MAPPING

One of the easiest and most popular uses of textures is to paint a picture directly onto a surface, like applying wallpaper or a decal. To apply a picture to a surface, you first specify the picture you want drawn. This picture is commonly called a *texture map*, or simply *texture*. The process of applying a texture is called *texture mapping*, or *texturing*. An example of texturing is shown in Fig. 7-1. You tell the computer to which surface the texture is to be applied (the billboard on the left). Part of this process involves explicitly telling the computer where and how the texture should be drawn. The result is texture upon the surface, as in the right-hand billboard. In this example flat texture is applied to a flat surface, but you will see later that almost any surface, flat or curved, can be textured.

Just putting a picture on top of a surface is called *picture mapping*, or *picture texturing*. It will be helpful for you to understand exactly what is happening when you apply a picture texture, because that understanding will serve as a basis for using other kinds of texturing. The first step is to provide the texture map, or picture, which is a grid of values, like a picture in a frame buffer (in fact, many people use textures that were either hand-drawn or digitized into a frame buffer).

7-1. Picture of a billboard, before (left) and after (right) a texture has been applied. (Image courtesy of Digital Arts.)

Suppose you have the texture of Fig. 7-2A. You need to identify points on the texture. A good approach is to put a two-dimensional coordinate system on the texture, for example, lines of latitude and longitude. This is a fine idea, but "latitude" and "longitude" are rather unwieldy names for the axes. And you don't want to use X and Y; those labels have already been used for the three-dimensional coordinate system where you build your models, and using them again in a different context would be confusing. The names for the texture axes are conventionally called U and V; U is the horizontal axis and V is the vertical axis. In some systems the origin is in the lower-left corner of the textures, as in Fig. 7-2B, and in some it is the upper left, as Fig. 7-2C. Almost always the values of u and v are 0 at the origin, and 1 at the opposite corner (the points are named in the order (u,v), so $(1,0)$ is the lower-right corner in Fig. 7-2B).

If you want to map this picture onto a polygon, you need to specify the values of the texture at the vertices of the polygon. This activity is called *parameterizing the surface*, since you are specifying texture coordinates (or parameters) for the surface. After a polygon has been *parameterized*, the texture will be appropriately stretched to fit the polygon. For example, Fig. 7-3 shows a textured polygon with four different parameterizations. Compare these coordinates with the texture itself in Fig. 7-2A and you can get an idea of how the texture is manipulated to fit the surface. You will probably want to do some experiments like this on your own system because the actual mechanisms for warping the texture can vary from system to system. Some systems do not allow you to assign arbitrary parameters to all the vertices; in such cases you usually get to pick the texture coordinates at only three or four vertices, and the computer fills in the rest.

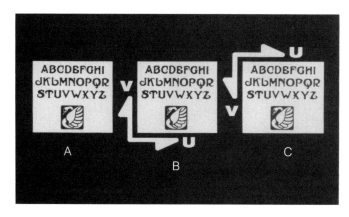

7-2. A texture and its coordinate systems. *Left*, the texture; *Middle*, that texture in a left-handed coordinate system; *Right*, a right-handed system. (Image courtesy of Digital Arts.)

7-3. A texture map and a polygon. Note how the texture is automatically distorted to match the parameterization. The left-handed (U,V) parameterizations for each polygon, reading clockwise from lower-left, are:

(0, 1), (0, 0), (1, 0), (1, 1)
(.6, 1), (.5, .8), (.6, .8), (.7, .9)
(.3, 0), (.7, 0), (.7, .7), (.3, .7)
(0, 1), (.2, .1), (.7, 0), (1, .3)

(Image courtesy of Digital Arts.)

Since the texture itself only has data from (0,0) to (1,1), you might think that you are restricted to these values as parameters on the surface of the polygon. But there is a handy wrap-around convention that proves useful when modeling with textures. If you specify a coordinate bigger than 1 or less than 0, extra copies of the texture are placed side-by-side and top-to-bottom with the original until one copy contains your texture coordinates; the result is the color that is used. For example, Fig. 7-4A shows a texture, and Fig. 7-4B shows how to find the color used if you specify (−2.3, 1.8). The computer does not actually replicate the texture, but that is the effect. If the texture is carefully designed so that opposite sides merge seamlessly, then you can put many copies of the texture on the surface without noticing the replication, as shown in Fig. 7-4C.

To see how picture mapping works in practice, suppose you are shading the polygon shown in Fig. 7-3, and you want to find the shade at a particular point. Now recall that part of your description of the polygon's material included colors for the surface color and body color, as well as reflectivity and transparency. For simplicity here, assume that the polygon is opaque, so you are only interested in the surface color. But rather than use the color specified for the polygon, you instead find the texture's (u,v) coordinates at that point, and then look up those coordinates in the texture. You get the color at that point, and that is the color you use to compute the reflected light. In effect you have completely ignored the surface color you specified with the polygon when you defined its material; the texture map specifies the color to use on a point-by-point basis.

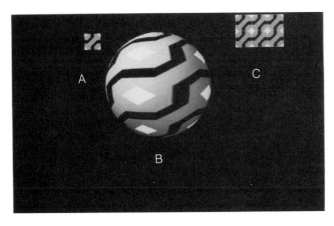

7-4. Texture values outside the range (0,0) to (1,1) can be found by replicating the texture until it contains the desired point. (Image courtesy of Digital Arts.)

One reason to keep the polygon's original surface color in your model is to use it to *modulate* the texture map. For example, suppose you have a model for a book and you want to texture-map the front cover. Your texture might consists of black writing on a white background. If you render the cover using a white polygon, you will get black writing on a white background, just like the texture itself. But if you render that cover texture onto a green polygon, it would be like viewing the texture through a green piece of glass: you get black writing on a green background. This technique is convenient for using one texture in many places and having it look a little different each time. Modulation is something you need to specify as an option; normally the color of the object is ignored when picture mapping.

TRANSPARENCY MAPPING

I have shown that a texture map can be used to specify the color at each point on a surface. Another interesting use of a texture is to control the transparency of the surface, a method naturally enough called *transparency mapping*. Such a map might look like a picture, but the computer would not interpret the contents of the map as colors. It would interpret them as values that describe the transparency of the surface at each point. For example, Fig. 7-5A shows one way to make a transparency map. In this system, each entry in the map may be a number between 0 (meaning fully opaque) and 255 (meaning fully transparent). Values in between these extremes represent in-between transparencies.

Fig. 7-5B shows a transparency map applied to a surface.

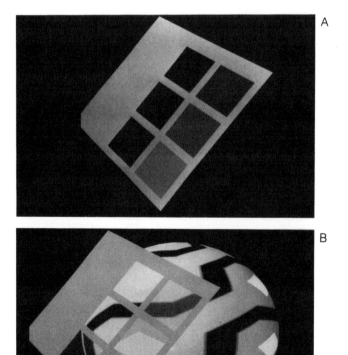

A

B

7-5. An example of transparency mapping. (Image courtesy of Digital Arts.)

MATERIAL MAPPING

The two types of texture mapping already described, picture mapping and transparency mapping, are really just special forms of the more general idea of *material mapping*. Recall the eleven parameters necessary to describe the material properties for a material (though not all eleven are necessary for all substances):

Reflection: surface color, diffuse coefficient, specular coefficient, surface roughness coefficient, metallic coefficient, and

Transparency: body color, body density, diffuse coefficient, specular coefficient, internal roughness coefficient, index of refraction.

Nine of these properties are just single values; the other two are colors. Picture mapping is a technique for specifying just the surface color at each point on the surface. Transparency mapping is a technique for specifying just the amount of transparency at each point. In both cases, the other parameters remain unchanged.

However, you can use eleven different maps if you like, one for each parameter. In fact, using several textures simultaneously is a popular technique.

An even more powerful technique is to use one map to *multiplex*, or choose, among several different complete materials. For example, suppose that you wanted to make a picture of a birthday present wrapped in fancy paper. You decide that your model will be a white box, and you'll use texture to make the wrapping paper. The paper you decide on has alternating stripes of very different material: one set of strips is a shiny, silver-colored foil, and the other set is fuzzy blue felt.

The important point is that the two different stripes have very different optical properties. Both are opaque, but one is almost completely diffuse (the felt), while the other is almost completely specular (the foil). Additionally, both have different colors, and if the felt is a bit reflective then they'll have different reflective highlight values as well. You could make your wrapping out of three different maps: one each for color, reflectivity, and reflective highlight.

Using three separate textures would work, but it would not be very easy to change. If you wanted to widen the stripes, or use curvy stripes instead of straight ones, then you would have to modify all three texture maps.

A more powerful approach uses a single *material texture*. Such a texture can be used in several different ways. In the example, you want to have two different kinds of texture on the present. So you specify the two textures to the system and assign them the numbers 0 and 1. Then you build a material texture map; each point in the map contains either a 0 or 1, telling which material is to be used to specify the property of that point. When the computer shades a point, it first consults the material texture at that point to find the correct material to use, and then uses that material. To change the stripes you simply change the pattern of 0s and 1s in the material map.

You can use more than two materials if you like. Suppose that your material texture map can hold values from 0 to 255. Then 256 different kinds of materials could be used on just one surface. Alternatively, you can say that 0 represents material 0, 255 represents material 1, and values between 0 and 255 represent mixtures of the two materials. So, using a material map and a model of a tuba, you can render that tuba as if it was made out of a new material composed of fifty percent wood and fifty percent metal, smoothly blended together!

Fig. C-3C shows a plain white box, and a Fig. C-3A shows a material map for a bee inlay. The result is Fig. C-3B, a box apparently made of ivory and two different kinds of wood. Notice that when the material map selects the background wood, the system then finds the wood texture corresponding to that material.

BUMP MAPPING

The last few sections show how you can apply a texture map to a surface and modify any or all of its material properties. But the surface itself does not change. There are actually two ways to apply a texture to a surface that seem to change its shape. I say ''seem'' to change its shape, because only one technique actually deforms the surface. Here we will look at a technique that does not actually change the shape of the surface, but only makes it look changed. This technique is called *bump mapping*, and it is basically a trick, an illusion.

Recall that the shading of a surface is intimately connected with the surface normal. The more the normal at a surface location points towards a light source, the brighter is the illumination arriving at that location from that light. Why does a smoothly shaded sphere look round? Its silhouette is just a circle, so that does not give any clue to its being a three-dimensional shape. The clues come from how the shading changes across the surface of the sphere, and those changes result from how the surface normal changes.

Now suppose that you want to shade a particular location on a smooth sphere. Interrupt the shading process right after computing the surface normal at each location. Take the surface normal, and give it a little nudge in some particular direction. Then finish the shading process as before. The result is that the surface of the sphere will look as though it were bumpy, since the shading appears to be that of a bumpy surface. Fig. 7-6A shows a smoothly shaded sphere. Fig. 7-6C shows a texture map; the amount by which the normal is redirected at each point is derived from the texture value at that point. Figs. 7-6B and 7-6D show the result of this normal manipulation on the sphere. In both cases the texture is interpreted as indicating height. In Fig. 7-6B a base value of black was used, so that a higher altitude is indicated by a whiter pixel; in Fig. 7-6D this interpretation is reversed.

This kind of texture is called a *bump* (or *perturbation*) *map*, because it describes the bumps on a surface. When the bump map is applied to a surface, you usually have control over how high the bumps are to appear. Fig. 7-7 shows four bump-mapped spheres; the map was scaled so that about a quarter of the texture map covers the sphere. In Fig. 7-7A and C the bump scaling factor is small, so the surface looks only slightly rough. In Figs. 7-7B and D, the bump scaling factor increases significantly. The bumps in A and B look like intaglio—depressions. By scaling the bumps with a negative number the reverse effect is obtained in C and D, where high spots become low spots, like relief.

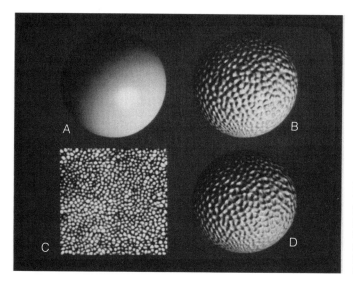

7-6. Bump mapping on a sphere. The original sphere is in the upper left. The bump map is in the lower left. Interpreting the white regions as hills over a black terrain gives the result in the upper-right; reversing the interpretation gives the lower-right image.

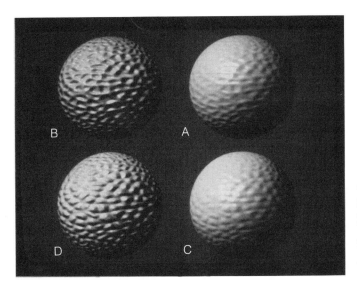

7-7. The scale of the bumps may be changed to control the amount of apparent distortion of the surface. These spheres are textured with only a piece of the bump map in Figure 7-6. The spheres on the left show deep bumps; the spheres on the right show shallow bumps.

The texture used for Figs. 7-6 and 7-7 was originally a very stark black-and-white image, like that shown in Fig. 7-8A. Using this map directly would have made the bumps appear to be channels with sharp walls. So the map was blurred first, as shown in Fig. 7-8B. Blurring a bump map before you use it is a common trick to give the edges of the bumps some width, and thus make them a little more noticeable.

You can use any texture as a bump map. Since you are adjusting, or perturbing, a surface normal, bump mapping is sometimes also called *normal perturbation mapping*. Fig. 7-9 shows a face mapped onto a sphere, where again white indicates height. The result has some interesting characteristics from the combination of shading and shape in the original photograph.

The advantage to using bump maps is that they are generally fast, and they are able to model all kinds of surface detail without your really doing it. Imagine how many polygons it would take to model a golf ball with real dimples! If your surface variations are small, then bump mapping is just what you need.

But problems arise if you try to model big changes in a surface with bump mapping; for example, the silhouette. Since you are not really changing the surface shape, only how it is shaded,

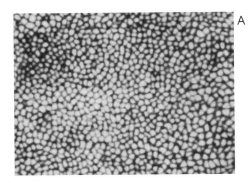 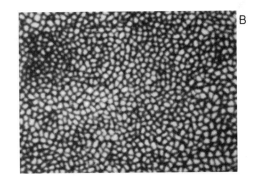

7-8. The bump map, both before (left) and after (right) blurring. Blurring a bump map helps spread the bumps out, giving them more visual interest.

7-9. Any image may be used as a bump map.

the silhouette does not change. A sphere, no matter what texture you apply to it, still has a circular outline. Fig. 7-10B shows a "backwards" golf ball, with rather large dimples that are raised rather than sunken. Notice that the silhouette is still a circle, which looks odd and gives away the fact that there is something wrong here. And because the silhouette doesn't change, shadows cast by or upon this object will also be free of the surface distortion.

When you want to model small features on a surface, bump mapping works well. But when the features get too big, bump mapping fails because the unchanged silhouette gives the technique away. Incidentally, it is not just the silhouette that fails when surface features are large. Look toward the outside of Fig. 7-10B, but within the sphere, and you will see that the dimples near the edge fail to hide the surface behind, as they would if they were really there. When the dimples are small you do not notice that; when they are big, it begins to look strange.

DISPLACEMENT MAPPING

To actually distort a surface, you may use the technique of *displacement mapping*. A displacement map contains a single value. It is consulted at the same time in the process that a bump map would be consulted: just after computing the surface normal. But a displacement map specifies that the bit of surface that is being shaded should be moved before it is drawn! The movement is performed in the direction of the surface normal, and the amount is given by the displacement map. Thus, the silhouette changes, and shadows cast by and upon this surface show the change. Fig. C-3 shows displacement mapping used to round the corners on a box, and to pull in a strip around the outside to represent the gap between lid and box.

The drawback to the technique is that displacement mapping really only works in systems that are built especially to give you this kind of power; many computer graphics systems are not designed that way. And since displacement maps move surfaces around, it becomes difficult to determine which surfaces are in front of others. Displacement maps are mostly useful for small-scale movement of the surface. Because of how they work, big displacements can look odd, and might even cause your object to develop cracks and gaps in its surface. You should not be surprised if you do not have displacement mapping in your system; you are probably getting your pictures somewhat faster than if you did (and not just some of the time, but all the

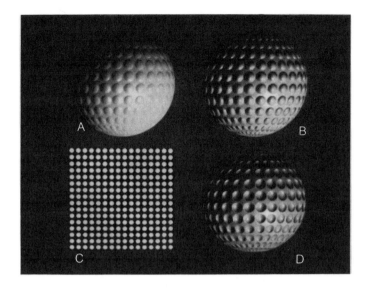

7-10. A golf ball may be simulated with a bump map of dimples. Look closely at the bumps on the sphere; they do not really change in appearance as they would if the sphere were really dimpled. Also notice the silhouette of the upper-left sphere; despite large apparent bumps, the silhouette is still a circle!

time). If you do have displacement mapping, you may find it a powerful tool for creating small but real surface distortions that you don't want to actually model with explicit surfaces.

CASCADING TEXTURES

Sometimes it is useful to have one texture modify another texture, rather than modify a surface's material properties. For example, suppose you want to draw one side of a house from the outside, where the wall contains two windows. One picture map contains the siding on the house, while the other contains the inside of the house seen through the windows. By *cascading textures* (or applying one texture to another), you can apply a transparency map to the siding picture, to make that picture transparent where the windows are, and also a transparency map to the "inside of the house" picture so that that picture is invisible except at the windows.

Another useful combination of textures is to use one after the other. For example, you might use a bump map to move a surface normal, and then use a displacement map to adjust the surface along this new normal, giving you more freedom in how the shape is manipulated.

Still another use of cascading textures is to override defaults. Suppose you wanted to wrap a birthday present as described before, but you wanted to write the words "Happy Birthday" on the package in red paint. You could make a new map that contains 0 wherever you want writing, and a 1 wherever you want wrapping. This is really just another material map the computer consults before consulting the material map describing the wrapping. When this map is 0, the system uses the "red paint" material; otherwise it consults the wrapping map as before, and selects either the foil or the felt as appropriate.

MULTIPLE TEXTURES

It is often very effective to use multiple textures on a single object, as shown in Fig. C-3. You can also use multiple textures to add complexity to an image. Fig. C-4 shows bump mapping on the bark of vines, and picture mapping on the leaves. The petals are Gouraud-shaded with color interpolation in addition to shade.

SPACE TEXTURES

So far I have discussed textures as two-dimensional maps somehow wrapped onto three-dimensional objects. That wrapping model is good for all sorts of things, such as writing on a piece of paper. But for other situations, this kind of "gift wrapping" of texture is not a good solution.

Suppose that you want to make a wooden form consisting of a block of wood with a sphere on top. Your first step is to model a block and then a sphere. You then need to get a wood texture. So you digitize the image of a piece of wood, and you have a lovely picture of wood grain. But if you wrap that single image of wood grain around the block and the sphere, you'll get the results shown in Fig. C-8A. There are two problems with this approach. The first is that the grain obviously looks bad on each individual object. The second problem is that when you bring these two objects together, the texture will not flow smoothly from one object to the other, and the form will not look as if it were carved from a single piece of wood. This problem of *texture alignment* is difficult enough when you have two objects touching, but the problem becomes almost impossible when there are many objects.

The solution to the texture-alignment problem is to use a *space* (or *spatial*) *texture*. In some ways, a spatial texture is even easier to use than the texture maps already described. A spatial texture is a three-dimensional table that contains a texture value for every point in space. To texture a point with a two-dimensional texture map, you first find the (u,v) parameters on the surface at that point, and then look up those coordinates on a two-dimensional map to find the texture value. To shade with a spatial texture, take the (x,y,z) coordinates of the point in space and look them up directly in the texture.

Any texturing operation can be done with values from a spatial texture rather than from a two-dimensional texture map.

For example, consider a spatial material texture. Imagine a block composed of sheets of laminated wood. These are parallel sheets of different kinds of wood of varying thickness, stacked up one on the other; each layer is a different material. Now suppose you build a three-dimensional table, where each point in the table indicates which material is present at that point. To shade a point, then just look it up directly in the table and use that material value. Fig. C-8B shows the result on the block and sphere. Fig. C-8C shows how several primitive surfaces can be combined into a single form where the wood grain flows smoothly between the surfaces.

This technique neatly eliminates the problems of getting textures to merge and of getting the wood grain not to look odd when "wrapped around" a sphere. In effect, the sphere is sitting in a space that contains wood grain. What you see on the surface of the sphere is just the grain at that point, in just the same way as if the sphere had been carved out of real piece of wood. Other surfaces are the same, and the grain matches naturally because every point where two surfaces touch is the same point.

Fig. C-9 shows a marble vase and Fig. C-10 shows a wood-burl teapot, both created with spatial textures.

A spatial texture does not have to be very large because you can replicate it in three dimensions just as the two-dimensional texture in Fig. 7-4 was replicated.

Given a spatial texture, you can experiment with it. Rather than adjust the parameters on the surface to move the texture around, move the texture itself (since you do not have any surface parameters for a spatial texture, just the position of the surface point itself). For example, you could tilt the spatial texture with reference to the world of the objects. When rendered again, the texture will appear tilted.

How can you make a spatial texture? You can draw or digitize a two-dimensional texture map, but these three-dimensional tables seem a different matter. Probably the easiest way to make one is to write a program. A neat part of this solution is that you do not need to use the program to build the texture and then exit. Rather, the rendering system can call on the texture program for a texture value whenever it needs one. In effect, instead of looking up the texture value in a stored table, the renderer calls up a program that computes a new texture value. The advantage is that you can use gigantic textures that are very expensive to compute, and yet they don't really exist; the texture values are only computed when needed and then thrown away. The disadvantage is that you have to write the program! If you really want to avoid the programming, you could build up a spatial texture by drawing in the bottom-most slice of the three-dimensional texture table, then the next slice, and so on.

Spatial textures are most popular when used as material textures, but you can use them for any texturing operation. They are especially useful for rendering things that are supposed to be carved out of real materials, such as wood or marble.

SUMMARY

The process of texturing (or texture mapping) involves taking a source texture (or texture map) and applying it to a surface to make that surface more interesting.

Picture mapping modifies the color of an object and depends on a picture map with an associated coordinate system with axes called U and V. Each surface to be textured is parameterized, so that every point has an associated (u,v) coordinate. When a point is ready for shading, the computer finds the (u,v) values at the shading point and finds the corresponding color in the texture map. That is the color used for shading calculations. The new color need not replace the old one; it could, instead, simply modulate or filter the original color.

Another technique is called transparency mapping, and it makes use of a transparency map. When shading is performed, the value for the transparency of the surface at the shading point is determined by the value stored in the transparency map.

More generally, you can create a material map that specifies which of many complete materials is to be used at a point. This map is then able to multiplex, or choose among, different materials, and even blend different materials together.

Some small-scale changes can be simulated on the surface of the object with bump (or perturbation) mapping. The texture, called a bump map, specifies how the surface normal is to be nudged at the shading point. By nudging the normal in careful ways, you can stimulate the effect of small-scale deformations of the surface. This technique begins to break down if the deformations are made to appear too large, because other effects begin to conflict with the apparent shading and ruin the illusion.

Small-scale changes can also be made with the technique of displacement mapping, which actually pushes small bits of the surface along the surface normals, by a distance dependent on the value in the displacement map. This technique also breaks down when the movements of the surface get too large, but since the surface is actually moved there are no conflicts with other image features.

Textures can modify textures when they are cascaded, or used one after the other. You can also choose multiple textures for a surface, which allows you to control several different aspects of the surface simultaneously with different texture maps.

Two-dimensional textures wrapped around three-dimensional objects can work well in many situations, but they are not suitable for all applications. Surfaces that are to appear carved out of solid material need a texture that looks appropriate everywhere on the surface. If several primitive surfaces are combined, and it is desired that they are to appear of one piece, then the texture alignment problem must be solved: How can the textures be made to flow smoothly from one surface to the next? With two-dimensional textures, this can be an almost impossible task.

Space textures are three-dimensional tables that contain texture values for points in space. Rather than using a parameterization to find a texture value, a shading point's (x,y,z) coordinates are used directly to find a value in the texture table. Using a space texture means that textures align naturally, since they come from a single, three-dimensional source of texture values.

8 FRACTALS

This chapter presents a method for model-making that works not by specifying shapes, but by specifying rules and a single starting shape. When carefully chosen, these rules give rise to a class of objects called fractals.

Fractals are useful shapes because they can be as complex as you like. This complexity helps make a shape interesting to look at. You can build two-dimensional fractals to use as textures, or three-dimensional fractals to use as modeling primitives. Part of the expressive power of fractals comes from their ability to mimic some of the features of the natural world. Fractals have been used successfully to create images of mountains and clouds, which would normally be very difficult to build.

The word "fractal" is used in several different ways in computer graphics: to describe a modeling technique, an algorithm, and the shapes produced by those methods. The most common use is to describe the objects themselves; thus one typically speaks of a "fractal mountain," though it may have been created with a "fractal program" that implements a "fractal algorithm" based on "fractal geometry."

Fractals are new to the world. They represent a new system of mathematics, and its results, which have been used to describe the structures of mountains, coastlines, galaxies, and much more. Previously, it was generally believed by mathematicians and scientists that such complex natural phenomena were almost beyond rigorous description. After all, a mountain looks so jagged and wild, it seems impossible to capture the essence of its shape with the clean and elegant tools of mathematics.

But fractal geometry works differently than the geometrical tools I have presented so far. It can be thought of as a collection of rules that tell you how to build an object, rather than as a description of the object itself. Like a blueprint, these rules are not the object itself, but rather a complete description of how to build a copy of the object if you wish.

Fractals can be thought of as objects built by rules that obey certain patterns and conditions. Fractal objects mimic natural structures in a nonspecific way. For example, fractal techniques in general cannot be used to build a copy of any particular real mountain that you have seen; rather, they describe how to create a shape that looks like some mountains. So if you want to model Mount McKinley precisely, you still have to do it by hand. But if you just want something that looks like a mountain, without worrying about just which mountain it is, fractals provide a quick and easy modeling technique.

Fractals are also useful for making objects other than natural structures (discussed later). But always remember that when you use a fractal, you get the shape that you must get according to the rules. You can modify those rules if you want, or even use random rules, but it would be a lot of work to make rules that generate a shape that matches any specific object you had in mind.

The use of fractals is one technique for getting an effect called *database amplification*. A useful analogy is an audio amplifier: a little bit of signal comes into an amplifier, and a lot of signal comes out. The use of fractals is a geometric technique that simulates that amplification; you put a little bit of database (a flat triangle representing the base of a mountain) into a fractal system, and you get a lot of database (a craggy mountain) out, with no more work on your part.

The following example may help to explain what fractals are and how they can help you make pictures.

Imagine you are flying in an airplane high above the coast of France. If you look out the window at the coastline, you could sketch it on a small pad. As the plane then started coming in for a landing at a coastal airport, you would see the coastline grow larger and larger in your window, and you could keep re-sketching what you see as the plane descends. Note that the large features you saw from a high altitude are still visible close up, but there is ever more detail visible in the coastline as you approach the airport. Fig. 8-1 shows a set of coastal sketches you might make.

8-1. Sketches of a coastline from a descending airplane.

If you wanted to simulate this sequence with a computer, you would run into trouble modeling the irregularity of the hills and the coastline. Most of the objects I have discussed so far have been precisely defined. Polygons are flat and bounded by straight edges, and the curved surfaces presented in Chapter 9 are all smooth by definition. Imagine how difficult it would be to model such a rocky, craggy coastline out of polygons.

Even if you were intrepid enough to start on a polygonal model of the coastline, there would still be a problem. To make an animation following the sketches just described, you would need enough polygons to describe the coastline for each frame in the film. The coast would have to look craggy from a great height, requiring some large features, but there would also have to be enough small detail so that when the plane is landing the coastline still appears rugged. Even when you are far from the coast, the computer has to draw all the little details that are really too far away for you to see, because the description of the coastline will not change over time (it is a static model, as defined in Chapter 1). Therefore, if a polygon is in the model at the end of the film, it is there at the beginning as well.

The result is that a lot of computer time is wasted when you are very high up drawing little details that usually will not make a difference on the screen, as well as when you are close to the ground (because the computer processes all the polygons in the coastline, which means all the little polygons currently out of view). Of course, you could have several coastlines defined, and you could draw different ones when the plane is at different altitudes, but designing those several coastlines and figuring out ways to switch between them smoothly would also require much hard work.

SOME CHARACTERISTICS OF FRACTALS

It would be very convenient if you could somehow get the computer to draw rough objects like the coastline automatically. There are certain properties that objects created by the computer should have in order to be really useful. The first is that craggy objects (such as a coastline) should be *self-similar*. For example, if the coastline is very rough and jagged when viewed from far away, it should be just as rough and jagged close up. In other words, the details when viewed close-up should have the same general kind of shape as the overall structure seen from far away. Another important requirement for your applications is that the computer should generate *appropriate detail*, or only as much detail as is needed. For instance, you do not want fine details in your coastline from high up, but you do want them when you are close to the ground. Lastly, there should be some *general controls* over the shapes that are made: where they are located, how big they are, and so on.

To consider another application, suppose you want to animate a scene in outer space that includes many asteroids flying by on the screen. Asteroids are very rough and craggy, and it would be a time-consuming and difficult task to create a large number of different ones. What you really want is a computer program that can automatically generate asteroids for you, each one different. From far away they should look like craggy rocks, and as the asteroid approaches the screen, increasing amounts of detail should become visible.

If you asked a programmer ignorant of fractals to write a program to "make asteroids," you would probably have a long time to wait. And then you might very well end up with some kind of random shape, roughly round, and certainly craggy, but as unlike an asteroid as a child's random scribble is unlike a coastline. Certainly natural objects have some kind of natural order to them. Although a coastline appears random to some extent, not every random scribble looks like a coastline.

HOW COMPUTER GRAPHICS FRACTALS ARE MADE

It is important here to distinguish between fractals in general and the particular objects I present here and that you normally use in computer graphics. The word "fractal" describes a class of mathematical shapes, and they can get complex and subtle. To use the properties of fractals in pictures, I ignore many of the fine points of the theory and concentrate on making believable or visually pleasing pictures.

One kind of two-dimensional fractal has been known for a long time; it is called a *Koch curve* (even though it is made entirely out of straight lines!). The basic idea in this fractal construction (and indeed, in most fractals), is that you take a starting shape and change it in particular ways until it starts taking on the appearance you want.

Fig. 8-2 shows the starting shape (a single straight line), and another shape, called the *generator*. The first step is to take the starting shape (step 1) and replace it with the generator (step 2). Looking closely at the result, you can see that there are now four lines; each of these is just a rotated and scaled copy of the original shape. So you take the generator and apply it to each of the these smaller lines, rotating and scaling the generator as needed to make it fit,

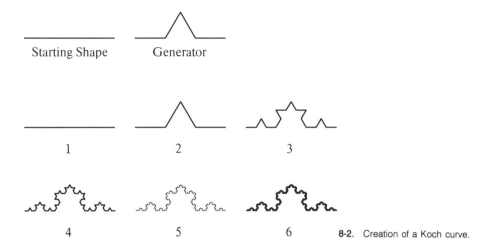

Starting Shape   Generator

1   2   3

4   5   6

8-2. Creation of a Koch curve.

as in step 3. You can repeat this operation again and again, as shown. Fig. 8-3 shows the result of building Koch curves on all three sides of a triangle; this shape is often called a *Koch snowflake*. Each time you apply the generator, you create a new *generation*.

There are two important observations to be pointed out about the shapes made this way. The first is that they are all self-similar. If you examine any section of a particular figure, it bears a strong resemblance to the whole. In other words, the crinkly shape when viewed extremely close up is like the crinkly shape when viewed from a distance. Thus, the details faithfully reflect the overall structure of the original form.

The other observation is that you can control just how much detail you want in the evolution of the Koch curve. This control is helpful for the kind of situation described earlier in the imaginary airplane flight. When the shape is far away (and thus small on the screen), you only want the rough shape to be rendered by the computer, so you stop creating a shape after a small number of generations. Additional detail would not show up when the coastline is small and would just make the computer's job harder (meaning a longer wait for the picture). On the other hand, when the coastline is close up (and thus large on the screen), you want more detail, which you can get by applying the generator again and again. Note that new detail is added to the old; it's not as if you invented new, random shapes every time you wanted more detail. The advantage

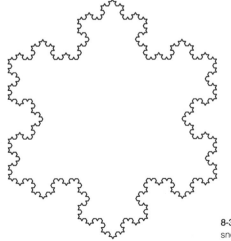

8-3. A fifth-generation Koch snowflake.

here is that as you get closer to such a shape and add detail, the shape itself does not change radically. It just picks up more and more detail as needed. This kind of control is called appropriate detail, as previously mentioned.

Another line fractal can be seen in Fig. 8-4, where the starting shape is a line and the generator is a pair of lines that form the other two legs of a right triangle with it. Fig. 8-5 shows this construction carried out eight times; it is often called a *C curve* because the shape it makes looks something like the letter *C*. In this construction, the orientation of the lines is important, so in Fig. 8-4 I have included arrowheads in the construction diagram, although they are not part of the C curve itself. Fig. 8-6 shows almost the same construction, but the generator's lines are oriented slightly differently (note the directions of the arrows). The result is called a *dragon curve*, and Fig. 8-7 shows the result after several generations.

Thus far, the fractals have been built by replacing one bit of shape with another, more complicated piece of shape. One way to make this happen within a program is to use a technique called *subdivision*. Each time you add a little more detail to the image, you subdivide one more time. The number of times you subdivide to make a figure is called its *level of subdivision*; this is a synonym for generation.

Starting Shape   Generator

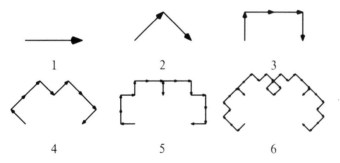

8-4. Creation of a C curve. (The arrows are not part of the curve, but they help show how it is built.)

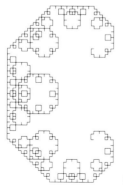

8-5. A fifth-generation C curve.

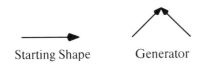

Starting Shape   Generator

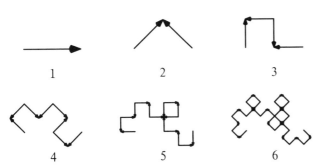

1   2   3

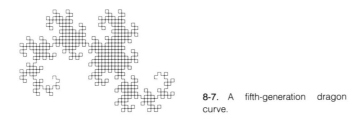

4   5   6

8-6. Creation of a dragon curve. Note that a generator is used with exactly the same shape as for the C curve (Fig. 8-4), except that the orientation of one line has been reversed.

8-7. A fifth-generation dragon curve.

FRACTALS IN THREE DIMENSIONS

Two-dimensional techniques can be generalized from lines to surfaces, and although it gets more complicated, it is really just more of the same. If you want to create a three-dimensional object, such as a mountain or asteroid, you create a three-dimensional polygonal object and do a more complicated kind of subdivision on it, as sketched in Fig. 8-8. Often this kind of subdivision is done with some randomness, so things look a little less regular than the two-dimensional examples.

In the hands of talented programmers and artists, fractals can be used to create computer-generated pictures that were previously almost impossible because of their complexity. Fig. C-11 shows a small range of fractal islands as seen from the air. Note that the coastline looks jagged and irregular, as you would wish.

Fig. C-12 shows a fractal moon and planet. The planet in the background was modeled as bumpy fractals wrapped around a blue sphere. Then the surface of the sphere was pushed out a little bit until about half of the bumps were above the surface and half were below. Some color was added to the bumps above the surface to make them look like land masses in ocean. The moon in the foreground shows mountains and craters built with fractal techniques.

Fractals are also useful for abstract work; Figs. C-13A and B show some three-dimensional fractals that would be very hard to create directly. These two images were created with very little information from the modeler except some starting values.

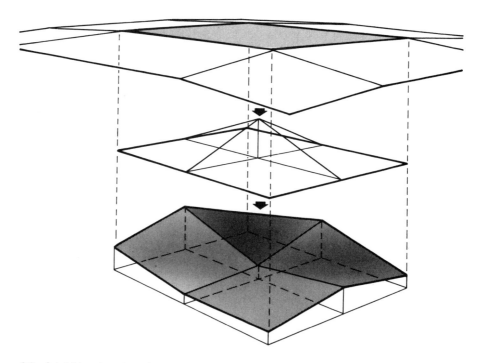

8-8. Subdivision of a polygon into several smaller polygons to build a three-dimensional fractal.

SUMMARY

Fractals are a class of objects described not by their primitive surfaces, but by rules that construct those surfaces. Fractals are useful for database amplification, which allows you to turn a small amount of modeling into rich, complex objects.

One useful property of fractal objects is self-similarity, which means that a fractal object looks substantially the same whether viewed from close up or from far away. It is this feature that allows the addition of appropriate detail, so that you have just enough detail in your model for a particular image.

The model is based on general controls. In my examples, this consists of a starting shape and rules that describe how a generator is to be applied. By making random changes to the generator, a regular construction can begin to look craggy and rough.

Two-dimensional fractals can be constructed by using a Koch curve (culminating in a Koch snowflake), a C curve, or a dragon curve. By repeatedly applying the generator to the shape being built, the generation, or level of subdivision, of the figure is increased.

The fractal technique can be extended easily to three dimensions, where instead of replacing a line with a new set of smaller lines, a bit of surface is replaced with a new set of smaller surfaces.

Fractals are not generally useful for exactly replicating some particular object. The power of fractals is that they can create many different objects, each of which is similar in its properties to some class of objects (such as mountains or coastlines). A single particular object still needs to be created by hand.

9 CURVED SURFACES

Previous chapters discussed using polygons to model curved surfaces by manipulating the shading to make the polygonal surfaces appear round. But this approach has its drawbacks. Silhouettes are still polygonal, and if the object gets close to the screen then the silhouette may become very visible and ruin the illusion created by smooth shading. Another problem comes from intersections: when two polygonal models intersect, the underlying polygonal structure is obvious and, again, the illusion is ruined.

Curved surfaces solve these problems because they are really curved. There are many kinds of curved surfaces and, although they are sometimes harder to work with than polygons, they are often more appropriate. This chapter introduces a variety of curved surfaces and some of their properties.

SHADING AND DEFINITION

Recall from Chapter 6 that there are several methods for shading polygons, each with advantages and disadvantages. Having more than one shading technique for polygons enables you to make a polygonal surface look like a smooth surface by interpolating the shades and surface normals.

For the curved surfaces commonly used in computer graphics, the surface is defined by a mathematical expression in such a way as to guarantee that the surface is already smooth. To shade a point on a curved surface, you find the surface normal at that point and compare it to the various light sources. You can also texture a curved surface, changing the material parameters or nudging the surface normal, just as for mapping polygons. There are various kinds of curved surfaces that have proven useful in computer graphics. Most of them require some mathematical sophistication to create.

PATCHES

A general class of open curved surfaces can be grouped under the category *patches*. I have not used patches in this book, but you may encounter them in other people's models, so it will be helpful to you to have some idea of what they are.

The basic concept is that the user defines a small section (or patch) of a larger curved surface. An object may be created out of many patches placed next to one another, as Fig. 9-1 illustrates. For example, a barrel might be considered an object built up of many patches, where each patch is one of the staves. The definition of a patch is very broad and includes many different kinds of shapes. In fact, even polygons may be considered a type of patch, although they would be the simplest. Most patches actually have some curvature.

A. Patch.

B. Shape.

9-1. Patches are small pieces of curved surface.

Some systems let you specify a polygonal model as a starting point for a patch-based model. The idea is that the polygonal surface is considered just an approximation to the curvy surface, and the computer fills in the curvy surface for you. To adjust the curved surface, you can adjust the polygonal model from which it was derived. Fig. 9-2 shows two models, the first built with polygons and the second built with patches derived from those polygons.

Recall the discussion of splines from Chapter 3, which described two general classes of splines: interpolating and approximating. The same distinctions hold for patches derived from a polygonal model. In this situation each polygon is called a *basis* (or *control*) *polygon*, and the patches are created polygon by polygon. If the patch passes through the vertices of the control polygon, it is called an *interpolating patch*; if it merely passes nearby, then it is an *approximating patch*. Examples of these types include *cubic patches* (an interpolating patch), and *Bézier patches* (an approximating patch).

9-2. A polygonal model can be converted into a patch model. Each polygon becomes a control polygon for one patch. (Image courtesy of Digital Arts.)

The mechanics of just how patches work varies greatly from system to system, because there are so many different kinds of patches and they may be used in many different ways.

QUADRIC SURFACES

A *quadric surface*, or *quadric*, is formally defined as the surface that is a solution to a *quadric equation*. Typical quadrics are *spheres, cylinders*, and *cones* as illustrated in Fig. 9-3. Other quadric surfaces are called the *paraboloid*, the *saddle*, and the *hyperboloid*, also shown in Fig. 9-3; these are sometimes more difficult to work with than the first group of quadrics named.

Spheres are completely defined by a center and a radius, as shown in Fig. 9-4. A cylinder is defined by a central axis, radius, and the position of the top and bottom of the cylinder along the axis. Fig. 9-5 illustrates a collection of cylinders of different parameters. The central axis controls in which direction the cylinder lies. The radius controls how thick the cylinder is, and the top and bottom indicate where the cylinder ends. A cone is defined as shown in Fig. 9-6.

Drawing a cylinder on the screen requires care. The mathematical definition of cylinders (and of several other quadrics as well) originally specifies them as having infinite length, which is usually not what you want. Instead, you have to tell the computer to *clip* the cylinder off at certain points, or *bind* the surface. You also have to enter *bounds* for the surface, or indicate that it must be *bounded*. Bounds are limits on the extent and size of the shape of a surface, beyond its initial mathematical definition. Fig. 9-7 shows several cylinders with the bounds that must be included when you actually draw a picture: the lower and upper limits of the cylinder. Cones also need these limits, as shown in Fig. 9-8.

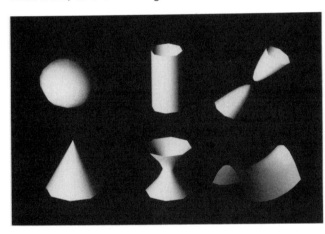

9-3. Quadric surfaces as approximated by polygons. *Top row*: sphere, cylinder, paraboloid. *Bottom row*: cone, hyperboloid, saddle. (Image courtesy of Digital Arts.)

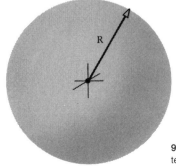

9-4. A sphere is defined by a center and a radius.

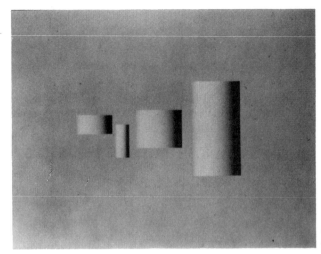

9-5. Cylinders of different parameters.

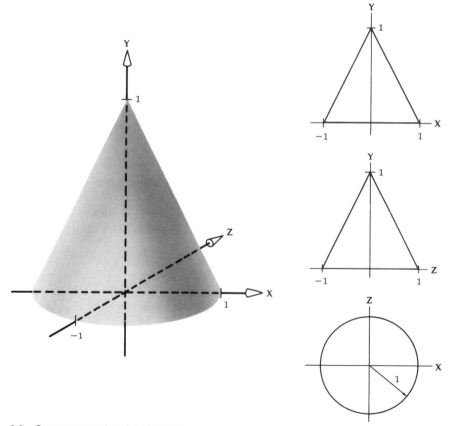

9-6. One prototype orientation of a cone.

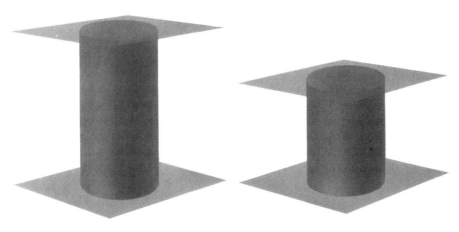

9-7. Infinite objects, such as cylinders, require bounds to set top and bottom limits.

9-8. How to bound cones.

SURFACE PARAMETERIZATIONS

To apply a two-dimensional texture map to a quadric or patch, you need some kind of coordinates on the surface with which to specify texture map location.

Patches are typically parameterized just like polygons: You specify texture coordinates at each vertex of the polygon underlying the patch.

It makes the process easier that most quadrics have common, or *natural*, parameterizations. Fig. 9-9 shows parameterizations for the quadrics of Fig. 9-3. For those surfaces with natural parameterizations, you can still exert some control by specifying *offset* (or *translation*) *scaling* and *rotation parameters*. The idea is that when a point is looked up in the parameterization, you assume that the origin has the value (0,0) and that the maximum value of both the U and V axes is 1. But you can specify a different value for the origin if you like, which has the effect of sliding the texture around on the surface, as shown in Fig. 9-10B. You might also multiply the values

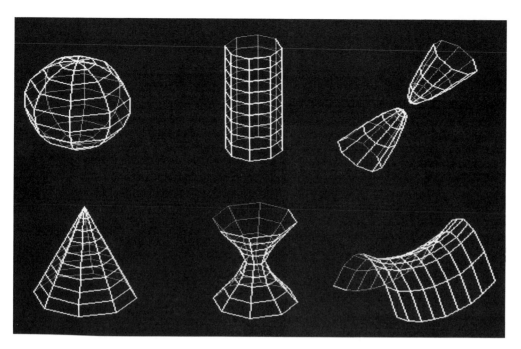

9-9. Quadric surfaces from Fig. 9-3 with their natural parameterizations. (Image courtesy of Digital Arts.)

A

B
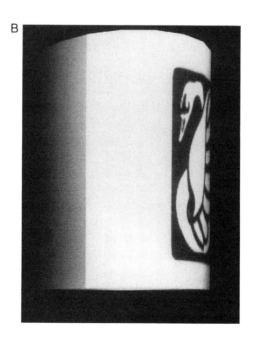

C

D

9-10. The effect of modifying the natural parameterization of a cylinder. The original texturing is shown in top, left; translation, top, right; scaling, bottom, left; and rotation, bottom, right. (Image courtesy of Digital Arts.)

of U and V, with the result that the texture is either stretched or compressed on the surface, as for Fig. 9-10C. If you rotate the U and V axes a bit, the result rotates the picture, as shown by Fig. 9-10D. Notice that in all of these operations, the surface and the texture are unchanged; only the surface parameterization is different.

SUMMARY

Polygons are suitable for many applications, but sometimes it is best to model with real curved surfaces. Perhaps the most straightforward curved surface is the patch, which is a small bit of curved surface. A patch is usually derived from a basis (or control) polygon, which influences the patch's shape the way knots influence the shape of a spline. Like splines, patches can be interpolating (meaning that they go through the vertices of the control polygons) or approximating (meaning that they only come near the control polygon's vertices). A common interpolating patch is the cubic patch; a common approximating patch is the Bézier patch.

A quadric surface is one class of objects that satisfy a quadric equation. Common quadrics include the sphere, the cylinder, and the cone. Less common but still useful are the paraboloid, the saddle, and the hyperboloid. Many of these quadrics are defined as having infinite extent; normally you will want to clip or bound the surface with bounds that set limits on how far the object extends in space.

To apply two-dimensional texture maps, the surfaces must be parameterized. Patches are parameterized just like polygons, by specifying (u,v) pairs at the vertices. Quadrics have "built-in" natural parameterizations that derive from their definitions. To control these parameterizations you can specify offset (or translation) parameters to move the texture and scaling parameters to change its size, and rotation parameters to rotate the texture around its natural origin.

10 BASIC MODELING

I mentioned several times in this book that simple surfaces may be combined to create complex objects, but, so far, I have not discussed any of the techniques involved in building big objects out of simple models. This chapter presents the techniques for organizing the simple pieces in a model that can greatly simplify both the design and the mechanics of entering the model into the computer. If the model is later to be animated, then one of the approaches here will prove to be a convenient structure for later posing and manipulation.

DESCRIBING A COMPLEX OBJECT

The first step in prepared model making is to prepare a drawing of the model. The drawing serves to identify the primitive surfaces used to make the model and, perhaps, also describes the materials out of which they are made. Once you have an idea of what surfaces are best to use and how they are to be combined, then you can enter them into the computer. This chapter concentrates on organizing the geometry of the model (the shapes), rather than the appearance (the materials).

To understand the approach, imagine a list of *nested coordinate systems*. The outermost coordinate system is often called the *global* (or *world*) *coordinate system*. This is the one absolute coordinate system that you cannot change. Everything you do will ultimately happen with reference to these global coordinates. But there will be smaller coordinate systems within. Recall the discussion of a model within a shoebox in Chapter 2. The model is described relative to the shoebox, but the shoebox is described relative to the global coordinates. Thus, the description of the shoebox is nested within the global coordinates.

One way to think of nested coordinates is to begin with the objects. When you specify an object (for example, a cone) in your model, that object begins life in your model as a copy of a *prototype*. A prototype object is specified with respect to its own coordinate system, like the object within a shoebox. Part of your specification of the object is to tell how the object's coordinate system sits within the global coordinates. This information allows you to move the object around without changing it. On the other hand, you can change the object's coordinate system to allow you to change the object without moving it. For example, imagine a shoe in a regular-size shoebox. You can move the shoebox around, which changes the location of the shoe within, but the shoe itself is unchanged. However, if you double the size of the shoebox, the shoe inside will double its size as well. If you did not move the shoebox when you enlarged it, then the shoe was enlarged without moving.

When you are modeling, you can typically tell the computer that you want to *pop*, or move up, the list of nested coordinate systems. This specification allows you to deeply nest many systems within others, and then jump all the way back to the beginning of the list for a new object. For example, suppose you want to model an octopus. You define the head, and then model the start of the first arm; nest that system to design the next piece of the arm; nest that system to design the next piece; and so on, until you reach the tip of the arm. You can easily add suction cups to the bottom of each arm as you define it, since each time you nest a coordinate system you have a logical origin to work with. When you reach the end of the arm, you pop all the way back up to the top of the list and start on the next arm. Sometimes the act of creating a new coordinate system is referred to as *pushing* the current coordinate system onto the nested list.

To see how modeling with nested coordinate systems works, refer back to Fig. 9-6, which shows a prototype cone, and its relation to its own, private coordinate system. (I chose a common orientation, but there are several "standard" prototype coordinate systems for most objects.) When you first create a new cone, it originally arrives in this prototype form: The center of the cone goes up the Y axis. The coordinate system for this new cone would sit within the coordinate system in which it is nested; if you have just started building a model, then the axes and origin of the cone will be in the same location and orientation as the axes and origin of the global coordinate system.

To use this technique, first recall from Chapter 2 that you can manipulate an entire coordinate system with transformations such as translation, rotation, and scaling. Each of these may be applied to any coordinate system, affecting everything within. For example, see Fig. 10-1. It shows a global coordinate system (labeled g_x, g_y, g_z) , and a new, temporary coordinate system created by the user (labeled n_x, n_y, n_z). The mechanics of telling the computer that you are defining a new coordinate system vary with each implementation, so I do not go into this activity in detail. It suffices to say that you instruct the computer to take the "current coordinate system," create a new copy of it, and manipulate that new copy, leaving everything that was done before unchanged. When you begin defining your model, the global coordinate system is the current coordinate system.

Consider designing the model in Fig. 10-2 (this diagram is in a left-handed coordinate system). It consists of two spheres of different sizes and two cones. To create this object, create a new instance of each primitive (each one within its own coordinate system), move that system into position, rotate and scale the axes, and then tell the computer to "draw an object within the current axes."

Place the small sphere first. Give the command "create a new sphere." The sphere is created within its private coordinate system (although not yet drawn; this is only modeling now, not rendering). The origin of the sphere is at the origin of its local coordinate system, and its radius is one unit in that system. The sphere's system sits within the current system when it is first created, so this sphere is originally at the center of the world. Then move the sphere's private coordinate system 100 units in the negative Y direction, as illustrated in Fig. 10-3A. (These directions are

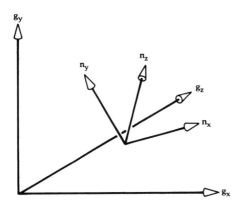

10-1. A new coordinate system (nx,ny,nz) created within the global system (gx,gy,gz).

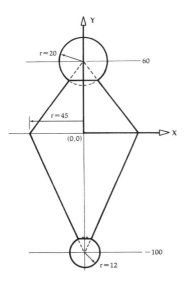

A. A model plan.

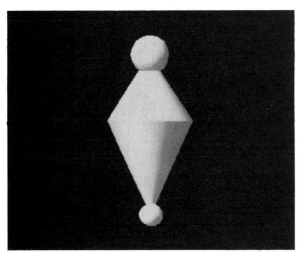

B. An image of the model.

10-2. A plan for a model and its rendered image.

with respect to the system in which the sphere's coordinate system was created; in this case, the global system.) Scale all the axes of the sphere's system by a factor of 12 (Fig. 10-3B). Now one unit in the sphere's system corresponds to twelve units in the global system. If you then say "draw the sphere" as in Fig. 10-3C, the sphere is drawn within its own system with a radius of 1. But since you have moved and scaled that system, in the global system the sphere is centered at (0, −100, 0), and has a radius of 12.

Now, place one of the cones. As for the sphere, issue the command "create a new cone" to create a new coordinate system containing a cone. First move the coordinate system (Fig. 10-4A) so that the origin of the new set of axes (the center of the base of the cone) is in the correct place. Then rotate the axes so that the tip of the cone lies on the Y axis (Fig. 10-4B). The last

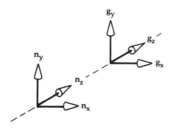

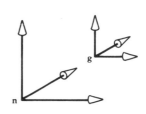

A. Create a new coordinate system.   **B. Scale this new coordinate system.**

C. Draw the sphere.

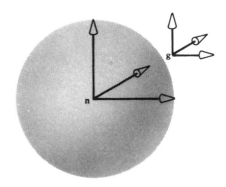

10-3. Steps in modeling a sphere in space.

step involves scaling the *X* and *Z* axes by 45, and the *Y* axis by 100, as shown in Fig. 10-4C. Remember that you are giving commands to manipulate the cone's own local system with respect to the global system. Since you have already spun the cone around, scaling it by 100 in *Y* will put the tip of the cone at $(0, 0, -100)$. Scaling in *X* and *Y* by 45 will result in a forty-five-unit radius of the cone.

Repeat the modeling process for the second cone and the second sphere, and the description of the geometric model is complete.

One way to make the preceding operations happen is to type all the information into a file, called the *modeling script*. This file is just a sequence of commands that tells the computer how to assemble your model. When you have typed the entire file and saved it, you then give it to the computer to interpret. The computer reads the script, executes the commands, and eventually produces your image. Alternatively, you can use an interactive system to build the model on the screen piece by piece, just as if you were assembling a real object.

INSTANCING

Suppose you want to create the model shown in Fig. 10-5. Note that this is simply three copies of the model in Fig. 10-2 placed in different positions and orientations. You do not have to define the model three times. First, specify one copy of the model using the previously described procedure. This model is relative to the current coordinate system, which, unless it has been previously modified (as you will do now), is the global coordinate system.

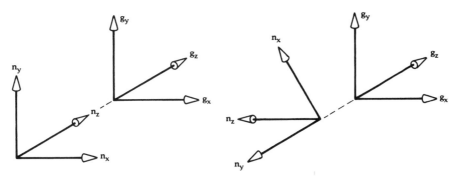

A. Translate a new coordinate system.   B. Rotate it.

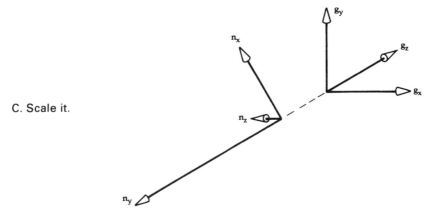

C. Scale it.

10-4. Steps in modeling a cone in space.

When this single unit of the model has been made, you can give it a name. Usually almost any sequence of characters is allowed; you can call this object SIMPLEROBOT. If you save the file with that name, then from now on SIMPLEROBOT can be treated like any other built-in surface. When you request that the computer "create a new SIMPLEROBOT," it comes into being relative to its own coordinate system (which is the global system at the time it was defined; Fig. 10-2 is the coordinate system that the object begins with). Then you can move, rotate, scale, and otherwise manipulate this new copy of SIMPLEROBOT until it is just where you want. Then create another new copy, position it, and so on. Creating many copies of something that has been previously defined is called *instancing*, and each copy is an *instance* of the original.

Note that each sphere in SIMPLEROBOT is now three levels deep; the sphere is within its own system, which is nested within the SIMPLEROBOT system, which is within the global system. Think of shoeboxes within shoeboxes.

The first step is shown as Fig. 10-6. You ask for a new SIMPLEROBOT whose origin begins right at the global origin, and whose axes are aligned to the global axes. Then move this copy of SIMPLEROBOT to where you want it, as in Fig. 10-6A. Then scale and rotate the axes (Fig. 10-6B). If you stop there and tell the computer to draw the object, you get the composite object drawn where you last left the new coordinate system, as shown in Fig. 10-6C.

10-5. A composite model, made of three copies of Fig. 10-2.

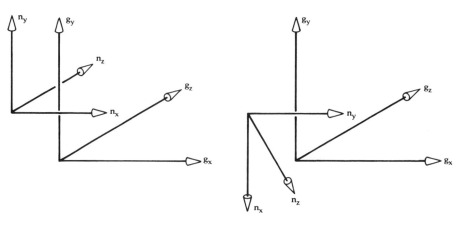

A. Create new, translated axes.   **B. Scale and rotate.**

C. Draw a model.

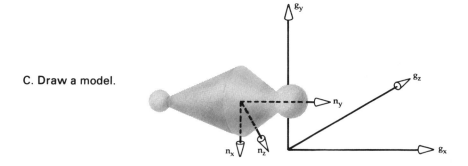

10-6. Modeling with an instance of Fig. 10-2.

Then, repeat this process two more times, moving a set of axes into position and drawing the model called SIMPLEROBOT instead of just simple surfaces.

The model definition of this larger model is now complete. As mentioned before, one way to make all of this happen is to create model scripts ahead of time. Fig. 10-7 shows two different ways to create scripts for Fig. 10-5. Fig. 10-7A shows two scripts, one for SIMPLEROBOT and one for the composite model. Compare the script for the SIMPLEROBOT model to Fig. 10-2. Fig. 10-7B shows one large script in global coordinates that does not make use of instancing.

```
Scriptfile SimpleRobot          Scriptfile ThreeRobots2
Push                            Initialize
   TranslateY -100              Screen = -200 -200 200 200
   Scale 12                     Push
   Sphere                          TranslateX -60
Pop                                Push
Cone -100 0 0 45                      TranslateY -100
Cone 0 45 60 0                         Scale 12
Push                                   Sphere
   TranslateY 60                    Pop
   Scale 20                         Cone -100 0 0 45
   Sphere                          Cone 0 45 60 0
Pop                                Push
End                                   TranslateY 60
                                      Scale 20
                                      Sphere
        --------                   Pop
                                Pop
                                Push
Scriptfile ThreeRobots1            TranslateX 120
Initialize                         Push
Screen = -200 -200 200 200            TranslateY -100
Push                                  Scale 12
   TranslateX -60                     Sphere
   "SimpleRobot"                   Pop
Pop                                Cone -100 0 0 45
Push                               Cone 0 45 60 0
   TranslateX 120                  Push
   "SimpleRobot"                      TranslateY 60
Pop                                   Scale 20
Push                                  Sphere
   TranslateZ -20                  Pop
   RotateZ -75                  Pop
   "SimpleRobot"                Push
Pop                                TranslateZ -20
Render                             RotateZ -75
End                                   Push
                                      TranslateY -100
                                      Scale 12
                                      Sphere
                                   Pop
                                   Cone -100 0 0 45
                                   Cone 0 45 60 0
                                   Push
                                      TranslateY 60
                                      Scale 20
                                      Sphere
                                   Pop
                                Pop
                                Render
A                             B End
```

10-7. Two equivalent ways to create Fig. 10-5. *Left*: two modeling scripts separate the work; *right*: all the objects are placed directly.

ARTICULATION TREES

Another way to describe the whole picture of Fig. 10-5 is through the use of a *tree*. The name comes from the similarity of the structure, illustrated in Fig. 10-8, to an upside-down tree. Each splitting point is called a *node*, and each line is called a *branch*. The top node is called the *tree's root*, or just the *root*, while the bottommost nodes along any path are called *leaves*, or sometimes called *external* (or *terminal*) *nodes*. The root is at the top, and the leaves are at the bottom. Branches and internal nodes are encountered along the way. You can use this kind of a tree to help describe and organize your models.

The basic idea is that each node represents a coordinate system, each branch represents a transformation, and each leaf represents an object (leaves always contain objects; some internal nodes may as well). To draw an object, start at the root, and *descend the tree* by the shortest path until you reach that leaf. Along the way, you build up a complete coordinate system in which you will draw the object. The following is a sample descent.

Start at the root, which always holds the global coordinate system. Then move down the tree, starting along the appropriate path to reach the leaf in which you are interested. The first branch you follow contains a transformation of the coordinate system, for example, a rotation or scale. Apply that transformation (creating a new system), and then store that new, transformed system at the node just below the branch. Then you come to the next branch, apply its transformation to the system just built, and store the composite at the next node. In this way, you accumulate transformations down the tree until reaching the leaf. When you store the composite coordinate system in a leaf, you then automatically draw the object at that leaf in the coordinate system stored there. The internal nodes can contain objects as well; when you store into such a node, you draw its objects with the current coordinate system the same as is done for a leaf.

Each leaf may indicate a simple surface to be drawn, or it could contain the name of some other complex surface. This could be an instance of another object (such as SIMPLEROBOT), which might itself be described by a tree. The act of descending a tree in the way I have just described is also called *traversing the tree*.

This kind of modeling tree is also called an *articulation tree* (one definition of articulate is "to unite by joints"). Models that fit into this kind of scheme are called *articulated models*. These

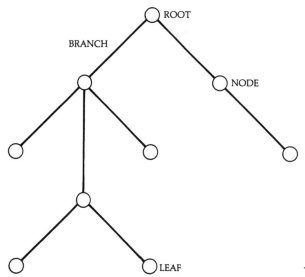

10-8. A simple model tree.

kinds of models are very popular because they can embrace many mechanical and natural assemblies. Bodies and hands are natural objects for articulation trees. Articulation trees are also well-suited for creating keyframes, or poses, of objects for animation.

Surfaces indicated by leaves may be as complex as you like. That is, a surface may contain (or use) a surface that contains a surface that contains a surface, and so on. The only requirement is that no surface contains a surface above it on the same path (but it is all right if the object is on the path to another node). This procedure can get confusing, because when you have trees pointing to trees, it is not always easy to decide if a particular object includes some other object which is also above it in the complete tree.

Fig. 10-9 provides an example. It shows a tree that violates the rule. Fig. 10-9A shows a tree called "dollhouse," which includes several other trees as terminal nodes. When the computer reaches one of these trees, it starts following it until finally reaching the terminal node of every tree in the picture. But notice that one of the leaves of "dollhouse" is "room," and one of the leaves of "room" (Fig. 10-9B) is "dollhouse," implying that in a dollhouse you might have a bedroom with a dollhouse inside it, which contains a bedroom, which contains a dollhouse, and on and on.

The problem is the *loop* between the dollhouse and room. This kind of tree is called a *self-referencing tree*. If you try to follow this tree, you never come to an end; you just go around the loop again and again forever. Sometimes this is called an *infinite loop*. Some computer systems will not detect this error for you, and they may run for quite a while, burning up computer time and resources going around and around the loop that has been accidentally created. Obviously, try to avoid creating self-referencing trees.

Fig. 10-10 shows a tree for a robot arm. Each branch contains an instruction to perform a rotation. Each node but the root contains a little bit of the arm or hand. For example, the node right under the root causes the forearm part to be drawn. The leaves take care of the joints at the end of the fingers. By changing the amount of rotation specified at each node, you can cause the arm to move around and to open and close its fingers.

Notice that if you change the amount of rotation applied to the forearm, then all the objects beneath the forearm in the tree are also rotated so that they still line up; this is a natural result of the fact that the transformations accumulate as you descend the tree. So you can specify different positions for the whole arm naturally, in the sense that you can work your way down the tree as though you had a physical model in front of you. If you bend the arm at the elbow, everything beneath the elbow responds similarly even though it is not explicitly moved. Fig. 10-11 shows an articulation tree and the model it describes.

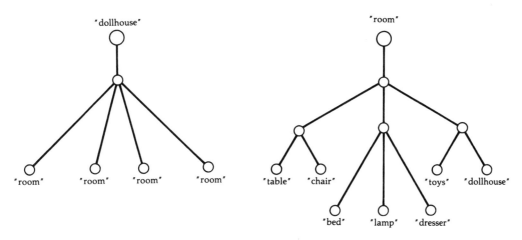

10-9. A recursive tree. Note that *dollhouse* contains *room*.

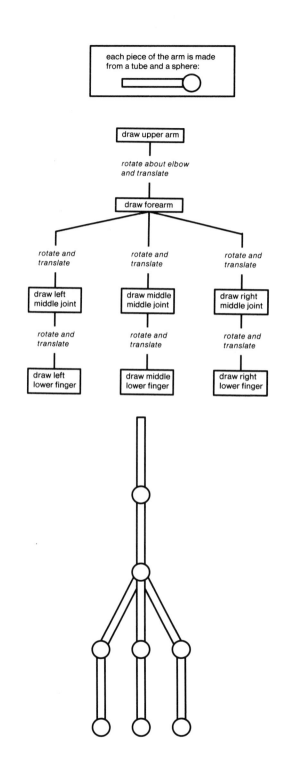

10-10. A robot arm and its model tree.

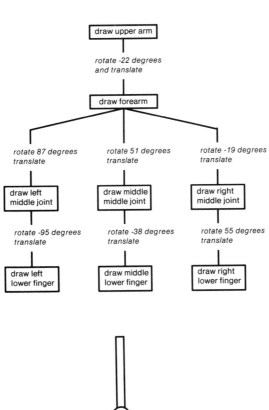

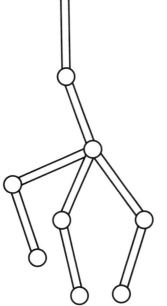

10-11. The model of Fig. 10-10, but with parameters at the nodes.

SUMMARY

A complex object can be created from several simple surfaces. The description of such an object is made easier when each primitive is defined with respect to its own coordinate system. These systems are then nested within one another, so that each system is defined with respect to the system within which it is nested. Ultimately, the global coordinate system, which is never nested, is reached.

When a new instance of a primitive is first created for use in a model, it begins as a copy of a prototype that is an unchanging description of the object in its own coordinate system. When the object is instanced, the object's private system is automatically nested within the current coordinate system. That system is said to be pushed to make room for the new system. Later you may wish to pop back up to some previous level. A complete set of commands may be issued by typing them into a file called the modeling script and handing that to the computer when you are actually ready to have the model built.

Complex objects can be used just like primitive objects through the use of instancing. Each complex object is given a name, and then a new copy, or instance, can be created at any time by issuing the name of the complex object, just like issuing the name of a primitive object.

One implementation of nested coordinate systems may be found in the use of trees for modeling. A tree is an abstract connection of parts, beginning with a root that is connected by branches to internal nodes (or just nodes). A node with no lower branches is called a leaf (or external node or terminal node). The global coordinate system is represented by the root. Each branch represents a transformation. Objects reside in the nodes.

When you descend (or traverse) the tree, you accumulate transformations as you work down from the root. Each transformation takes place on a copy of the coordinate system stored at the node above the branch, and the result is placed in the node below. If any node contains an object, then that object is drawn in the coordinate system written into that node.

Care must be taken to avoid creating a self-referencing tree that can lead to an infinite loop in which the computer could run forever in circles.

The tree structure used for modeling is called an articulation tree and the model is called an articulated model. Articulated models are very easy to pose and manipulate when designing an animation.

11 PRINCIPLES OF RENDERING

All image synthesis techniques share a common ground of basic ideas and some basic problems. Almost all rendering algorithms start with a few steps that make later steps simpler, and they all must look out for difficulties caused by the very act of creating images on a computer.

This chapter discusses these common themes, setting the stage for later discussions of specific rendering algorithms.

OBJECT SPACE AND SCREEN SPACE

When an object is described geometrically, it is always in relation to some coordinate system—that is, an origin and a set of axes radiating from it. The three-dimensional objects presented so far have all been described in relation to a three-dimensional coordinate system.

An object drawn on the screen has only has two dimensions. The third, depth, gets lost in the drawing because the screen has no depth. The term "objects" is often used to refer to both three-dimensional objects in space and two-dimensional images of those objects on the screen. Using a single word for both can be confusing. To specify which object you mean, think of "mathematical objects in space" as inhabiting a three-dimensional a world called *object space*, and "objects drawn on the screen" as inhabiting a two-dimensional world called *screen space*. Fig. 11-1 shows an object and its representation in both spaces.

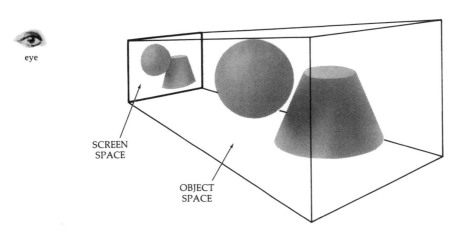

11-1. Screen space and object space.

Not all objects in a scene description will make it onto the screen in the final image. Some objects will be blocked by others, and some will simply not be visible from some points of view. It is helpful to know which objects can potentially make it to the screen and which cannot. To help you find out which objects could be visible in the final image, you create a three-dimensional enclosure that is guaranteed to contain at least a small piece of all visible objects. This object is shown in Fig. 11-2; it is a four-sided pyramid called the *viewing pyramid*. This pyramid contains the *viewing volume*, or that volume of space you can see. The pyramid is constructed with the viewer (normally drawn as an eye) at its tip (or *apex*). The four walls of the screen form the four walls of the pyramid. The *screen* itself is often called the *viewscreen*.

There are an additional two walls to the viewing volume that make up the bottom and top of a cut-off section of the pyramid, as shown in Fig. 11-3. All six of these planes are called *clipping planes*, because if something touches them or goes through them, it gets "clipped" by the pyramid to only allow that part within the pyramid to be seen. The four walls are called *boundary walls*. The near wall to the eye is called the *hither* (or *near*) *clipping plane*, and the far wall is called the *yon* (or *far*) *clipping plane*. As indicated in Fig. 11-4, the viewscreen itself is often the near clipping plane.

Sometimes it is useful to draw only those objects that are on the "other side" of the viewscreen, opposite the eye. In that case, the viewing pyramid loses its pointy top (since you cannot see anything nearer than the viewscreen, you cut anything nearer out of the viewing volume), and instead it becomes a sort of box with a small side and a big side. This "pyramid with the top

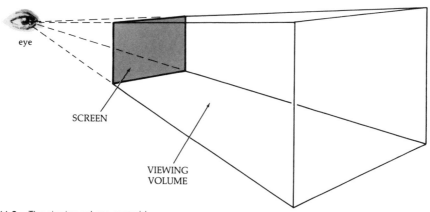

eye

SCREEN

VIEWING
VOLUME

11-2. The viewing volume pyramid.

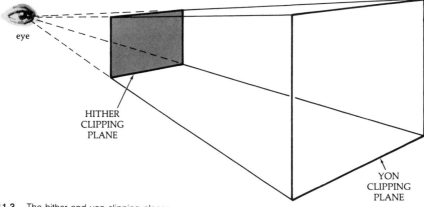

eye

HITHER
CLIPPING
PLANE

YON
CLIPPING
PLANE

11-3. The hither and yon clipping planes.

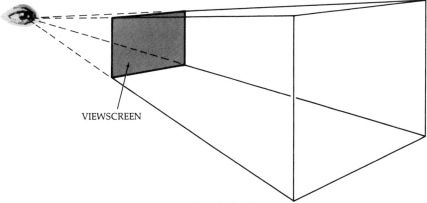

11-4. The viewscreen is often placed at the hither clipping plane.

cut off'' is called a *frustum*, so sometimes the visible world is said to lie within a *viewing frustum* formed by the hither and yon clipping planes and the four boundary walls.

PROJECTIONS AND PERSPECTIVE

Objects in the viewing volume are three-dimensional, and those on the viewscreen are only two-dimensional. You need a consistent way of getting those three-dimensional objects onto the screen that simulates the way a real camera would do it. This kind of operation is called a *projection*, and there are many ways of doing it. Following are descriptions of two projections.

The first, called *orthographic projection*, is illustrated in Fig. 11-5. Lines are drawn from the object to the viewscreen, intersecting the viewscreen at right angles. This kind of projection is often used to produce engineering and drafting illustrations, but it does not usually produce pictures that look as if they were photographed.

Another kind of projection, called *perspective projection*, does create a photographic effect. Note in Fig. 11-3 that the size of the yon clipping plane grows larger as it recedes from the eye. The objects farther away from the eye must appear to shrink if the entire yon clipping plane is to fit on the viewscreen. This shrinking of distant objects accounts for the phenomenon of *perspective*, a characteristic of photographs taken with a real camera or images seen with the human eye. A viewing volume with a large yon clipping plane is said to have a more extreme perspective than one with a smaller-sized clipping plane, as in Fig. 11-6.

The sizes of the clipping planes are not usually specified explicitly. Instead, you usually specify these values for the viewing pyramid by the distance of the hither clipping plane along the Z axis, the distance of the yon clipping plane along the Z axis, and the *half-angle* of the apex of the pyramid. This last parameter is called a half-angle because it specifies the angle between one wall of the pyramid and the line going through the center of the viewscreen from the eye. If it is more convenient, sometimes you can specify the *full-angle* instead, which is the angle from wall to wall, as shown in Fig. 11-7.

You might notice that in Fig. 11-7 the Z axis was assumed to be receding from the eye, with the eye at $Z = 0$. This is a common technique in creating images; before rendering, the computer automatically transforms the world so that the X and Y axes are in the viewscreen, and the Z axis goes away from the eye perpendicular to the viewscreen. This modification of the coordinate system is called the *viewing transformation*, and it is done to make the actual rendering easier to understand and program. Some systems prefer to use a viewing transformation that puts the viewscreen, instead of the eye, at $Z = 0$.

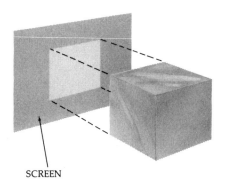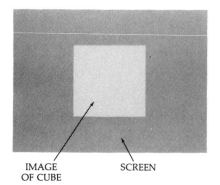

SCREEN

IMAGE OF CUBE   SCREEN

11-5. Orthographic projection.

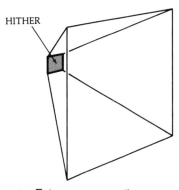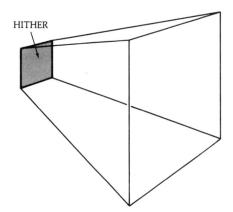

HITHER

HITHER

A. Extreme perspective.

B. Small or moderate amount of perspective.

11-6. The viewing frustum for both extreme and moderate perspective.

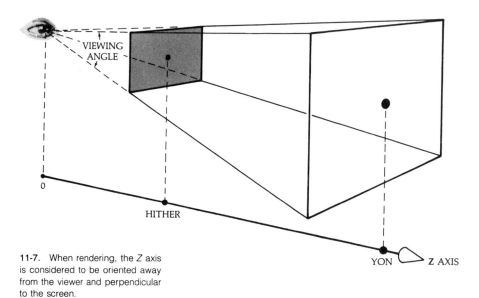

VIEWING ANGLE

0

HITHER

YON   Z AXIS

11-7. When rendering, the Z axis is considered to be oriented away from the viewer and perpendicular to the screen.

TYPES OF RENDERING ALGORITHMS

Many popular rendering techniques work by filling in one pixel at a time, line by line. Since each horizontal line on a raster monitor is called a *scan line*, rendering techniques that work by filling in lines pixel by pixel are called *scan-line algorithms*.

There are some rendering techniques that do not work very well as a scan-line algorithm. This is because the mathematics for a scan-line version of the technique can be very slow, very expensive, or simply unknown for some classes of surfaces. Some of these difficult surfaces can be handled with another approach of rendering technique, based on *subdivision algorithms*. The name comes from the mathematical technique used to produce the picture.

Another class of techniques is made up of *random-sampling algorithms*. Generally, these techniques work by finding the color of the image at arbitrary points on the screen, independent of any other screen locations.

Lastly, there are *preprocessing algorithms*. This class of techniques helps a rendering systems by examining the model and adding information that will help the final picture look better in some way. The resulting model can then be rendered by any rendering technique.

ALIASING

Before examining any image generation algorithms in detail, it is helpful to consider a few ideas that are important to understanding any rendering technique. The first such idea is a class of problems called *aliasing*. To ''alias'' is to masquerade, or to appear as something else. Mathematicians have studied aliasing in a variety of fields, and it recently has become an important issue in computer graphics.

Without detailing the mathematics of aliasing, its effects can be generalized as artifacts visible in an image or animation resulting from cutting something into pieces that are too large.

For example, you usually draw your pictures in a frame buffer. The frame buffer only has a limited number of pixels. When computing the color for a particular pixel, you sometimes color the entire pixel with the color of the object that is seen by the center of that pixel. Thus, sometimes small objects will slip between *pixel centers*, as shown in Fig. 11-8. If this object is moving within an animation, or the camera is moving around a static scene, this object might *flicker* on and off as it variously hits and then doesn't hit pixel centers.

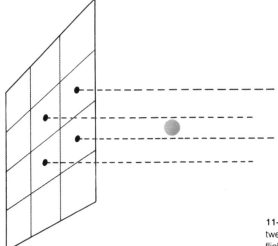

11-8. Small objects can slip between pixel's centers and cause flicker.

Fig. 11-9 shows a narrow cylinder to be drawn on the frame buffer. Note that you need only be concerned here with whether or not the center of each pixel can "see" the cylinder. So some pixels are completely filled in with cylinder, and the others are completely empty. This condition gives rise to the *jaggies*, or *edge staircasing*. For any high-quality images, from stills to film and animation, it is quite important to eliminate these annoying effects.

The cure for aliasing is called *anti-aliasing*. There are many anti-aliasing techniques, some simple and some sophisticated. Again, you need not be overly concerned with how anti-aliasing can be done, but the results can be seen in Fig. 11-10, which shows a pair of objects with and without anti-aliasing.

Although there are many mathematical techniques for doing anti-aliasing, they all result in what appears to be the same effect: a slight *blurring* of small pieces of the image in a very controlled, particular way. Blurring is not always bad: The blurring in Fig. 11-10 is very slight and carefully controlled.

Fig. 11-11 shows a closeup of Fig. 11-10, to illustrate how sharp edges are gently blurred to smooth them out. Note that several shades of gray are now used, no longer just black and white. Note also that this image is not being blurred indiscriminately; a transition between two differently colored regions is carefully built. Just how to make this transition is determined by the geometry of the regions and the mathematics of anti-aliasing. The idea is that from a distance one color appears to smoothly fade into the other color. From even a short distance, the "fuzzing" of edges becomes unnoticeable, and the human visual system, fortunately, interprets what it sees as a crisp edge.

Anti-aliasing is also very important when you want to display text on a frame buffer. If you want to draw very small characters, you might find that there are not enough pixels to allow you to draw a good-looking character. The result is a choppy letter or number, which is uncomfortable to look at. Fig. 11-12 shows how anti-aliasing can be applied to a large character to shrink it to a smaller size. The original letter "B" is 190 by 122 pixels, while the final result is only 30 by 21.

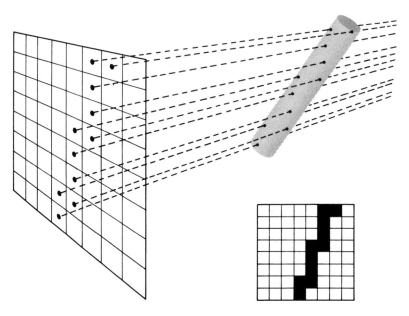

11-9. A jaggy cylinder resulting from some pixels being completely filled in with the cylinder and some being completely empty.

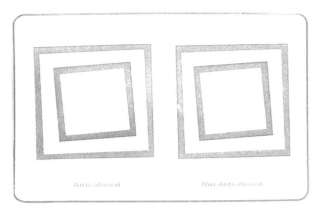

11-10. Objects with and without anti-aliasing. (Image by Paul Sholtz. Used with permission of IBM Corp.)

11-11. An enlargement from Fig. 11-10 showing how anti-aliasing smooths out sharp edges. (Image by Paul Sholtz. Used with permission of IBM Corp.)

Bodoni Book Italic - 18 point

Original Character   Filtered Character

11-12. Anti-aliasing applied to a large character (left) for reduction. The character on the right is only 20 pixels high (it is enlarged to better show the pixels).

Unfortunately, anti-aliasing is often a slow procedure. But the surprising thing about anti-aliasing is the quality improvement you get when you apply it.

As previously mentioned, aliasing results from cutting something up into pieces that are too large. In Fig. 11-9, cutting the screen into pixels that are too big means that staircasing and jaggies become noticeable. One solution might be to use many, many more pixels, but that would require waiting much longer to have your images generated. Although it is not a good idea in general, you can use that approach for quick-and-dirty anti-aliasing. The idea is to create your image at some resolution much higher than you want it, and then average down the high-resolution picture. For example, suppose you wanted to make a picture 512 pixels on a side. If you render the picture using a grid of pixels that is 1,024 on a side, you can then average two-by-two blocks of pixels into a single pixel in your final image. This approach will help reduce some aliasing effects, but it is not a very good method for picture-making in general.

MOTION BLUR

Motion blur occurs as a result of how conventional film is shot. Each frame of film passes in front of the camera lens, gets exposed, and is then moved away from the lens and eventually back into the film can. But, if when the film is being exposed, objects in front of it are moving, the film records the motion as a blur. If the motion is small enough during the exposure, then the blur will be slight. The faster the movement of an object, the greater its blur. Figs. C-14 and C-15 show examples of computer-generated images including simulated motion blur.

It can be very difficult to create motion blur in computer-generated images. Most rendering algorithms effectively "freeze" the world at the moment of rendering. For example, in a three-dimensional scene, the positions of the various objects are determined and then they are drawn. No information is kept about where the objects are going or how fast they are moving.

Because motion blur is the result of an object moving, to truly simulate that effect you need to know everything about an object's motion throughout the exposure of a frame. This extra information usually makes rendering programs both bigger and slower.

There are other problems similar to motion blur, which happen when objects are moving at fast speeds on the film, but the speed is changing. For example, think of a scene shot in extreme perspective, consisting of a spaceship flying from the center towards the viewer's right shoulder. As the ship gets closer it gets bigger, and it also appears to be moving faster because of perspective. Without motion blur, the ship will appear to *jump* abruptly from frame to frame. But there is another effect visible in such a situation. When you see a fast-moving object, your visual system predicts where the objects will be in a moment. But because you are using a great deal of perspective (which you're not used to), the prediction made by the visual system at one frame will not match where the spaceship actually appears in the next frame. Not only does the ship appear to jump, but you actually see both ships for a moment; you obviously see the ship on the screen, but you also "see" the one your visual system predicted for you. This kind of double-exposure is called *strobing*. Strobing is greatly reduced when each image is correctly motion-blurred.

It is important to get motion blur into your animations if you can. A great deal of work has gone into methods for making each individual computer-general image look realistic. Some systems are set up to support techniques for handling motion blur in a general way. But it is still a difficult problem because so much information must go into each frame to get the streaking to look right. Some systems do not support motion blur at all, and the ones that do may run slower than the ones that don't.

What if your system doesn't support motion blur? The first option is to ignore motion blur completely.

If you do want to simulate motion blur in three-dimensional animation, there is a simple trick that is sometimes helpful. When you finish rendering a frame of animation, add behind your image a copy of the previous frame, while greatly lowering that previous frame's contrast. It is as though you drew the current picture in the frame buffer without the previous frame having completely faded. Often people will add the previous two or three frames, with greatly diminishing contrast for each. Fig. 11-13 shows motion blur simulated with this technique. It does not always work well (and sometimes can be really bad), but it can be better than nothing.

Another approach, only useful in video production, is called *animating on fields*. This approach effectively shows new pictures to the viewer twice as often as usual, and can reduce the problems introduced when motion blur is lacking. Recall that a video image is typically drawn using interlaced scanning, so each frame is really built from first the odd scan lines, and then the even ones. Typically you *animate on frames*; you render a frame for time t, and then render another showing the world at $t + \frac{1}{30}$, then another a thirtieth of a second after that, and so on (for film work the interval is usually $\frac{1}{24}$ second. When animating on frames, you first render just the odd scan lines at time t, and then render the even scan lines at $t + \frac{1}{60}$. Then render the next set of odd scan lines at time $t + \frac{2}{60}$, then the even ones at $t + \frac{3}{60}$, and so on. The result is that images are shown twice as fast frames. The drawback is that each image is only a half-image. This technique can often work fairly well, but not as well as incorporating motion blur into the animation.

In the context of animation, motion blur fits the definition of aliasing as ''cutting things up into pieces that are too large.'' During animation, each frame of film is spanning too long a time. (That statement is not a very precise analysis of the problem, but if you were able to show, say, 100 frames per second, then the movement on the screen would be updated so rapidly you would not need motion blur.) Considered in this way, it could be said that motion blur is a result of not taking a large enough number of exposures of film in time, therefore it is aliasing in time, which is also called *temporal aliasing*. Sometimes people use this term to emphasize the mathematical way of looking at the problem of motion blur.

11-13. Motion blur may be simulated by adding in previous frames at lowered contrast. (Image courtesy of Digital Arts.)

SHADOWS

Some good techniques for handling shadows have begun to find acceptance in commercial products. There are no overall principles to those techniques; in fact, new shadow techniques are still being invented.

Shadows are an important part of the visual world. They indicate where things are, what is in front of what, and the shapes of surfaces. Shadows are usually an important part of making a picture look realistic, but they are not always necessary or appropriate. Sometimes you get shadows where you do not want them, and they obscure an important detail. And sometimes shadows are simply distracting from what you really want to focus on. But even though you might not always want shadows in your images, they are an important part of most realistic images.

Shadows have been a subject of much interest in computer graphics. They present a problem in that shadows themselves are not really objects and they surely are not light sources, and that exhausts the list of things we have seen. Shadows are a sort of in-between object. They have some three-dimensional components (if one object casts a shadow on another, anything you move into the space between them will also get shadowed), but you only really see a shadow when it is cast upon a surface.

Generally, a shadow is made of an *umbra* and a *penumbra*. The umbra refers to that part of the shadow that is completely dark; the penumbra is the fuzzy region at the edges of the shadow. Fig. C-14 shows an example shadow including both of these regions. Directly under the center chair is a region of umbra. The fuzzy area around it is a penumbra.

If you could shine a perfect, point light source, placed at infinity, onto a perfectly smooth sphere with a perfectly flat plane behind it, you would see a perfectly round, black disk on the plane. This disk is the shadow image of the sphere, and, since it is all perfectly dark, this disk is all umbra; those points on the plane are in the umbra of the shadow. If you are in the umbra of a shadow, you can see none of the light source that is casting that shadow. This situation is shown in Fig. 11-14.

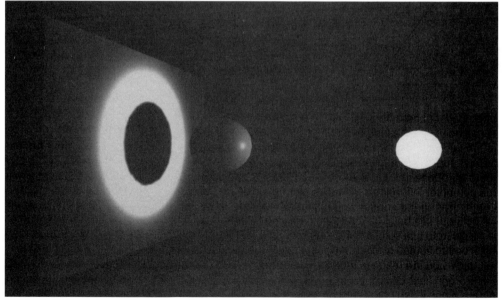

11-14. A shadow cast by a sphere onto a polygon. The black disk in the center is the umbra, which is surrounded by the fuzzy penumbra region. (Image courtesy of Digital Arts.)

Now think of the same sphere and plane, but this time illuminate them with a long fluorescent tube from not too far away. There will be points on the plane where the sphere blocks some of the tube, but not all of it. Thus, those points receive only some of the light from the tube; they are somewhat darker than the points that are completely lit, and somewhat brighter than those that receive no light at all. Those points are in the penumbra of the shadow. If the light source is big enough, you have only penumbra and no umbra.

Some systems that render shadows only include the umbra portions. In such a system, all shadows have crisp edges, regardless of the actual size of the light source. Other systems support penumbras as well. (It seems unlikely that there would be a system that would provide only penumbras!) Most shadows in everyday interior scenes are very fuzzy, since the lights are near and relatively large; this is where penumbras are very important. Most outside scenes are lit by the sun, which for most practical purposes can be considered an infinitely far point light source; in this type of scene, penumbras are not as critical as for indoor scenes.

Other effects come into play when you generate shadows. When objects (or details upon them) are very small, *diffraction effects* begin to appear (a diffraction effect occurs when some light seems to "creep around" the outside of an object that seems to block it). Most graphics systems do not support these (usually subtle) diffraction effects.

Shadows can certainly come in colors; the shadow cast by a stained-glass window is colored by the glass. Some systems do not support this effect because it can be complicated to program and slow to run.

SUMMARY

All three-dimensional objects live in a three-dimensional world called object space, but a rendered image of an object appears on the viewscreen in screen space. The part of object space that is directly visible from a particular point of view lies in the viewing volume. When the screen is a rectangular, the viewing volumes is a viewing pyramid, with the eye at the apex. The four sides of the pyramid are called boundary walls; the far side is the yon (or far) clipping plane. Most systems allow you to use a hither (or near) clipping plane as well; this is often set to the position of the viewscreen. Together, these walls are called the clipping planes. If those objects (and parts of objects) that lie nearer to the eye than to the hither clipping plane are ignored, then the pyramid becomes a frustum; so the viewing pyramid becomes a viewing frustum.

The act of converting an object from a three-dimensional shape to a two-dimensional image is called projection; when the projection is intended for rendering it is called the viewing projection. The engineer's orthogonal projection draws an image by sending every visible point in the viewing volume to the screen along a line that intersects the screen at a right angle. A more realistic projection includes perspective, leading to the perspective projection. To control the sharpness of a perspective you can specify the half-angle or full-angle at the tip of the pyramid; a larger angle gives a greater perspective.

From a user's point of view, there are only a few major classes of techniques for rendering. Scan-line algorithms work by filling in pixels one after the other across a horizontal scan line; they often derive much of their efficiency by reusing information from pixel to pixel as they work. Some curved surfaces can only be rendered with subdivision algorithms, which divide the object into small pieces to make it easier to render. A random-sampling algorithm works on each point (or pixel) on the screen independently, so different pieces of the screen can be rendered by entirely different machines. All of these techniques may be preceded by a preprocessing algorithm, which enhances a model with additional information before rendering to improve its quality in some respect.

All rendering techniques must take into account the aliasing problem. One way to think of aliasing is as the result of cutting something up into pieces that are too large. One common aliasing problem is flicker, visible in animation. This is caused by objects sometimes being rendered (because they are seen by pixel centers) and then sometimes not rendered, so they flash on and off on the screen. This problem shows up in still images as the jaggies, or staircasing, when tilted edges turn into choppy staircases because the pixels are too large to represent a smooth edge. No matter how small the pixels get, they will still be too large to correct this problem; anti-aliasing techniques must be used.

Anti-aliasing can be roughly considered as a carefully controlled type of blurring. It is based on mathematical theory and an understanding of the human visual system, so that when an image has been properly anti-aliased, all the edges will appear crisp and clean from a distance.

When a photographed object is moving quickly, it typically leaves behind a blurry trail on the film. This trail is called motion blur, and it is an important effect in making animated films appear realistic. Without motion blur, objects may appear to jump from frame to frame, or they may appear to be in two places at one time, an effect called strobing. Some systems provide accurate motion blur as part of the rendering process, by far the best solution.

There are two quick-and-dirty ways to simulate motion blur. One is to add in one or two previous frames at much lower contrast to each frame of film. Another is effective only in video production, where frames are drawn one field at a time. You typically create a film by animating on frames, meaning new images are created frame-by-frame. By animating on fields you create a new picture for each field instead of each frame. This way you can show a new image (actually a half-image) every sixtieth of a second, instead of every thirtieth of a second.

Most realistic images include shadows. Shadows exist only with respect to a light source; a certain object can be in a shadow from one light but illuminated by another. Generally, a shadow is composed of two regions. The umbra is the darkest area of a shadow and consists of those points where the light source is not visible at all. The penumbra is a hazy or fuzzy region where some of the light source is visible, but not all of it. The penumbra usually appears when an object is lit by a light source that has a large radiator (such as a fluorescent tube or hanging globe) and that is not too far away. Indoor scenes typically have penumbras on most shadows. When objects (or features upon them) are very small, diffraction effects start to appear, but most systems ignore these effects.

12 RENDERING ALGORITHMS

Once you have built a three-dimensional model, set up your lights, and positioned your camera, you are ready to render the image. There are many types of rendering programs from which to choose. Each has its own advantages and disadvantages, and your choice of program will be guided by availability and appropriateness to your needs.

This chapter covers three popular techniques in some detail: Z-buffer, ray tracing, and radiosity. Most rendering algorithms share at least some of the principles used in these three; they represent a cross section of the popular and available methods.

Z-BUFFERS

Frame buffers are not limited to storing pictures. They are large pieces of computer memory that can hold one or more numbers for each point on the screen. The stored information may be a color number ultimately destined for a color map, it may represent the RGB components of the color at that point, or it may be something else. This "something else" turns out to be an extremely useful concept for actually generating shaded pictures, and special techniques have been developed to take advantage of it. The basic idea is that if you want to store information about a picture on a pixel-by-pixel basis, a frame buffer is a natural place to put it.

There is a popular rendering technique that uses this idea. It works in two main steps, which can be posed as several questions. The computer has chosen a point on the screen (often a pixel center) and wants to know if anything should be drawn there. It chooses an object and asks: "Is this object visible from this point? If so, is it the closest object to the eye, or is it blocked by some other object?" If the object is both visible and the closest to the eye, the computer then asks: "What is the correct shading (color) for this object at this point?" For convenience, these questions can be reworded and asked for each pixel:

- Is this object visible from this point on the screen, using the current point of view?
- Is it the closest object at that point that has been encountered so far?
- Given the closest visible point on the surface from this point on the screen, what color is the surface there?

Once you know the answer to the question about color (which is really a question of shading), that point on the screen is filled in with that color. Then, you move on to the next point (or pixel) and ask the sequence of questions again. Once you have gone over the entire screen for this object, you get the next object in the scene, go back to the upper-left corner, and start again, checking for visibility pixel by pixel. This process is repeated for every object in the scene.

The frame buffer can help determine whether a visible object is the one closest to you (from a given point of view). Imagine several objects arrayed in front of you in random ways. To make an accurate picture, those objects that lie closest to the eye should be visible; those objects behind them should not be in the final picture (ignore transparent objects for now, so assume everything in the scene is opaque). If two opaque objects both project to the same point on the screen, the closer one to the eye is the visible one, and the nearer object should be the one visible in the final picture. There's no problem if other objects are drawn on the screen while you build up the picture, because the final picture is all you are concerned about. It helps that the computer's picture (in the frame buffer) is completely erasable.

This set of ideas is the heart of the technique known as the *Z-buffer algorithm*. The Z-buffer algorithm allows you to build up first objects and then scenes by drawing them one simple surface at a time. The name comes from using a frame buffer to store some information instead of a picture. The information stored in this extra frame buffer is the *Z-depth* of the nearest visible object at that point, hence the name *Z-buffer*. As mentioned in Chapter 11, an automatic first step in many rendering algorithms is to transform the world so that the *Z* axis points away from the viewer perpendicular to the screen. Thus, two objects at the same point with different *Z* values are at different distances from the eye; the one with the smaller *Z* value is closer.

The Z-buffer algorithm first selects a simple surface and then finds any and all points on the screen where it is visible. It does not matter in what order the surfaces are selected from the total scene description. Choosing a different order of objects will cause the picture to look different as it is built up, but the final image will be the same no matter what order you take the surfaces in.

Two frame buffers are used to build up your picture. The first is called the *image buffer*. It holds colors and is where you draw your image. You can use any depth of frame buffer for this image buffer.

The first step in using the image buffer is to clear it to some *background color*. Your new picture will be drawn in the image buffer, and you should erase anything that might accidentally be in it at the time you start the new picture. For simplicity, assume that the image buffer has only eight bits at each pixel, so it uses a color map. Clearing the buffer then just means selecting a color from the color map that makes a suitable background color and setting every point in the frame buffer to the number that represents that color.

Now set up another frame buffer, which will not hold a picture. You are not interested in the color map, and whatever the frame buffer looks like is only of curiosity value. This second buffer is the *Z-buffer* and will hold numbers that represent not colors, but the distance from the eye of points represented in the image buffer. Typically, Z-buffers are at least sixteen bits deep. Thus, each entry in a Z-buffer is a single large number that represents the distance of the nearest visible surface at that pixel, along the *Z*-axis (Fig. 12-1). The Z-buffer is initially cleared to the

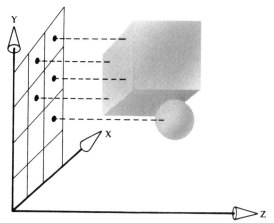

12-1. A Z-buffer holds the depth of the nearest object at each pixel.

largest value it can hold, which is often also the Z value of the yon clipping plane. Suppose that value is 500 units down the Z axis. Consequently, every pixel in the Z-buffer holds the number 500.

Now you are ready to render an image; you have chosen your first surface to render. Each pixel on the screen is examined and the computer checks (mathematically) to see if the surface is visible from that pixel's center. This activity provides the answer to the question: "Is this object visible from this point on the screen, using the current point of view?" The answer is illustrated in Fig. 12-2. If the surface is not there, then none of the following work is done and, instead, the computer just selects the next point on the screen and checks to see if the object is visible there. Suppose that the computer has finally found a point on the screen where the surface is visible, and say that this point is identified on the screen by the (X,Y) coordinates of (230,210) in the image buffer. Also say that this object is eighty-five units down the Z-axis from the eye at this point (if more than one point of the surface is in the line of sight, as in Fig. 12-3, then you need only concern yourself with the closest point of the surface).

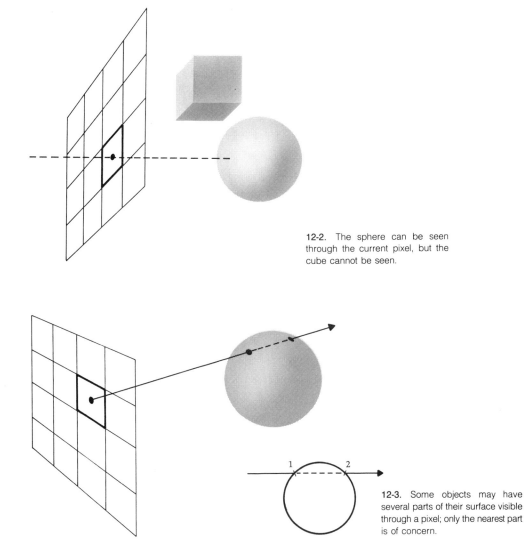

12-2. The sphere can be seen through the current pixel, but the cube cannot be seen.

12-3. Some objects may have several parts of their surface visible through a pixel; only the nearest part is of concern.

Now you know that the surface projects to this point, and you ask the question: "Is it the closest object at that point that has been encountered so far?" In the Z-buffer algorithm you ask, "Is this object closer to the eye than whatever object is currently represented in this pixel?" You know the distance of this object from the eye at this pixel; the computer determined it when it calculated the projection of the object on the screen (in this example it is 85). Now you need to know the depth of the object currently represented on the screen at this pixel.

To find the Z-depth of the visible object here, look at the value in the Z-buffer for this pixel. It contains the number 500 (the yon clipping plane, to which it was initialized). The pixel of interest on the sphere has a depth of eighty-five units, which means it is closer than the object currently in the image buffer at that point so it *obscures* (or covers up) the image there. So now you know that coordinate (230,210) sees this new object in front of what it saw before. Shade the object by answering the question: "Given the closest visible point on the surface from this point on the screen, what color is the surface there?" Put the resulting color in the image buffer at (230,210). The contents of the Z-buffer at (230,210) are replaced with the value 85. Now any other objects that project to (230,210) will have their Z values compared to the new value of 85. Only if their Z values are less, will the new color be placed in the image buffer, and the Z-buffer changed. Otherwise, you know the object lies behind some other object at that point, and you just move on to the next pixel on the screen. An illustration of a new object coming into the Z-buffer is given in Fig. 12-4. You can then finish the object. If there are more surfaces to be drawn, handle them in the same way. Note that it does not matter what order the objects are taken. The closest object at each pixel will always be the one remaining there in the end, after all surfaces have been rendered.

As you watch a Z-buffer picture being built up, it will frequently look wrong as surfaces are rendered one by one. But over time the closer surfaces will cover up and obscure farther surfaces, and the final image will look correct.

Figure 12-5 shows three different sequences for building a dumbbell out of two spheres and a cylinder. A snapshot was taken of the screen right after drawing each part in each sequence. Notice that the final images are exactly the same, regardless of the order in which the objects were drawn.

Although the Z-buffer is not intended to be a picture, it does hold an image of some kind. Often it holds an attractive moiré pattern that bears a resemblance to the picture in the image buffer. A picture of a Z-buffer is shown in Fig. 12-6.

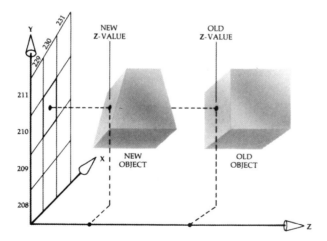

12-4. The new frustum will be drawn at the pixel because its *Z* value is less than the one stored for the cube.

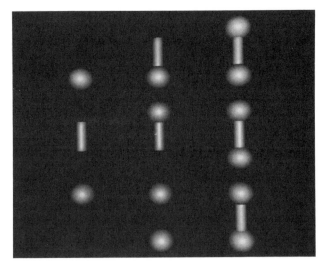

12-5. The order in which objects in a Z-buffer are rendered does not affect the final image. Each row shows a different order of rendering. (Image courtesy of Digital Arts.)

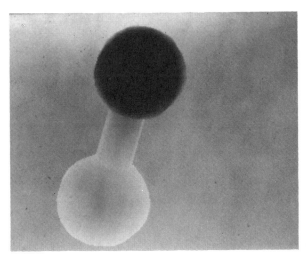

12-6. A Z-buffer (seen with a linear ramp for a color map).

Z-Buffer Algorithm Problems

The Z-buffer algorithm is valuable for its speed and generality in rendering. However, it has its problems, just as everything else does.

Transparency is not handled in the algorithm as described. It can be incorporated with a sorting step and then a variation of the painter's algorithm discussed in Chapter 4. The extra programming necessary to sort the objects before drawing becomes an expensive addition to the algorithm, resulting in both a larger program size and longer rendering time.

Reflections are not modeled in the Z-buffer algorithm at all. Mirrored surfaces require programs to be written to create textures that are applied to surfaces to make them look at all reflective. If many surfaces are reflective, then this algorithm becomes very unattractive. Z-buffers are also particularly prone to aliasing problems, since they typically only look down pixel centers (or else a small number of fixed locations within a pixel). It is hard to make good-looking motion blur with Z-buffers. It is also not obvious how to make good shadows with a Z-buffer.

With enough effort and some clever programming tricks, though, most of these limitations with the Z-buffer algorithm can be overcome. As an example, I show in a following section how to include shadows in a Z-buffered image. But as more and more effects are added on to the algorithm, it begins to lose its simplicity.

In the terminology of Chapter 11, Z-buffer techniques would be called scan-line algorithms. Although in theory they could work independently for each pixel, in practice most systems get an efficiency boost by sharing information among the pixels in a scan line. For that reason Z-buffers almost always draw their images one scan line at a time.

Z-Buffer Algorithm Advantages

Perhaps the strongest points in favor of using the Z-buffer technique are simplicity and speed. It is easy to program, it is simple to understand, and, with some care, it can work fairly quickly. There are even special pieces of commercial hardware devoted to doing nothing but implementing Z-buffer rendering, which can make it very fast.

Another advantage of Z-buffer techniques is that they allow you to make pictures with as many objects as you wish. Many other rendering techniques require the computer to hold in memory all the objects that will eventually make it to the screen. Since computer memory is limited, so is the number of objects that you can render with such a technique. But the Z-buffer algorithm draws each object one at a time, and needs no information about previous or following objects. Thus your pictures may contain an arbitrary number of objects.

The Z-buffer technique also permits many different kinds of objects to appear in a single picture. Each object is rendered independently, so there may be different programs for each kind of object. To correctly render an object, a program needs only to get to the picture buffer and the Z-buffer. Thus, a modeler may draw 5,000 polygons, followed by 100 curved surfaces, followed by a fractal mountain range, and then add more polygons. Each of these sections of the picture can be created by totally independent programs. Being able to use independent programs is helpful when you want to add a new kind of object to your computer's primitive object repertoire. You need only write a new program; you do not have to make additions and changes to existing programs, which can be much more difficult.

Z-Buffer Shadows

Although it is time-consuming, the Z-buffer algorithm can be extended to create a picture with shadows. The technique for using Z-buffers to draw shadows requires a large amount of storage and time, and it can only cast shadows from "infinite" light sources.

Suppose you are sitting inside a light source, looking at the scene. Here is the heart of the algorithm for including shadows with the use of Z-buffers: Anything that you can see will receive light from you. Anything that you cannot see will not receive light from you, so it will be in shadow with respect to your light (although it might be getting light from some other source). Take a look at Fig. 12-7 and imagine what you could see if you were standing at different points on the two spheres.

To use this observation, imagine that you are about to render an image with one light source. First you render the entire image from the point of view of that light source. You can ignore the image, but you will want to keep the Z-buffer, which is called the *illumination* or *shadow buffer* for that light. Any point that is farther away from the light source than the nearest point in a particular pixel (as found in the shadow buffer) is blocked by that first point and is thus in shadow.

If you have more than one light source, then you render the picture once for every light source, saving each individual shadow buffer. When you have rendered the picture once from each light's point of view, you are ready to draw the final picture from your eye's point of view. The computer

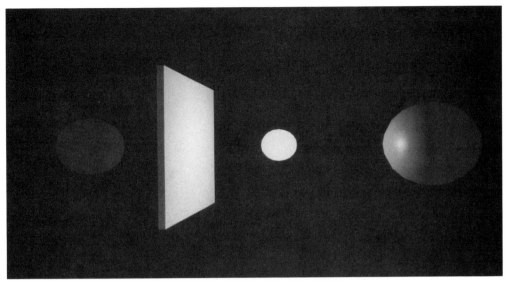

12-7. Points on the left sphere are in shadow because the polygon blocks them; points on the right side of the right sphere are also in shadow. (Image courtesy of Digital Arts.)

will proceed as usual with standard Z-buffer techniques, until it finds a visible point on a surface. It then wants to find the shading, and that is where the shadow buffers come in.

For this point, shadow information is computed on a light-by-light basis. First compute what pixel this point would be in if viewed from the light source, and then calculate its distance from that light source. Now check the shadow buffer that you saved for that light. Look at the point you want to shade and find its distance from the light. Then find from which pixel in the shadow buffer that point is potentially visible from the light source. If this object is at the distance stored in the shadow buffer at that pixel, then it must be the one receiving light, and you add in the illumination from that light source. But if the distance for this point is greater than the one stored at that pixel, it must be further away than the nearest object and is thus blocked by that object; that arrangement puts that point in shadow. So you do not add any illumination from that light. Then proceed to the next light source and repeat the whole procedure. Of course, all the mathematics are handled automatically by the computer. Fig. 12-8 shows three shadow maps, which were used to create the image in Fig. C-18.

The fact that the Z-buffer algorithm can be used to create shadows is important, but remember that you must save all the shadow buffers, which can take a great deal of storage. You must also render the entire image once for each light source for each frame, which can take a lot time. Thus, if you have five light sources illuminating a scene, it will take at least six times longer to draw the final picture than without shadows (once for each light, and then one more time for the final picture).

Another drawback is that the technique just described will not let light fall through transparent or translucent objects, so that some objects are only partly in shadow. It essentially forces all your objects to be fully opaque.

So Z-buffers are very simple in their basic form, and they can generate some realistic pictures, but their power is limited. If you want anything more (such as shadows or transparency) than what they easily provide, then their use becomes complicated. If you want fast pictures with lots of objects and fairly good results, Z-buffers may be your best choice. But if you want more realism, and you are willing to wait for it, you may find yourself attracted to one of the techniques of ray tracing or radiosity instead.

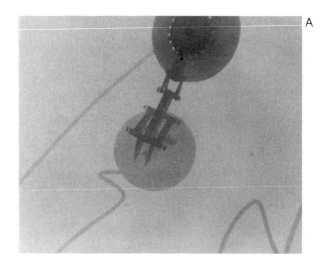

A

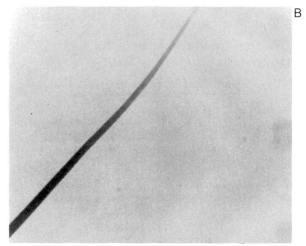

B

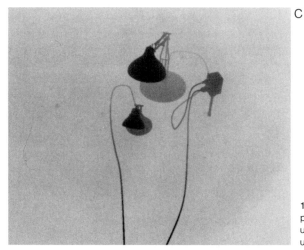

C

12-8. Three shadow maps computed for the three light sources used to create Fig. C-18. (Image used with permission of Pixar.)

RAY TRACING

Ray tracing is another type of rendering algorithm and it is, perhaps, the oldest rendering technique discussed in this book, although it has recently become widespread and popular. Ray tracing is often considered a random-sampling rendering technique because every pixel can really be thought of as a completely different problem.

Ray tracing is not a modified form of Z-buffer rendering. The whole process of generating an image works differently with this technique. The goal of ray tracing is to explicitly use the well-known physics of light to help you draw a picture. The image is based on the laws of light and optics that have been used for years to describe how prisms, lenses, and other objects affect light.

Imagine a light source as the originator of a huge number of light rays. Each ray starts at the light source and travels in a straight line until it hits an object. The object may then absorb the light, reflect some of it, or perhaps also allow some light to pass through if the object is somewhat transparent or translucent.

If you followed every light ray from the light source, as it bounced and reflected throughout a three-dimensional scene until it hit your viewscreen (if it ever did!), you would be able to build up a complete picture on your screen. Unfortunately, this technique is not suitable for practical purposes. First, there are far too many rays coming out of any light source for you to be able to follow them all with a computer in any reasonable amount of time. Second, most of those light rays will not reach the screen. You can spend a great deal of time following light rays that just disappear into nowhere and don't help you make a picture at all. For example, imagine creating a picture of a living room; all of the light rays that go out of an open window are useless to you for the purpose of making a picture, but if you didn't know that beforehand you would have to follow them anyway.

The scheme can be modified simply by tracing the rays the other way. Instead of following rays from the light source to the screen (and then, implicitly, the eye), you can trace them from the eye back to the objects in the scene. That way you know that every ray you trace will somehow contribute to at least one pixel on the screen, because that is where it started.

Ray tracing is one of the slowest rendering algorithms used in computer graphics today. So why does anyone use it? The reason is that ray-traced pictures can easily contain many of the optical effects previously noted (reflection, transparency, shadows), as well as in incorporate straightforward anti-aliasing for still images and motion blur for animation.

Figure 12-9 shows a viewing pyramid, with the eye looking right down the center and the screen located at the hither clipping plane. A ray is drawn from the eye, through a pixel on the

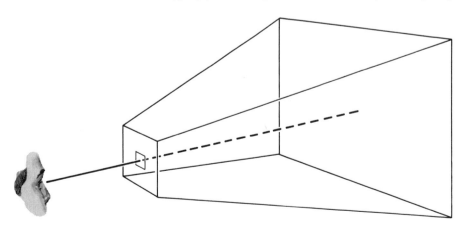

12-9.   An eye ray entering a viewing pyramid.

screen, and traveling into the viewing pyramid, where a three-dimensional model is located.

You need to know what happens to the ray when it hits different objects, because it is those interactions that will create your picture. Fig. 12-10 shows an example of a ray hitting an opaque, matte-finish (i.e., diffusely reflecting) sphere. Remember that this ray is really the path that light will follow away from the sphere and back to the eye. The sphere has a dull surface, so it does not reflect much light back to the eye (there is no highlight), and because it is opaque, no light passes through the surface of the sphere into the inside (and then perhaps out the back of the sphere). The light leaving the sphere along this ray is made up of the color of the incoming light from the light sources, modified by the material making up the sphere.

Fig. 12-11 shows a ray hitting a sphere that is both shiny and transparent, like a crystal ball. The ray bounces off the surface of the sphere as a reflected ray, and also passes through the surface of the sphere as a transmitted ray. Note that the transmitted ray has bent as it passed through the surface of the sphere (remember the discussion of refraction in Chapter 4).

Fig. 12-12 shows a ray entering a more complicated scene. Note that when a ray hits an object, that ray stops and two new rays (a *transmitted ray* and a *reflected ray*) begin. It is the effect of these rays that gives transparency (the transmitted ray) and reflection (the reflected ray). Sometimes you tell the rendering program that you only want to follow the original ray from the

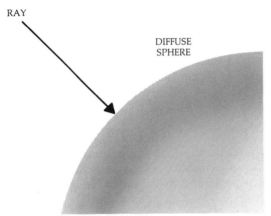

12-10. A ray striking a diffusely reflecting sphere.

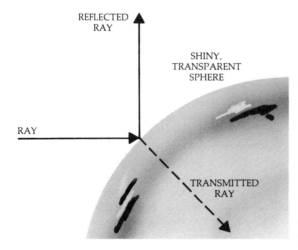

12-11. A ray striking a shiny, transparent sphere.

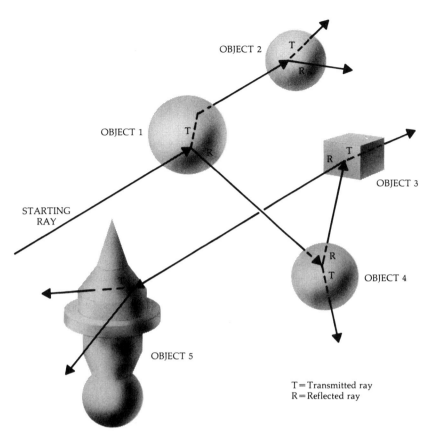

OBJECT 2

OBJECT 1

OBJECT 3

STARTING RAY

OBJECT 4

OBJECT 5

T = Transmitted ray
R = Reflected ray

12-12. A ray entering a complex scene.

eye (called the *eye ray*) until it has bounced some number of times. In this context, the word *depth* is used to describe the number of bounces, because you can associate with each ray an abstract picture of a tree, as shown in Fig. 12-13. Each row of the tree has more rays than the previous row; the exact number of new rays is dependent on how many light sources are illuminating the scene.

After several bounces you can quickly have many rays going at once. This situation will cause the computer to run slowly when it is rendering a picture, since each ray can take a while to follow. One typical approach to limiting the time you must wait for a picture is to impose a limit on the depth of the tree before you begin.

But you cannot limit the tree too much. It is difficult to identify a universally good point for stopping the tree, but a least value can be established fairly easily. Fig. 12-14 shows a ray going through a wine glass, hitting a mirror, and returning, along with the tree for this picture. To get the ray back to the eye from the mirror you need at least six levels to the tree, so six is certainly a minimum depth for the tree for this image. More complicated pictures may need much deeper trees, so they will take much longer to render.

The ray-tracing scheme is very good at handling hidden surfaces. The mathematics of ray tracing indicates easily which object is the first to be hit by a ray. You do not need a Z-buffer, but you do need to keep all the different objects present the entire time you are drawing a picture. You should also note that, although the viewing pyramid is important in ray tracing for determining perspective and hither/yon clipping planes, you might end up seeing objects outside of the pyramid

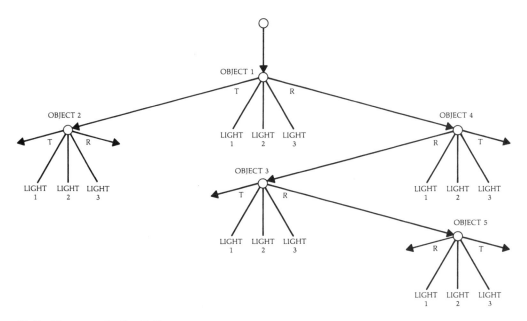

12-13. The ray tree for Fig. 12-12.

12-14. At least six levels to the tree are needed to follow a ray through the glass and reflecting from the mirror.

itself, because they could be reflected in objects that you can see directly. Fig. 12-15 shows a sphere reflecting the image of a sphere outside the viewing pyramid. Although rays from the eye cannot hit this "outside" sphere directly, the sphere can certainly be seen in the picture. Thus, the model can exist in a large volume of space, much more than just the viewing pyramid.

Since models can occupy an unlimited region of space, the computer has no way of "knowing" when a ray has passed outside of a model. It is easy to imagine a ray missing all

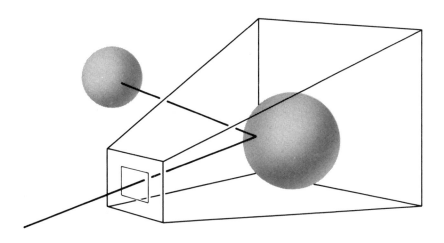

12-15. A ray can strike an object outside the viewing pyramid.

the objects in a scene and traveling off into infinity. You certainly would not want to trace that ray forever! To stop rays from shooting off into space forever, most modelers place a *bounding* or *world sphere* around the universe of the eye and the model, as illustrated in Fig. 12-16. This sphere is colored with some background color for the picture. If a ray hits this background sphere, it stops and assumes the color of the sphere where it hit.

So you have seen how ray tracing begins with a ray starting at the eye, passing through a pixel, and continuing into the world of the model. You have seen how that ray can be absorbed, reflected, and transmitted off of objects, and ultimately hit the bounding sphere. How, then, is all this information used to actually create a picture?

The technique actually consists of two steps: first you build up the tree of rays, and then you process the tree. You have seen something of how transmitted and reflected rays come about, but in the illustrations of trees you have also seen rays going off to light sources. What are those rays for?

Those rays are sometimes called *illumination* (or *shadow*) *rays*. To shade a point, one important piece of information needed is the color and intensity of the illumination arriving at that object directly from the light sources.

You find this illumination by considering each light source, and determining if it is indeed illuminating the point in question. If some opaque object is between the point and the light source, then no illumination will reach that point, and no illumination from that light source is added. If there is nothing between the point and the light source, then you calculate the light falling on the point as before. Notice that this gives shadows automatically; since some points will not have illumination from the light source added in, they are effectively in shadow. You can handle penumbras if you determine just how much of a light source is visible from a point. As more of a source is visible, that point will receive more light. So the amount of light you add to the point can be proportional to the area of the light source that is visible.

How do you determine if there is an object blocking the light between the light source and a point on a surface? To make things simple, assume you are only using point light sources. The essential step is to realize that if light can arrive at the surface directly from the source, then it must have followed a straight line. If there are any (opaque) objects along this straight line, then the light will be blocked, and the point will be in shadow. To see if you are blocked, you can start a ray at the light source and send it towards the object you are trying to shade. If you reach that object before hitting anything else, that point is illuminated; otherwise it is in shadow.

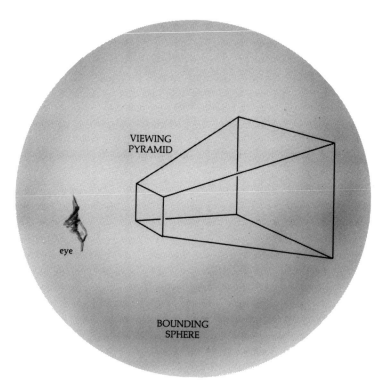

12-16. Surrounding a model with a bounding sphere to keep rays from traveling off into infinity.

In practice, it is usually easier to start the ray at the point being shaded and to follow it back to the light source. If the line between the point and the light source is not blocked by any objects, then it makes no difference which way you originally followed that line. Light will still travel from the source to the object along that path.

Now that you have seen how to shade objects, you are ready to start the actual business of rendering the picture, which is the second step of the create-the-tree/process-the-tree procedure mentioned before.

The central issue lies in the computation of the light leaving a point in a certain direction. To find the outgoing light, you need to find the incoming light. In ray tracing, you break that incoming light into three pieces: the direct illumination, the light that is ultimately reflected by the surface, and the light that is ultimately transmitted by the surface.

I have shown that you can find the direct illumination by tracing rays from the point to the light source and determining if they are blocked by any other objects. But what light is reflected and transmitted by the object? Ignore diffuse effects and simply consider specular reflection and transmission for now.

If you assume that the surface is perfectly flat, then there is only one direction from which light will come in order for it to be specularly reflected back into the direction in which you are interested. It might help to look at the situation from the point of view of the object being reflected. Imagine that a small peanut is being reflected off a mirror, and you (the observer) are looking into the mirror at a particular point. If you want the peanut to be reflected off of that point and back to your eye, you have to hold the peanut in such a way that the reflection will go into your eye. In general, there is only one direction, although you can get nearer and farther from the mirror to make the peanut look larger and smaller. But if you move the peanut off to one side, you no longer see the reflection.

Physicists have known for years how to determine that single direction in which you can see a reflection. In ray tracing, you find that direction, and then go looking to see if there are any objects out there. If you find an object in that direction, then that object would be reflected off the mirror and into your eye. So now you know the object that is being reflected and what point on the object is being reflected by the shading point on the surface. You then shade that point on the other surface; when you know the color leaving the other surface towards the mirror, you can add it into the color of the light leaving the mirror.

You might have noticed that in order to find the color leaving the other object, you do the same thing you did for the mirror. In fact, every point on every surface will go through this same sort of procedure.

To handle transmitted light, you follow essentially the same steps. Pretend that, instead of a mirror, you are looking at a piece of glass. Find the direction from which light must come if it is going to pass through the glass and into your eye. If there are any objects in that direction, find the color of the light leaving that object towards the glass and add it to the light leaving the glass (on the other side).

You find out with reflection and transmission rays if there is an object either being reflected or transmitted. For example, you build a reflection ray to find out if there are any objects reflecting off of the shading point. This ray begins at the shading point and travels in the direction from which reflected light would come. If the ray hits an object, then that is the reflected object. The transmitted ray does the same thing for transmitted light.

So these rays are traveling backwards to the direction that the light will really follow. You follow these rays because they help to quickly find the object that would send light back to the shading point. Then you find the light leaving those objects (which travels from the object back to the shading point), and when you combine this with the light coming directly from the light sources, you are finished finding the light both arriving and leaving the shading point.

Figs. C-20 and C-22 show images created using the basic ray-tracing technique. There is some mathematical theory that explains how to extend the technique to include anti-aliasing of almost all the aliasing phenomena: jaggies, strobing, motion blur, penumbras on shadows, and so on. This extended technique is called *stochastic ray tracing*. The term "stochastic" refers to a carefully controlled random process that lies at the heart of the anti-aliasing methods. To use the extended techniques of stochastic ray tracing, you need not know much more about ray tracing than I have covered here; your computer will do the appropriate extra work and you will get better pictures.

Ray tracing can be very slow (some of the computations can be quite difficult), but it is versatile because of the special effects it can handle and the wide range of objects that can be used in the models being rendered.

On the other hand, ray tracing does have its limitations. For instance, shadows do not always work completely right. Remember that if you hit an object, you assume that you are in shadow. That statement is valid for an opaque object. If an object is transparent, then the light should pass through and continue to the next surface; ray tracing has no good way to handle that effect. You can see some ray-traced pictures with shadows that appear to pass through slightly transparent or colored objects, but these are usually hand-tuned by the programmer or artist.

Another problem is caused by lenses, which are responsible for an optical effect called *caustics*. When you hold a magnifying glass over a piece of paper at just the right height, you get a very bright, focused spot of light, a caustic. This same effect causes rippling lines at the bottom of a swimming pool. Most ray tracing programs cannot handle caustics very well.

Perhaps the biggest problem with ray tracing results from *diffuse inter-reflections*. Ray tracing cannot handle this phenomenon at all. However, there is another rendering technique that has been specially designed to cope with diffuse inter-reflections: radiosity.

RADIOSITY

To determine the color of light leaving a surface in a given direction, you need to know both the properties of the surface and the color of the light striking that surface. Finding the properties of a surface are easy: They are provided by the modeler as part of the material description.

Perhaps the most straightforward way to calculate shading is with a technique such as ray tracing: you send rays to the light sources and the other surfaces in the scene to find what color light they are sending towards the point in which you are interested. That procedure works well for specular reflection and transmission, since you can generally find out just which objects are being reflected or transmitted.

But diffuse reflection and transmission are not so easily handled. If you are indoors right now, look up into a ceiling corner of the room. Unless you are in a very brightly lit or specially designed room, it is probably a little bit darker in that corner than on the flat surface of the wall. In fact, the junction between two walls is probably also a little bit darker than the wall, but not as dark as the corner. You can really see this effect if one wall is dark-colored (say, dark red) and one is light-colored (say, white). Right where the walls meet, the red wall will look a little lighter and the white wall will look a little pink.

This effect is caused by *diffuse inter-reflection*. Consider the red wall: Light strikes the wall and is then reflected. If the wall is painted with matte paint, there is probably little specular reflection (no highlights). But the wall does reflect diffusely and it is this diffusely reflected light that you see when you look at the wall. Since you see red when you see the wall, the light leaving the wall is red-colored. But just at the edge of the red wall is a white wall, and a little bit of the diffusely reflected red light is striking the white wall, tinting it red or pink. This is not a specular effect; it does not matter where you stand or where you look from, the effect (also called *color bleeding*) is still visible.

If you try to simulate diffuse inter-reflection with ray tracing, it will go very slowly. The problem lies in not knowing just from where diffusely reflected light might be coming. Since it can really come from anywhere, you have to shoot lots of rays, in all directions, just to see if any objects are reflecting diffusely towards you. This is a very time-consuming procedure, and it might not even work very well if you don't take enough rays.

Another way to solve the diffuse inter-reflection problem is with a technique called *radiosity*. This preprocessing technique is based on the principles of *energy transfer*, which has been studied by engineers and physicists. The basic idea is this: you break down the world into many, many little pieces, called *elements*, and then you find the contribution of reflected light from every piece to every other piece.

What does "many, many little pieces" mean? That is hard to say, exactly, and often systems require the modeler to help out and choose how many elements are needed. For example, you might use one big polygon to model the wall of a room. That is probably going to be much too big a piece if you are rendering a scene within that room with radiosity. The computer will want to divide that polygon into a dense grid of smaller polygons. Taken together, they still have the same shape as your wall (you won't get any cracks or overlaps), but now you can look at smaller sections of the wall one at a time.

Once everything in the scene is chopped up into small polygons (or elements), you then process those elements. One way to proceed is to work in two steps.

The first step involves determining just how much of each element is seen by every other element. The amount of element A that can be seen by element B is called the *form-factor* relating A and B. The form-factor is a purely geometrical piece of information, based on how much of one element can be seen by another.

If A and B are very near one another and parallel, the form-factor AB will be nearly 1, indicating that almost all the light leaving one surface will arrive at the other. If A and B are very far apart and edge-on, the form factor will be nearly 0. At other orientations and distances the form factor will be a value between 0 and 1 indicating how much the two surfaces are able to see of the other. If A and B are very near each other but *C* completely blocks them, again AB will be 0, although AC and CB may be large.

The second step is to *balance* the energy absorbed and radiated by each element by calculating its radiosity: the sum of the light that is emitted by object (if it is a light source) plus the light that is reflected. Perhaps the best way to see how radiosity works is to follow an example.

Suppose you have three small, rectangular elements in your scene, called A, B, and C, as shown in Fig. 12-17. The light source is A (say, a rectangular light source), while B and C are small pieces of wall painted with a matte paint. You begin by calculating the form-factors relating each pair of elements: AB, AC, and BC. You can store those form-factors away somewhere, for use later. The essential point is that these form-factors are just geometrical values and have nothing to do with the lighting. As long as the elements are not moved, the form-factors will not change.

Now you start the *balancing loop*. First calculate the *emittance* of each element; only A has any emittance, since it is the only light source. Next calculate the *reflectance* of each element, which is how much of its *incident* light each surface reflects. The first time through the loop, you don't know how much incident light each element is receiving, so assume that there is none. Consequently, the total radiosity of surfaces B and C is 0 because the sum of their emitted and reflected light is 0. The radiosity of A is equal to its emittance.

Now that you have a guess for the radiosity of each element (which describes how much light is leaving the element), you can find out how much of that light is striking each of the other elements. The amount of light falling on B from A is equal to the radiosity of A times the form-factor AB, which scales that light depending on the geometry relating A and B. You then find the light falling on C due to A, again by taking the radiosity of A and multiplying it by the form-factor AC. Now you are finished with the light leaving A, and you repeat the process to find how much of the light leaving B falls on A and C, and how much of the light leaving C falls on A and B.

Then you are ready for a second time around the loop. Each element now has a new value for its incident light, built from the radiosity of the other elements and the form-factors connecting them. So now you can find a new guess for the radiosity of each element; it is the sum of the emitted light (which is not changing) plus whatever incident light is reflected. With these new radiosities, you again calculate how much of the light leaving A falls on B and C, and so on.

It might seem that this would be a never-ending procedure, but, in fact, things begin to settle down after enough repetitions. At some point, the new calculation of the incident light at each element will cause no change in its reflected light; in effect, everything works out so that the whole system is consistent. At this point the system of elements is described as *balanced*, or the process

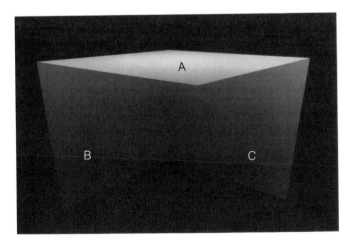

12-17. A small radiosity environment. The upper polygon (A) is a light source and emits its own light. The two polygons below it (B and C) absorb and reflect the light from A and each other. (Image courtesy of Digital Arts.)

is said to have *converged*. When the system has converged, you have a *solution*: a value for the radiosity of each element, taking into full account the light falling upon it from all the other elements.

At this point the diffuse inter-reflection problem has been solved, at least on the scale of the elements. Each surface, in addition to the color given it by the modeler, has also been given some extra color by the radiosity process to account for the reflections of objects among each other. If you render the scene now, you have a complete picture showing all the direct illumination and diffuse inter-reflection (and transmission) in the scene.

An added bonus of using the radiosity technique is that the form-factors give automatic shadows with umbras and penumbras. The job of finding out how much light is transferred from one element to another was handled when you computed the form-factors, and from then on it was a built-in part of the process. And these shadows are not only those due to the light sources; you also pick up shadows caused when one object sits between two other objects that are reflecting light back at each other.

These subtle effects can greatly improve an image. More importantly, perhaps, they provide a better simulation of reality. This kind of approach to making an image not only makes a better-looking picture, but it makes a picture more true to the real world. Figs. C-19 and C-21 show two images created with radiosity methods.

Since the form-factors depend only on the geometry of the scene and not the lighting, you can change the emittance of some objects to adjust the lighting on the scene. The expensive work of breaking the world into elements and then calculating form-factors need not be repeated; only the relatively quick balancing loop need be performed to create a new picture showing the new illumination.

Note that the radiosity method is independent of viewpoint. It does not include any information about specular reflections and transmissions; only diffuse reflection and transmission is solved for in radiosity. When you are ready to draw your model with a rendering technique, the changed colors of the model will automatically account for the diffuse inter-reflections; the rendering technique itself will need to handle specular effects.

SOME COMPARISONS

The three rendering techniques in this chapter, Z-buffers, ray tracing, and radiosity, are by no means a complete list of rendering methods, but these three do span the range of most available techniques.

Recall that Z-buffer techniques are primarily scan-line methods, ray tracing is a random-sampling method, and radiosity is a preprocessing method. Why are they so different? And why use one instead of the other?

These three algorithms are so different because they are really trying to do different things. Z-buffer techniques are best for quickly making images that convey a three-dimensional scene for which realism is not so important. You can make Z-buffer images look very realistic, but extra work is required. Some people think of Z-buffer algorithms as a "brute-force" image generation technique because there is just enough work going on to produce a reasonable three-dimensional image.

Ray tracing tries to match some of the real world more carefully than the Z-buffer technique. Specifically, ray tracing is ideal for scenes that include reflective and transparent objects and for when special effects such as good shadows (including penumbras) and motion blur are important.

Radiosity is a little different than the other two techniques because it is not really a rendering method. It is, rather, a technique to enhance your model and to add to it new coloring that takes into account the subtle effects of diffuse inter-reflection. But it can also create excellent shadows and can even account for those shadows between inter-reflecting objects (which ray tracing cannot do).

No one of these three methods is best for all purposes. Z-buffers are the fastest, ray tracing is best for shiny and transparent objects, and radiosity is a boon when you have many diffuse inter-reflections, which is common for indoor scenes. All three share the strengths of supporting different modeling techniques (including texturing). None of these techniques generates images that are completely realistic; the physics of the real world are very complicated, and computer graphics programs have barely begun to scratch the surface.

Then what does make a realistic image? Probably it is a combination of the quality of the geometric model, the richness of the materials chosen to apply to the surfaces, and the physical accuracy of the rendering. If your models are built crudely, then there is no need for super-realism in the rendering (incidentally, there is nothing wrong with crude models; they can sometimes convey more meaning than very accurate copies of real things). If your surfaces are very simple, then again there is no need for true-to-life rendering; wood grain, rough textures on walls and chairs, and subtleties of shape geometry are part of the real world, and if they are not in the model, no rendering technique will save your image. But if you have detailed models and rich surfaces, then you might want to try for realism; in which case you have to resort to the programs that simulate physics (ray tracing, radiosity, and maybe some other techniques) and aim for the lofty goal of photorealism.

If your goals are to create stylized or new kinds of images and animation, then you might find the strict physics of the techniques needed for photorealism to be too restrictive. You would then probably be drawn to one of the simpler techniques (such as Z-buffers) that allow you the freedom actually to tinker with the works and change how things look.

A couple of quick examples might suggest the possibilities offered by these simpler, but more accessible, techniques. Try rendering your picture halfway through, then clear the Z-buffer back to the yon clipping plane (but don't touch the image buffer!) and continue rendering. Switch the comparison in the Z-buffer test: only write a new pixel if the Z-value is greater than the one already stored (initialize the Z-buffer to the hither clipping plane for this one). Or, render a scene into a Z-buffer and then use the Z-buffer as a bump map in another scene (or even the same scene, re-rendered!). These procedures all produce interesting but totally unrealistic effects.

So the techniques that favor realism are useful when you want to simulate the real world, but the simpler techniques can offer more flexibility and experimentation.

SUMMARY

There are a number of techniques for rendering images. One of them is the Z-buffer algorithm, which is of the scan-line algorithm variety. This technique makes use of a frame buffer called the Z-buffer that stores on a pixel-by-pixel basis the Z-depth of the nearest object encountered so far at that pixel. That object appears in the image buffer, which is originally cleared to a background color. The Z-buffer itself is initially cleared to the Z-value of the yon clipping plane.

The basic Z-buffer technique does not support transparency, reflections, or shadows, although all of those qualities can be added at the cost of extra rendering time and program complexity. The advantages of Z-buffers are their simplicity and versatility, and the fact that they can handle an unlimited number of objects.

Shadows can be added to the Z-buffer method by rendering the scene once from the point of view of each light source. The result is stored in an illumination (or shadow) buffer for that light. When rendering the scene from the eye's point of view, points may be transformed to the point of view of each light, and from there compared with the appropriate value in the shadow buffer for that light. This comparison can reveal whether or not a point is in shadow with respect to that light. One drawback of this scheme is the great increase in rendering time and storage requirements demanded.

Another rendering technique is ray tracing, which is of the random-sampling variety. Ray tracing begins with an eye ray that starts at the eye and travels into the scene through the viewscreen. When the ray strikes an object, a transmitted ray and a reflected ray are sent out into the environment to determine the color of the light that will be reflected and transmitted by this object back to the observer. Each of these rays follows the same process of striking an object and sending out additional rays. The result is a ray tree of some depth, or number of bounces. You may choose to limit the depth of the ray tree before rendering to increase speed at the expense of some shading quality. If a ray never hits an object it will eventually strike the bounding sphere, which gives the ray a background color.

Shadows are created through illumination (or shadow) rays. These travel from the shading point to a light source. If an object blocks the ray before it reaches the light, then the shading point is in shadow with respect to that light; otherwise that light's illumination is added in to the incident light at the shading point.

Once the ray tree has been built, it is shaded from the bottom up, eventually ending with a color for the eye ray, which is placed into the appropriate pixel on the screen.

Anti-aliasing can be handled with an extension of ray tracing called stochastic ray tracing. Problems that cannot be resolved with this method are caustics (bright spots of focused light) and diffuse inter-reflections.

To handle diffuse inter-reflections (or color bleeding) the preprocessing technique of radiosity may be used. Radiosity is based on the principles of energy transfer, which describes how light bounces among parts of an environment.

The scene is initially broken down into small elements, which together form the original model. Each pair of elements is examined, and a form-factor is calculated from their relative geometry. The form-factor describes the percentage of light radiated from one surface that will strike the other. Once the form-factors are computed, you can begin to balance the light in the environment.

This operation takes place in a balancing loop. The first step is to find the emittance (or self-generated light) of each object. Then a guess is made to estimate the incident light at that point, and from that value the reflected light is calculated. The total radiosity of that element is the sum of the emitted and reflected light.

Then each pair of elements in the scene is examined. The light leaving each surface is scaled by the form-factor and applied to the other as incident light. Once this has been done for all pairs of elements, each element has a new guess for its incident light. The computer recalculates the radiosity of each element, and the loop is repeated.

After a while the system converges, meaning that it has become balanced. At that point you have a solution, which describes just how much light is bleeding from every element to every other. The model is then modified to take these diffuse inter-reflections into account, and can then be rendered.

Part of this process is that objects cast shadows on other objects even when they are not in the direct path of a light source. Radiosity can greatly enhance the realism of a rendered scene by taking into account light balancing and shadows.

Ray tracing and radiosity are often the rendering algorithms of choice for photorealism, since they closely approximate the real world. But by the same token, they are also quite fixed in their approach. The Z-buffer technique, though far less realistic, is often more flexible, and can offer opportunities for new kinds of creative expression in rendering.

13 ADVANCED MODELING

Previous chapters introduced polygons and curved surfaces as modeling primitives, and presented some methods for building models from those primitives. There are many other types of modeling primitives available on most systems; some are explicit surfaces (such as polygons), and others are built from your instructions (such as fractals). Once you have your models, there are also some interesting ways to combine and modify them to make them more interesting.

This chapter introduces a variety of useful primitive surfaces and a few techniques for combining and manipulating those surfaces in sophisticated ways.

COMPLEX SURFACES

In the first part of this chapter I present some surfaces that are more complex than the polygons and simple curved surfaces (quadrics and patches) described in previous chapters. In general, though, there is nothing discussed here that you could not do with polygons and simple curved surfaces if you really wanted to. In fact, in many systems every modeling object is automatically converted into a very fine mesh of polygons before rendering. This way the program can be carefully designed to be extremely efficient at rendering polygons, yet still support more complex sorts of shapes.

So why not use polygons directly? Sometimes that approach is fine, but it is not a good use of your time as a modeler. Suppose you want to model a round ball. You could manually construct a spherelike surface from many polygons, but it would take a lot of work and you probably would not be sure how many polygons you would need for the ball to look round. It is much easier to just work directly with a sphere. This approach allows you to work more efficiently, describing your shapes the way you think of them rather than how the computer wants to see them.

The world is complex, and a complete set of tools for describing everything in simple ways is not yet available. Indeed, such tools may never exist. For example, the best way to describe the shape of a human hand may be to actually give a very detailed, point-by-point model of a hand. But there are other shapes that have some kinds of regularity or symmetry that can be exploited. Or else there is some other handle that we can get on the description that allows us to state it more compactly than a long list of points.

This section covers some of the techniques that are commonly used to describe complex shapes. It does not provide an exhaustive list; new techniques are invented all the time. But the ones described here have been available for some time and have proven to be useful.

Sweep Surfaces

There is a general class of techniques for making a model that works by taking some original shape and moving (or *sweeping*) that shape along a three-dimensional path. If the shape leaves a trail behind it as it moves, the result is a three-dimensional shape called a *sweep* (or *swept*) *surface*.

Generalized Cylinders

One class of sweep surfaces uses a two-dimensional contour as a shape. Imagine taking a long piece of stiff wire and straightening it out, and then fitting it into a crack in the floor so that it stands straight up. Then take a phonograph record and hold it so that the wire goes right up into the hole in the center. Focus your attention just on the rim of the record and let go, so the record falls straight to the floor. The rim of the record is circular, and it moved in a straight line. The rim just traced out a circular cylinder, which is a sweep surface.

You can generalize this experiment with the record and the wire by bending the wire into some unusual shape; the record will still follow the wire from the top to the bottom (you may have to help a bit by pushing it at some places). This technique generates a tube with a circular cross section, but bent like a piece of neon tubing formed into a sign (ignoring the kinks that this practical process puts into the glass). You can also change the shape of the record into something other than a circle; any flat shape will do. You can move a square, an outline of the letter S, or a silhouette of a car along the wire.

All of these swept shapes are called *cylinders*. Our familiar circular cross-section, straight-line path cylinder is just a special case, sometimes called a *right circular cylinder*. The three-dimensional curve along which you slide the two-dimensional curve is called the *path* (or *generator*), and the two-dimensional shape is called the *contour* (or *profile*). Sometimes shapes built this way are called *generalized cylinders* to emphasize the possible variations.

A special class of cylinder is the *generalized prism*. This is any two-dimensional contour swept along a straight path. The image of a guitar case can be made this way; choose the curvy shape of the guitar as your profile and sweep it for a bit along a straight line. If you want a slightly larger lid, enlarge the contour a little bit and start sweeping it from the top down, stopping before you go very far along the path.

Fig. 13-1A shows a two-dimensional contour of three intersecting circles. That contour may be swept along a straight line to generate the prism of Fig. 13-1B. In general, you may make any kind of transformation you wish to the contour as it moves along the generator. For example, scaling the contour as it moved resulted in Fig. 13-1C. You can also use a path more interesting than just a straight line; a piece of a circle resulted in Fig. 13-1D.

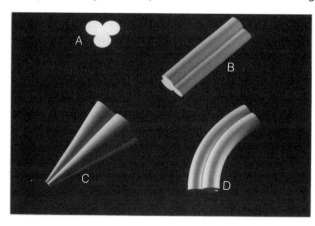

13-1. Sweep surfaces. *A*: a simple contour. *B*: *A* swept along a straight line. *C*: scaling the contour as it is swept. *D*: bending the sweep surface. (Image courtesy of Digital Arts.)

Another interesting variation is to rotate, or twist, the contour as it moves along its path, with a result like Fig. 13-2A. You can also combine transformations. In Fig. 13-2B twist and scaling are combined, and in Fig. 13-2C twist is combined with a curved path. Twist, rotation, and scaling together make Fig. 13-2D. All these cases use the same profile; only its path and transformations change.

Sweeping is a powerful technique for creating complex shapes from simple ones. Imagine a profile that consists of a hollow ring, like the letter O. If you sweep that profile along a short curved path, you get a piece of macaroni!

The modeler's job is to specify the three-dimensional path and the profile (and the transformations to the profile as it moves, if desired). The computer will do the work of sweeping the profile and keeping track of the three-dimensional shape generated by its moving contour.

Surfaces of Revolution

Another way to produce a sweep is to use a slightly different kind of contour. On a piece of paper, draw a straight line. On one side of the line, draw any curve you like, as long as it never crosses the line. Then imagine taking that curve and spinning it around the line in three dimensions for one complete revolution, sweeping out a surface as it goes. This surface is called a *surface of revolution*. The curve is also called a *profile* and the line is called the *axis of revolution* (or the *axis of rotation*). Fig. 13-3 shows a wine glass generated as a surface of revolution, the classic example of this technique.

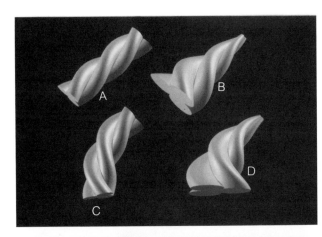

13-2. More sweep surfaces using the contour in Fig. 13-1. *A*: rotated (or twisted) as it is swept. Transformations may be combined while sweeping: scaling and twist (*B*); bending and twist (*C*); scaling, bending, and twist all simultaneously (*D*). (Image courtesy of Digital Arts.)

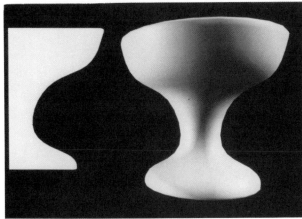

13-3. A surface of revolution. (Image courtesy of Digital Arts.)

Usually the profile you draw for a surface of revolution is not changed as the curve is swept around the axis, because you want the surface to join where it begins and ends. This procedure is similar to the operation of a lathe. As the piece of wood spins around, you cut into it with a tool; the cut is the same all the way around the piece.

Surface Sweeps

The discussion so far has been about two-dimensional profiles moving along three-dimensional paths. You can also move three-dimensional objects along three-dimensional paths. Imagine sweeping a sphere along a straight two-dimensional line. The result is a cylinder, but with round ends (the sphere at the beginning and end). Everywhere else, multiple copies of the sphere overlap and you end up with just a single round tube. Remember that for an opaque object you are only concerned with the surface that is generated at the outside of the sweep. What things look like on the inside of the surface is unimportant.

All of the two-dimensional sweep techniques can be applied directly to three-dimensional sweeps, creating *surface sweeps*. The three-dimensional object can be transformed in any way as you sweep, and you can use any three-dimensional path you can think of. Sweeping a sphere seems useful; it produces the same thing as a two-dimensional circular sweep except for the rounded ends. Generally, most objects are not practical for surface sweeps: What is the shape generated by a pair of scissors swept along a three-dimensional spiral? And, more importantly, why would you want such a shape? Surface sweeps may be an answer in search of a question, but they can create some interesting-looking surfaces.

Contour Sets

Some shapes are difficult to describe directly. Think of a mountain. How can its overall shape be described? The technique used by hikers and mountain climbers is to rely on topographical maps. A topographical map shows *contour lines*. Every point on a contour line has the same altitude. If you walk along a contour line, then you will not go up or down at all. Rivers tend to flow downhill as quickly as possible, so they cut across many contour lines as they travel down a mountainside.

You can follow this process in reverse to create a shape. You might construct an object by describing the shape of contour lines at various elevations, and then ask the computer to create the complete shape by joining the contours in some sensible way. Fig. 13-4 shows an example of building a complete object from contours.

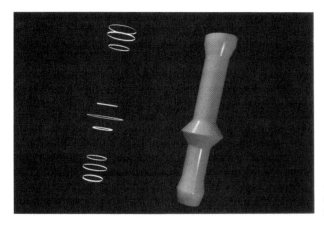

13-4. Turning a set of contours into a three-dimensional object. (Image courtesy of Digital Arts.)

This is a very common technique used in medical computer graphics, when doctors take X-rays or CAT (computer-aided tomography) scans of a patient. These techniques take a series of pictures representing different "slices" through the patient. If a particular bone is under scrutiny, then several cross sections of the bone are taken at slightly different locations. A doctor identifies the contours of the bone for the computer, and the computer determines the surface that best fits those contours, thereby creating a three-dimensional model for the bone that can be rendered later.

You can use this technique as a modeling tool because sometimes cross sections are the best information available. For example, suppose you want to model the hull of an ocean yacht. Often the only information known about a hull is the shape of several cross sections. You can enter these into the computer and ask it to compute a smooth surface that joins the contours. Of course, you can never be sure you guessed right. But for constructing a model rather than trying to reconstruct something real, you can change the contours (or add new ones or delete existing ones) until you like the shape you get.

Another example of the use of contour sets is a bottle design. Suppose you want to make a bottle that is hexagonal for most of the base,but round at the top so you can have a twist-on cap. It might be somewhat difficult to model all the polygons to make a smooth transition from the hexagon to the circular top, but you could do it with cross sections, using a hexagon at the bottom and the middle (so that whole lower half is hexagonal) and a circle at the top. The system will make a smooth change for you from the hexagonal cross section to the circular cross section, and you will have your bottle.

Blobby and Implicit Surfaces

This section introduces a new kind of modeling primitive, called a *blob*. Blobs are different from the primitives previously described because you do not actually model directly with them. For example, if you put a polygon somewhere, then that is where the polygon shows up in your rendered image. But blobs create models indirectly instead.

Starting with two-dimensional blobs makes the extension to three-dimensions easy. Fig. 13-5 shows two two-dimensional blobs approaching each other. A blob is a mathematical object that is extremely dense in the middle, and grows less dense at its edges. Density is shown here on a pixel-by-pixel basis, where the most dense part of the blob has value 1, which falls to 0 at the edges of the blob. In the figure the pixels are colored white for density 1, black for density 0,and grays for in-between values.

Blobs combine in an interesting way. If two blobs are placed close to each other, their values add together. Fig. 13-5 shows blobs some distance apart. Select the value 0.05 as a magic density

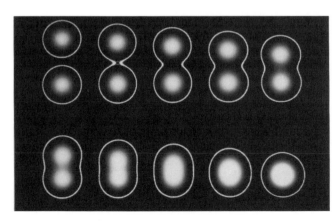

13-5. A pair of two-dimensional blobs approaching each other. The whiteness of a pixel indicates its density. A bright white line has been drawn at the density of 0.05, showing the isodensity contour at that value.

and color all pixels with that value bright white so that they are easy to find. Note that there is a circle around each of the blobs when they are far apart. Since the circles indicate the regions of constant density, they are called *isodensity contours* (the prefix *iso-* means ''the same''). The value you pick for the isodensity contour is sometimes also called the *blobbiness* of your blobs.

As the blobs get closer, the pixels between them start combining the densities of the blobs. As the blobs get closer, the two isodensity contours begin to stretch towards each other, and finally end up merging and becoming one big contour. If you have several blobs in the scene, the contours can have very interesting shapes.

The extension of this process in three dimensions is straightforward. Use three-dimensional blobs that are basically spheres or ellipsoids of ever-decreasing density, and draw the three-dimensional surfaces that correspond to those points that have some fixed density; these are called *isodensity surfaces*. With your blobs in some fixed position, different values for the density will give you different isodensity surfaces. These surfaces can have a lovely organic feel to them, different from most shapes in computer graphics, since they smoothly flow together when they get near to each other. When animated, blobs can move in lovely ways. Sometimes the isodensity surfaces are called *blobby surfaces*. Fig. 13-6 shows the approach of three-dimensional blobs. In this figure, the isodensity contours are each drawn at the same level as the blob centers approach each other.

Fig. 13-7 shows two fixed blob centers, with several isodensity surfaces around them, each at a different blobbiness value. Notice that each surface fits completely within the next larger one.

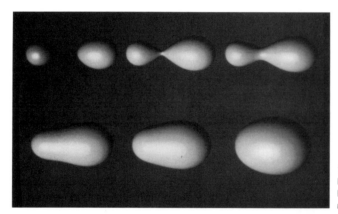

13-6. A pair of three-dimensional blobs approaching each other. Notice the stretching as they get near.

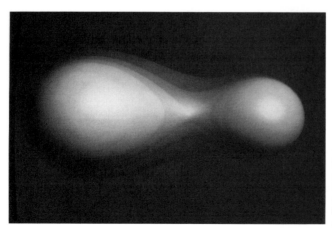

13-7. If the blob centers are left fixed, choosing different blobbiness values leads to different surfaces. Here six surfaces at different densities are shown at once. Notice how each blob neatly fits within the next larger blob.

Isodensity surfaces belong to a larger class of surfaces called *implicit surfaces*. This is a very large class because it contains all of those surfaces that are solutions to a very general form of mathematical equation. By choosing your equation carefully, you can create some interesting shapes, but quite a bit of sophistication is usually required to get that equation right. Fig. 13-8 shows an implicit surface. Notice the smooth region where the three prongs join.

Particle Systems

There are many objects in the world that do not seem to fit into the type of models described so far. For example, how would you model fire?

Probably the best way, given the techniques presented, is to construct some kind of three-dimensional flame-shapes (with polygons or some other surfaces), and then texture-map a picture of fire on those shapes, with a transparency map so you can see through and around the flames. But that is a very time-consuming solution, and in some ways it begs the issue. Where are you going to get all those pictures of flickering flames to map onto the three-dimensional flames? One answer is to draw them, but you would end up making hundreds of drawings for just a few seconds of animation. Surely there is a better way.

Another approach is to think of the flames as being made up of many little glowing particles, each of which begins at the fire source (a burning log, for example) and travels upwards, blowing in the wind, until it burns out. If you use enough of these particles and they move realistically, you begin to get something that looks like fire. This approach is an application of a modeling technique called *particle systems*. Particle systems do not create modeling surfaces such as polygons or blobs, but, rather, represent an approach to orchestrating the movement of many tiny surfaces (or particles). These particles are generally controlled by a few parameters that describe their typical lifetimes. A particle starts somewhere and travels with some speed in some direction. For fire particles, each particle would also be emitting a certain amount of light of a given color. The path of the particle is specified, as well as a description of how the light changes as time goes on. Eventually the particle fades out, and is said to "die"; that is the end of that particle. You do not usually specify all of this information for each particle individually. Instead, you give more general directions and let the computer build the individual particles. So to model fire, you might say that all the particles begin somewhere on the topmost log, they each have a color from red to yellow (although most of them are orange), and they travel upwards for two or three seconds on a twisting path until they fade out. Given this sort of general description, the computer will generate as many particles as you like, each one fitting these rules, but each one being different.

13-8. An implicit surface. (Image by Jules Bloomenthal, Xerox Palo Alto Research Center.)

The advantage to using particle systems is that you need only give the general rules for how particles behave, and the computer does the rest of the work. To make a stream, you need only generate water particles at the head of the stream. If a particle strikes the shore or a rock in its path, it will bounce off and continue on its way downstream. If the ground suddenly disappears from under the particles, they will shoot a bit past the edge because of their momentum and then drop downwards, creating a waterfall! Fig. C-16 shows a waterfall created with particle systems; the fire coming out of the dragon's mouth in Fig. C-27 was also created with particles.

Using particle systems you can make simulations of things that are normally very difficult to model. A cloud can be created from many little water-vapor particles, each of which is slightly opaque. As the wind blows past these particles, they move in response, and the whole cloud moves. In general, particle systems are ideal for things made of many little objects that obey some general rules. To make the best use of particle systems, you need to recognize those applications and then design good rules to specify how particles are born, how they live, and how they die.

Particles need not actually move to be useful modeling primitives. Fig. C-17 shows a forest built from trees created by using particles for leaves.

Cameras

In some graphics systems you have as much control over the "camera" used to image the scene as you have over a real camera. You can choose different lenses, focus on different objects, and set the aperture and the exposure time. This kind of power has the same drawbacks as a real camera: With all of these choices, you can ruin an otherwise good image by recording it poorly. Luckily, in computer graphics you can always shoot the image again and with a slightly different set of camera parameters.

Some systems have a function similar to the "autofocus" mode in a camera. You specify what object should be in focus and what the depth of field should be, and the computer determines the other parameters.

Blends

Blends are usually not something you model directly, but rather something you ask the computer to add into your model for you. Also known as *fillets*, blends are the little bits of extra surface that round out the joint between two sharp edges. Blends are particularly popular in *computer-aided design* (CAD) because they help a designer make a model that can be actually carved out on a milling machine.

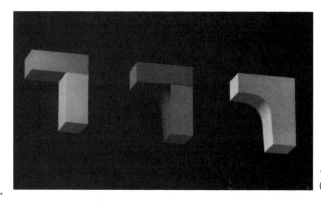

13-9. Adding fillets to a joint. (Image courtesy of Digital Arts.)

Imagine a machine equipped with a robot arm, and on the tip of the arm is a small, spherical drill. If you asked the drill to cut a rectangular box out of a piece of wood, it would not make a box with sharp corners. The tip of the drill is like a sphere; the best it can do is to hollow out a box with rounded edges and corners. If you wanted to design this model, you could create a block of wood with a rectangular hole in it, and then ask the computer to provide small blends in the edges and corners. It would insert small bits of rounded surface to smooth out these sharp transitions. Fig. 13-9 shows an example of a model, both before and after adding blends.

If you want a blend but your system does not support it, you can still create one by hand out of other bits of surface. For example, for the hollow box, a small quarter-cylinder could fit into the crack where two edges meet, rounding out the sharp joint. An eighth of a sphere could fit into the corner to round it out.

SHAPE CONTROLS

The preceding sections cover some new and unusual modeling primitives, which are essentially new ways to create shapes or surfaces. The next few sections describe some powerful ways to manipulate these shapes once you have them. These procedures enable you to make even more complex and interesting shapes, based on the surfaces you can build directly.

Constructive Solid Geometry

So far there has been only one kind of operator, called the *union* operator. If a node in a CSG tree contains the union operator (written + or ∪), then the two children are simply combined as they have always been combined; they simply accumulate and cohabit space. So if you wanted to, you could build a CSG tree for every model you have seen so far. The dumbbell illustrated in Fig. 12-5, for example, could be shown with a tree like the one in Fig. 13-10. So, all Fig. 13-10 tells you is that all three objects get drawn in the final image. Since the union operator simply keeps both objects in the scene, it does not matter which is the left node and which is the right. Remember that where the objects are positioned is still up to the model tree.

The interesting part about CSG results from the use of the two other operators: *intersection* and *difference*. If you take two objects and join them with an *intersection* (written & or ∩) node, then, as far as your model is concerned, you have just eliminated those two objects and created a new object in their place. Refer to Fig. 13-11, which shows a CSG tree for a face. Included at each node is a picture of the model represented by the tree below and including that node (called the *subtree* at that node). Find the intersection node that joins a pair of spheres; these two spheres and the intersection operation at that node above them make the nose. Fig. 13-12 shows the rendered result of Fig. 13-11.

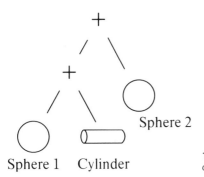

13-10. The CSG tree for a simple dumbbell.

tells you is that all three objects get drawn in the final image. Since the union operator simply keeps both objects in the scene, it does not matter which is the left node and which is the right. Remember that where the objects are positioned is still up to the model tree.

The interesting part about CSG results from the use of the two other operators: *intersection* and *difference*. If you take two objects and join them with an *intersection* (written & or ∩) node, then, as far as your model is concerned, you have just eliminated those two objects and created a new object in their place. Refer to Fig. 13-11, which shows a CSG tree for a face. Included at each node is a picture of the model represented by the tree below and including that node (called the *subtree* at that node). Find the intersection node that joins a pair of spheres; these two spheres and the intersection operation at that node above them make the nose. Fig. 13-12 shows the rendered result of Fig. 13-11.

The result of an intersection node is one or more new objects, which are just those parts of its children that overlap. If there is no overlap among its children, the result is no object at all, and the result is sometimes said to be *null* or *void*. In the example, the two spheres overlap just a bit, and that overlapping creates the shape for the character's nose in Fig. 13-16. You can combine any two nodes with an intersection node. The nodes are leaves (containing objects) in this example, so it is easy to see the result. But those nodes could represent some composite model made by some other CSG operations and you would get the same result. You could perfectly well ask for the intersection of a horse and a flower; the result might not be useful, but you can still do it! It also does not matter which object is on the left and which is on the right for intersection nodes.

The other operator is the *difference* operator (written −). Essentially, the difference operator takes everything in its left-child node, and removes from that model anything within its right-child node. For the face shown in Fig. 13-12, the top (or root) node contains a difference operator. The left subtree is the large sphere representing the head; it already contains the eyes and nose. The right subtree is a small rectangular block. The result is the head (with eyes and nose), with a groove cut into the sphere below the nose, where the block would have been. The difference operator is most useful for scooping out pieces of a surface, or for cutting holes. If you wanted to make a telephone dial, you could easily manage it by first making a large, thin cylinder, and then subtracting from it several smaller cylinders placed where you want the finger holes to be. The result is a dial with holes cut into it. Because the right-node object is subtracted from the

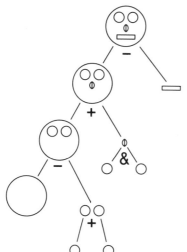

13-11. The CSG tree for a simple face.

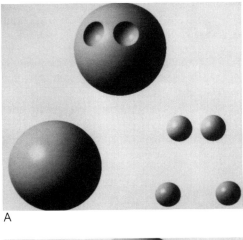

A

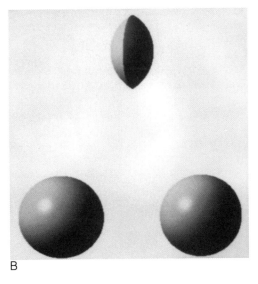

B

C

13-12. The rendered result of the construction indicated by Fig. 13-11.

left-node object, it matters a great deal which object is where. Subtracting a finger hole from a telephone dial is very different from subtracting a telephone dial from a finger hole (the latter would be a short cylinder with a slice missing in the middle).

Remember that the CSG tree only tells you how to combine those objects; where they are located is defined by the model tree. These two trees need not have anything to do with one another; for the face shown in Fig. 13-11, all the primitive objects could be immediately below the root node of the model tree. Yet their geometric result is derived from the CSG tree. To keep things straight, first follow the model tree to find the position of every object in the scene. Then follow the CSG tree to find out how to combine those objects into the composite model. Most of the models in in this book can be represented by a CSG tree with all union nodes.

Sometimes it is most convenient to build a small CSG tree, and then name the result so that you can use it several times. You need to be careful to avoid recursive CSG trees, just as you needed to avoid recursive model trees (as discussed in Chapter 10). So your leaves need not be the primitive surfaces indicated here; they might be other trees representing complex models.

It is sometimes helpful to write down a CSG tree, but drawing the whole tree on paper can take up a lot of space. Modeling programs often use a more compact notation (called a *CSG formula*) based on the following rule for writing down each node: Write down the contents of the left node, write down the operator at this node, and then write the contents of the right node (the value of a leaf node is the name of the object it contains; the value of an operator node is the result of applying this rule). As an illustration of this rule, assign names to the face shown in Fig. 13-11. Reading the leaves from left to right you have *head, left-eye, right-eye, nose-left, nose-right,* and *mouth.* Call the resulting tree FACE; this is the result of the root node.

One way to work out a CSG formula for the tree is to start with the root node and work your way down. The left node doesn't have a name,so temporarily call it *left1.* The right node contains an object called *mouth.* So you begin with a description that reads

$$FACE = (left1 - mouth)$$

Now to find *left1,* you apply the rule again. Neither of its children is an object, so you can call them *left2* and *right2*:

$$left1 = (left2 + right2)$$

You can write down the value of *right2* immediately:

$$right2 = (nose\text{-}left \ \& \ nose\text{-}right)$$

To find *left2,* you see that its left is *head,* but its right child is another node; call it *right3*:

$$left2 = (head - right3)$$

And, finally, you see that *right3* is built from the eyes:

$$right3 = (left\text{-}eye + right\text{-}eye)$$

So, substituting back up the list, you plug in the value of *right3* into the expression for *left2*:

$$left2 = [head - (left\text{-}eye + right\text{-}eye)]$$

and then working your way back up, you find you have *right2,* so you can make *left1*:

$$left1 = [head - (left\text{-}eye + right\text{-}eye)] + (nose\text{-}left \ \& \ nose\text{-}right)$$

Now you can plug that result into the root node to finally find

$$FACE = \{[head - (left\text{-}eye + right\text{-}eye)] + (nose\text{-}left \ \& \ nose\text{-}right)\} - mouth$$

The final expression for FACE is not a very simple result. But if you look at the expression and compare it to the tree, you see that it really contains the complete tree. The enclosure symbols help you to figure out which expressions are children of which nodes. Try working out the tree just from the CSG formula above; you should get the same results as for Fig. 13-11. Some modeling systems allow you to enter your CSG tree as a typewritten formula, just like the examples above. After some experience you will feel as familiar with CSG formulas as with graphical CSG trees.

CSG is a powerful tool because it does not matter what the contents are of the various nodes in the tree. You can have any kind of surface or complex model at the leaves, and the CSG operations will still work out properly. Polygons, quadrics, and other CSG trees can all be the contents of leaves. CSG is a natural tool for making all kinds of manufactured objects, created by gluing things together (union nodes), or scooping or drilling out pieces of material (subtraction nodes). Intersection nodes do not seem to have an intuitive physical counterpart, and so they are a little less common, although useful in some circumstances. And since the CSG tree is independent of the model tree, you can move around two objects in space that seem unrelated and get odd effects in the rendered image (for example, you might only render the intersection of the two arms of a robot).

Free-Form Deformations

Imagine that you have taken an object and immersed it into a block of flexible, transparent gel and that doing so makes the object flexible, too, and easy to manipulate. That process and capability is the basic idea behind *free-form deformations* (or *FFD*).

Fig. C-23A shows a starting model, which is just a collection of spheres and cubes. The model is already in the gel, which is represented by the small sticks and small spheres. The spheres are also called *handles*, because you grab and move them to distort the shape. When you move a handle, the gel and everything within it deforms, just as though you were pulling on a real piece of flexible material. Fig. C-23B shows what happens when the handles are pulled into some other position. (The handles are generally moved one at a time. The figure shows the result after moving them all). The result is that the gel and everything in it is deformed. When you have the shapes the way you like them, you then tell the system to remember the new shape of the object and to forget the gel and the handles. You then have a distorted object to place in your scene. Fig. C-26 shows an example of a bottle deformed with this technique. Note that the handles control the shape of the deformation, but the gel does not follow the handles precisely. In this example the shape of the gel relative to the handles is similar to that of an approximating spline relative to its knots.

You can put any kind of object you like in the gel, from a single polygon to your complete scene description. You can create all kinds of interesting and unusual effects. It is easy to make something melt, for instance, by pulling down on the handles near the bottom of the object more and more.

The technique of free-form deformation is primarily useful when you already have a model, and you want to make some stretches or bends that apply to the whole model. For that reason, it is said that FFD offers you *global control* over object deformations.

Free-Form Modeling

Another technique, called *free-form modeling* (*FFM*) allows you to interactively build a model by adjusting and tweaking bits of the surface. FFM offers *local control* over the shape of the object, since you can adjust one bit of the object without affecting the rest.

Suppose you start with some simple surface, to which you attach handles as for FFD. You can add or delete handles anywhere on the surface that you wish. When you grab a handle and move it, the surface moves with you, but in a very controlled way. Each handle has a specified *region of influence* on the surface, and nothing outside that region will change, no matter what you do with that handle.

The sequence pictured in Fig. 13-13A through I shows an example of this technique, starting with a simple flat sheet, which was textured to make it more interesting. Each step shows an adjustment of just part of the model, while the rest remains fixed. Typically, in such a system early steps make big changes, and then you add additional handles as you work to carefully refine small pieces of the surface. Fig. C-27 shows another character created with this technique.

A

B

C

D

13-13. Nine steps in the creation of a ram's head using free-form modeling. (Images © copyright 1988 by David Forsey and the Computer Graphics Laboratory at the University of Waterloo.)

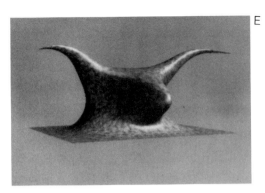

E

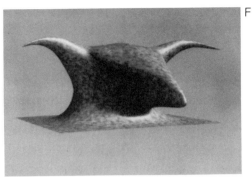

F

G

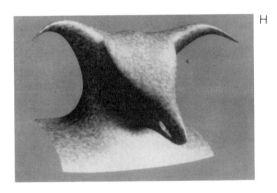

H

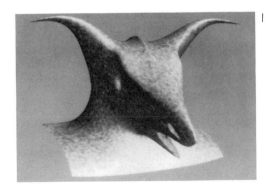

I

SHADING LANGUAGES

In Chapter 4 the way a surface can reflect and transmit light was broken down into smaller shading components, and I said that you could completely specify a surface by giving a value for each coefficient in the shading model.

That much was accurate, but that procedure applied to only one shading model. There are actually many different shading models, and each has its own strengths and weaknesses; I chose one that was both popular and powerful. But suppose that your surface is opaque, so that all the information about how much light it transmits, and how, is useless. In effect, the approach in Chapter 4 was to build a shading model with fixed structure and some blanks, and you filled in the blanks with colors and coefficients.

Unfortunately, not all objects and materials fit well into that shading model. Some structures, such as hair, have very unusual reflectance properties that cannot be described by the shading model given in Chapter 4. Trying to make good-looking hair with that model would be like trying to forge a dollar bill using nothing but a paint roller. If you have the wrong tool for the job, you cannot get really great results no matter how hard you work.

When the standard shading model won't do, one solution is to use a *shading language*. This is a specialized programming language that allows you to specify how your material interacts with light by creating a customized shading model. Thus, you can build your own shading scheme that involves only those operations that are useful, and that combines them in a particular way. Using such a scheme, you could invent various new shading rules.

Although shading languages are powerful, today's systems have a serious drawback: You have to be a programmer to use one! Writing a shading language program to describe a surface can be simple, or it can be every bit as complicated as writing a sophisticated computer program. Shading languages are ideal for special effects and material design, but until they are easier to use, they will remain the province of the programmer, not the artist or designer.

NATURAL PHENOMENA

One of the most difficult, but rewarding, modeling tasks is to try to simulate nature. Many of the techniques discussed in this chapter and elsewhere in the book resulted from people trying to make ever more realistic models of natural phenomena.

In general, it is very hard to do a good job at modeling nature. You end up making numerous complicated, one-of-a-kind objects, and doing much of the modeling by hand. It seems that you must also turn to the scientific literature on the subject, and learn about how trees grow, or how waves form, or how clouds move, in order to simulate them well. The advantage to such effort is that once you have a good model for how a tree grows, you can make forests very easily. If you have a scene that requires a few trees in the background, you can just pop them in; you won't have to painstakingly model each and every twig and leaf from scratch.

Many people hope someone else will one day build up a large library of natural shapes, each one carefully designed and constructed. Then you could make very complex scenes populated with natural-looking objects, without modeling individual objects by hand each time! But until that task is accomplished, natural modeling will remain an art form somewhere between natural science, mathematics, and sculpture.

Two examples of modeling natural phenomena are shown in Figs. C-24 and C-25. Each model is the result of months of work, but now that the structures are understood, the resulting three-dimensional models can be incorporated into new scenes and animated with relative ease.

SUMMARY

Model making requires creating and manipulating primitive surfaces to build complex objects. It would be ideal to have many kinds of primitives available, and many manipulation tools to adjust those primitives.

One powerful class of primitives belongs to the category of sweep (or swept) surfaces, also called generalized cylinders. These involve taking a two-dimensional contour (or profile) and sweeping it along a curved, three-dimensional path (or generator). Special cases include the right circular cylinder, the helix, and the generalized prism, the latter being a sweep surface using a straight line as a path. The contour may be transformed as it sweeps. If the contour is scaled, the result is sometimes called tapered sweep. If you sweep a three-dimensional surface along a three-dimensional path, the result is called a surface sweep.

Another technique spins a two-dimensional profile about an axis of revolution (or axis of rotation) to produce a surface of revolution.

Another way to specify an object is to supply a series of contours, which are cross sections of the object. The computer can interpolate the contours to create a whole object.

You can also model with blobs, which are three-dimensional density fields in which the density is high in the center and tapers off towards the edge. In two dimensions you can specify isodensity contours to create curves where the blob density is at some constant value; in three dimensions this procedure results in isodensity surfaces. The density value at which those surfaces are drawn is called the blobbiness. Blobs are a special case of a more general class of objects called implicit surfaces, which are defined in general as the solution to a form of mathematical equation. Implicit surfaces can be difficult to design, but they offer tremendous generality.

Modeling can also be done with particles, giving rise to a particle system. By specifying the general rules to be obeyed by all particles, the computer can create a large number of slightly different particles that move and glow under their own rules. Particle systems can model many different kinds of phenomena that seem to be made up of many smaller pieces acting independently.

When you specify your models, you can also specify the camera with which your scene is to be photographed. The camera may include as many controls as any physical camera, plus some others.

A blend (or fillet) is a small bit of surface that is added into a model to smooth out sharp corners and edges. Blends are very popular in computer-aided design (CAD) because they help make models that match what can be created by milling machines.

Once a model has been created, it is often useful to manipulate it. One technique for doing so is called constructive solid geometry (CSG). This technique builds a CSG tree, which contains an operator at each node. One operator is union (+ or $\cup$), which simply accumulates its two children without modification. A second is intersection (written & or $\cap$), which replaces its two children with a new object defined as just that part of the children where they overlap. If there is no overlap, then the result is said to be null or void. A third operator is difference (written $-$), which removes its right child from its left. The difference operator is routinely used to cut or scoop holes in an object. A CSG tree can be written textually as a CSG formula that contains the same information but in a form that can be written without diagrams.

Another way to manipulate an object once it has been created is to apply free-form deformation (FFD). The idea is that of an object embedded in a flexible gel represented by sticks and handles. By pulling on a handle you can deform the gel and the object within it as well. FFD exerts a global control over the model.

A technique related to FFD is free-form modeling (FFM). FFM is an interactive modeling technique that provides local control over the manipulation of your model. Each handle has a well-defined region of influence; any points outside that region are unaffected by movement of that handle. While modeling, you can add, remove, and adjust handles and their regions of influence to help you adjust the model.

Some materials are not well handled by standard shading models. To allow more control over the appearance of a material, a shading language can be used to create a special shading model appropriate for just that material.

One lofty goal of computer graphics techniques is to model nature. Natural phenomena present a challenge that spans disciplines and boundaries in the quest for understanding natural forms.

14 COMPUTER-ASSISTED ANIMATION

This chapter examines the process of creating conventional two-dimensional animation, presenting first the principles that explain why animation works at all, and then a discussion of how an animated film is designed and produced. It then discusses ways that the computer can help you create two-dimensional animation more efficiently and quickly. The techniques of two-dimensional animation underlie three-dimensional animation, so they are important from a background point of view. They are also important because much three-dimensional animation can be enhanced or supplemented with two-dimensional animation. (For example, if you have a three-dimensional scene of a living room, you might have a two-dimensional animation running on a television screen to simulate a program.)

The techniques of three-dimensional animation share some similarity with those used for two-dimensional animation, but they include a whole host of new problems. In two-dimensional animation you need only draw objects the way you want them to appear; three-dimensional animation requires that you first build a three-dimensional model, and then position it the way you want.

This chapter discusses how to create three-dimensional models that are easy to animate. It also covers animation techniques ranging from methods for which the animator bears the burden for every bit of motion in the frame, to those for which the computer essentially does the animation itself, and the in-between methods requiring that the animator and the computer share the job of creating motion.

When you see a film on television or in the theater, the motion usually appears smooth and continuous. But if you look at a piece of film (Fig. 14-1), you can see that it is not really smooth and continuous at all. Instead, movie film (and videotape) consists of a sequence of static images, flashed in rapid succession on the screen so as to give the illusion of movement. Because each picture is slightly different from the one preceding it, you perceive motion when these frames are shown quickly enough.

This illusion of smoothness exists because of a peculiarity in the human visual system. When you are shown a picture, it tends to be retained in your mind's eye for a very brief period of time; this effect is called *persistence of vision*. If the pictures are shown quickly enough, one after the other, then the new picture arrives before the old one fades, and you perceive a smooth movement. If the difference between successive frames is too large or the time between them is too long, then the illusion is shattered and the motion no longer appears smooth.

Persistence of vision is what allows conventional film, video, and animation to provide a successful illusion of movement. A rate of twenty-four frames per second has become standard for the film industry. Actually, the projection rate is forty-eight frames a second, but each frame is shown twice so only twenty-four pictures per second are needed. This rate turns out to be the best compromise between economy in the amount of film that must be projected and enough frames to give the illusion of motion. For comparison, video (television) images are broadcast at thirty frames per second.

14-1. A piece of film. Note that each image is static.

CONVENTIONAL TWO-DIMENSIONAL ANIMATION

The production of an animated film is a very time-consuming process, normally involving many people. For example, to create thirty minutes of film (to be shown at twenty-four frames per second) requires 43,200 different frames, each of which must traditionally be hand processed through a half-dozen or more steps! Here is what is involved.

The story is first written in script form. This script is then turned into a series of pictures that show important moments in the story or animation. Fig. 14-2 shows such a set of panels for a very short film. This set of panels is called a *storyboard* and can easily consist of dozens or hundreds of pictures, depending on the length of the film and the detail with which it needs to be worked out at this stage. A more complex animation will typically require more storyboard panels to plan than a simple animation. Storyboards help the writers and animators envision how they will tell the story, plan nuances of the character's features, and, perhaps, plan special effects and important moments in the film.

When the storyboard has been completed and refined, the actual work of production can begin. If there is a soundtrack, it is usually recorded first in a studio. The soundtrack is then measured and meticulously timed. Each event in the soundtrack that is related to what goes on up on the screen must be identified and timed. For example, if there is the sound of a door opening (and the door is on screen at that time), then the animators have to be sure to draw the frames so that they show the door opening at just the right moment to match the soundtrack. The same timing requirement applies to all the sound effects, music cues, and dialog. Every word must

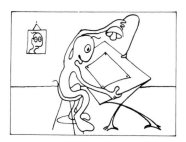

1. The artist works on a new film.

2. Wonders what to draw.

3. Gets idea.

4. And goes to work.

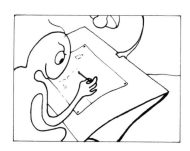

5. Zoom into drawing board.

6. to show the new film.

THE
END

7. The last board.

14-2. A short storyboard showing action and camera moves.

be identified with a starting and ending time. These times are typically marked by frame numbers, so the animator can refer to the chart and see (for example) that a particular character must start saying the word "Pshaw" at frame 365 and be done saying it by frame 378.

Once the soundtrack is recorded and timed, the animation process can begin. To understand the different steps, it is useful to understand how a complete frame of animation is created and photographed.

A single frame is actually a photograph of many *cels* laid over one another (cel is short for cellulose, the clear plastic material upon which frames of animation are drawn). Each cel in the stack is a piece of clear plastic with one character, or one piece of a character, drawn upon it. Fig. 14-3 shows several cels, and Fig. 14-4 shows how they are stacked to create a complete image. The advantage of this technique over drawing each frame individually is a savings in human labor and time. If a character is standing still and speaking, then that character might be reasonably animated with only the mouth and facial features changing. The cels showing his body need not be redrawn for every frame in this case. The illustrations show a simple example, but, in fact, this process is how most animation is created.

14-3. Many individual cels make up a character.

14-4. A composite frame made of the six cels shown in Fig. 14-3. Note that the eyes or arms can be easily changed without redrawing the whole character.

The major cost in producing an animated film lies in the drawing of the many thousands of cels necessary for even a short film. Each cel must be carefully hand drawn and hand painted, at a great cost in time and skilled effort.

The first step in creating the cels is the drawing of *keyframes*. These are frames selected by the master animators for their importance in the film, either because of the composition of the frame, a character's expression, the extremes of movement, or other important event. Fig. 14-5 shows two panels from a simple storyboard, and Fig. 14-6 shows some keyframes for this sequence. Note that the keyframes are much more closely spaced in time than the storyboard panels.

Once the keyframes are drawn, work begins on drawing *in-between frames*, as shown in Fig. 14-7. These frames, as their name suggests, are placed in between the keyframes. Generally, more skill is required for keyframe design than for in-betweening, and the animators with the most experience do the keyframe production, letting apprentices and less senior animators perform the in-betweening. Remember that I am simplifying here; in some situations, producing in-betweens can be just as creative and rewarding as producing keyframes.

You should note that in-betweening is not a completely mechanical process. For example, consider the sequence shown in Fig. 14-8, where you see a man raising his hand very quickly. The keyframes in Fig. 14-8 show the extremes of the movement, but they do not tell the whole story.

To make animation appear smooth and fluid, animators have developed a range of special techniques (these are not covered here because they are well described in many books on

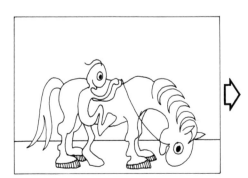

14-5. Two panels from a storyboard.

animation). An example of these methods is shown in Fig. 14-9, where the raised hand actually overshoots its final destination before stopping; it is also distorted by stretching on its way up.

There are no hard and fast rules for this kind of distortion; animation is an art, and the best animation is usually done by the best artists.

Once the outline of a cel is drawn in pencil on paper, it is transferred to a clear cel, where it is drawn with india ink (this is called *inking* the cel). Then the cel is *painted*, filling in the open areas with colored paint. Once all the cels necessary to a frame have been inked and painted, they are *stacked* and *photographed*.

14-6. Some keyframes for the sequence shown in Fig. 14-5.

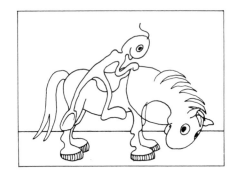
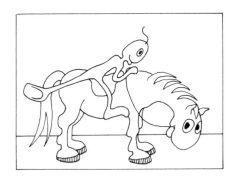

14-7. In-betweened frames for the first two keyframes shown in Fig. 14-6.

14-8. Two keyframes of a character raising its hand.

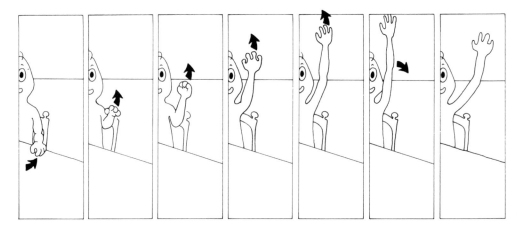

14-9. The in-betweens for Fig. 14-8. Note the distortion of the hand as it moves.

Several techniques exist for cutting down the time required to produce animation. One such technique is called *rotoscoping*, which involves the tracing of previously filmed live action onto animation cels. The cels are then inked and painted as usual, and then filmed. The time required to design the keyframes and in-betweens is eliminated. Rotoscoping is most often performed from live footage. For example, it would be difficult to traditionally animate a herd of running horses but with live footage of running horses to trace from, the animation can be produced much more quickly.

The results of rotoscoping have a fluidity and style not normally seen in conventional animation, but which looks better is often a matter of context and taste.

Two-Dimensional Computer-Assisted Animation

It seems reasonable to assume that, given sufficient information about keyframes and perhaps a few general distortion rules, a computer should be able to do most of the in-betweening in animation. This statement is true to a limited extent. Problems arise because the in-betweening process itself is surprisingly difficult in general, and there are really no good "rules" for the essential animator's principles that make animation look good. Thus, you have to carefully plan your animation if a computer is going to help you, and the results are usually somewhat mechanical looking. However, with enough time and care, this effect can be lessened.

Consider Fig. 14-10. There is no way the computer can, without help, properly produce the in-between frames. There is too much information that is usually taken for granted not explicitly given in the frames. Without this information, the computer cannot produce correct in-betweening.

Making elaborate three-dimensional models of the characters and entering them into the computer works in some cases, but the effort is tremendous. It is usually not worth the time and trouble if all you want is two-dimensional animation. (However, the situation is very different for three-dimensional animation, discussed later in this chapter). And as noted before, there is a good deal of style in animation that such well-defined models cannot easily perform.

So, how can the computer help? There are applications in two-dimensional animation where the computer can be of assistance to a greater or lesser degree. It is common to call this field *computer-assisted animation*, which is an appropriate name, because it implies that the computer helps the animator and that the animator also helps the computer!

A popular method in two-dimensional computer-assisted animation is called *stroke interpolation*. In stroke interpolation, the animator describes the keyframes to the computer with

A. He walks away but hears his name . . .   **B. And turns around.**

14-10.   A character turns around at the sound of a bird calling his name.

a tablet and pen, as described in Chapter 1. The frame is actually entered as a collection of curved lines. But since the word "line" usually means something straight, a frame is said to be built up of *strokes*. A stroke is the computer's representation of the motion of a pen from one place to another. A simple picture and one collection of strokes that defines it is shown in Fig. 14-11. So the computer has a picture of the frame in terms of the strokes that were used to draw it, each of which has a specific starting point, stopping point, and shape along the way.

Think about interpolating just between two keyframes. The animator enters both keyframes as a collection of strokes. The basic premise is that every stroke in the first keyframe will be turned into its corresponding stroke in the second keyframe. So both keyframes contain the same number of strokes, and they correspond: The stroke that makes the left eyelid is the same in both keyframes.

To make the in-betweens, the animator specifies the number of frames to be in-betweened. The computer then takes the first stroke of the first keyframe, and interpolates it into the first stroke of the second keyframe, producing as many in-betweens along the way as needed. It then does the same thing for the second stroke, the third, and so on. Fig. 14-12 illustrates this process. It is called *linear interpolation* because with just two strokes, the computer can do no better than place the in-betweens along a straight path from the first key to the second.

One problem with linear interpolation is that is can look choppy; there is no anticipation at all of what comes after the second keyframe. Imagine that the keys describe a hand throwing a ball. The entire motion should be smooth, but it probably won't be if linear interpolation is used. Typically, most systems provide interpolation that creates in-betweens between two keyframes, but looks at other keyframes while doing it to help the motion look smooth. These techniques use *nonlinear interpolation*, as discussed in Chapter 3.

Computerized in-betweening is far from perfect. Figure 14-13 shows a character starting a long jump. Given the first and last poses the computer generated the five in-betweens. In this drawing, each ellipse was entered as a single stroke. Note the distortion of the biceps of the near arm: It appears to shrink out of sight and then reappear! This effect occurs because the ellipse is rotating, so the points of the ellipse seem to pass through each other. It is an unfortunate result, but it is a perfectly natural consequence of simply interpolating strokes. One way to reduce this effect it to redesign the keyframes so that the ellipse appears to rotate, which might require breaking up the ellipse into several smaller strokes. Another option would be add another keyframe or two in the sequence, so that the distortions (which would still be there) would be less noticeable.

The process of linear in-betweening is quick, although the human element is missing in the in-between frames. A series of keyframes interpolated all at once can create a continuous sequence

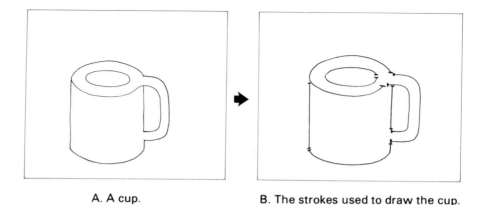

A. A cup.

B. The strokes used to draw the cup. (Strokes are marked for clarity.)

14-11. Breaking down a drawing into strokes.

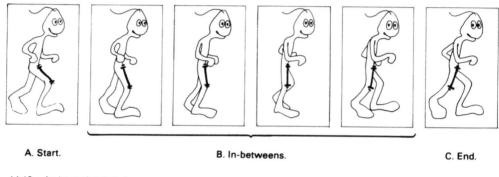

A. Start. **B. In-betweens.** **C. End.**

14-12. An interpolated stroke.

14-13. In-betweens for a running character. Each ellipse is one stroke; note the distortion of the biceps on the nearer arm.

of animation (although, as mentioned, if the interpolation is linear the result might look choppy). With practice in interpolation, a skilled animator can create high-quality animation in a fraction of the time otherwise needed for conventional animation, and with a fraction of the manpower.

Once each frame is drawn, the computer can help with the inking part as well. Computer-assisted *paint stations* are common in many production studios, and allow an artist to quickly fill in the colors for a character. There are also automatic systems that can do the filling-in for you. But they don't work perfectly all the time, and you have to check their output and correct any mistakes.

Another advantage to using a computer is that you can stack as many cels as you care to, one upon another. In conventional animation only a limited number of cels can be stacked, because even though the cels are drawn on clear plastic, that plastic starts to show up when too many cels are laid on top of each other. The colors on the bottommost cels begin to appear darker, and sophisticated color corrections must be made, either when painting the cels or when developing the film, to make the colors come out right. The computer has no such problem. It can digitally stack the frames on top of one another using mattes (which are covered in Chapter 15). The transparent parts of the image are perfectly transparent, and the colors do not degrade when additional cels are added. The computer can stack a virtually unlimited number of cels on top of one another with no loss of quality or transparency.

THREE-DIMENSIONAL ANIMATION

One popular way to create three-dimensional animation is to first build models designed specifically for easy manipulation and then use an animation system to design their motion.

Perhaps the most straightforward kind of model for this task is an articulation tree, as discussed in Chapter 10. An articulation tree produces a model described by a sequence of transformations and objects. If you change the transformation at one node, all the objects beneath are also affected. This chain-reaction effect is well-suited to many kinds of models, such as animals (including humans) and mechanical assemblies. Fig. 14-14 shows three poses of a figure built from an articulated model.

Three-Dimensional Keyframing

The general plan for three-dimensional keyframing is similar to that for two-dimensional keyframing. A series of three-dimensional frames is created that describes the position, structure, and other characteristics of each object in the frame (including the camera). The computer then creates in-between frames. Recall that in the two-dimensional example, the computer was given actual pictures to interpolate, although they were broken down into strokes. For the three-dimensional process you give the computer not the final image, but rather the model descriptions for each frame.

Consider Fig. 14-15, which shows a simple see-saw with a sphere on one end and another sphere on the ground. The whole scene is described by the tree in the figure (ignore the camera for now). You can call this the first keyframe. Then Fig. 14-16 shows the same tree, but with different

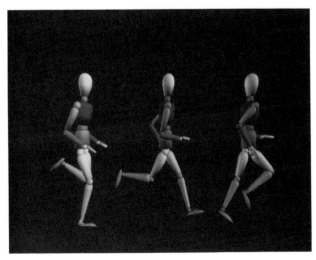

14-14. A three-dimensional robot in two different poses. (Image courtesy of Digital Arts.)

187

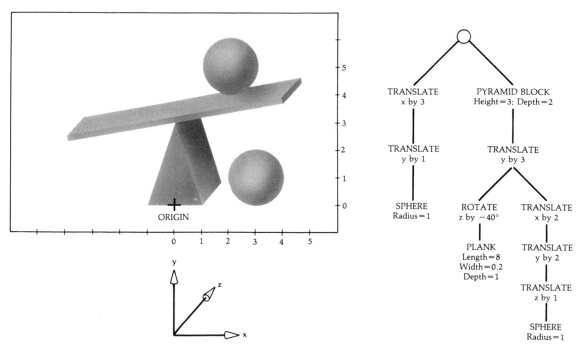

14-15. An articulated model and its tree.

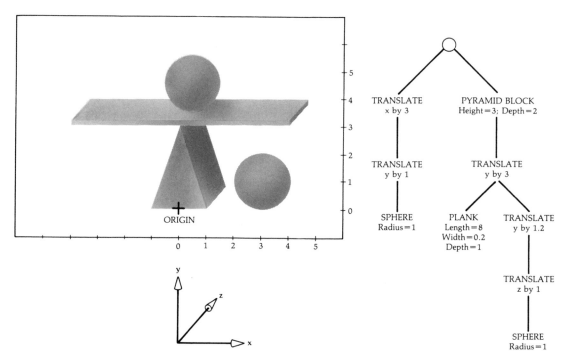

14-16. The same model as shown in Fig. 14-15, but with different parameters at the transformation nodes.

transformations at the nodes. The result is a model that appears different geometrically. This is the second keyframe. You can then ask the computer to produce in-between frames by interpolating the transformations at each node. The in-between frames will show the board swinging to horizontal and the sphere moving to the center. A model tree used as part of a keyframe is called a *pose* (or *keypose*) for that model. Note that the board will actually rotate as it moves, because what you are interpolating is the angle at a rotation node and not the board's shape. Contrast this to the shape interpolation of Fig. 14-13.

A keypose is frequently built by adjusting each parameter in each node throughout the tree until the whole model looks just right. Working with an interactive system, you can select a node and then a transformation within that node. You then use an interactive device to change the value of that transformation, constantly watching the resulting model on the screen. For example, you could select the left node of the root shown in Fig. 14-15, which contains a translation in X for the sphere on the ground. By adjusting the value of this translation you can move the sphere nearer and farther from the pyramid in the center. When this parameter is just right, you then move on to the next parameter, and then the next, going back and adjusting when you have to, until the whole model is exactly as you want it.

An advantage of this approach is that you have the opportunity to pose and animate just one character at a time. You can ask the computer to display only the first main character in a scene, and create all the key poses for that scene working with only that character. When the motion is right, you can temporarily erase that character and bring up just the second character, and build the entire motion for it. Then you can watch them both, with background, and make sure that everything works well together. If it doesn't, then you can fix either character or both to make to make things better. It can be very useful to be able to work with a single character at a time, something that would be extremely difficult to do when using clay or model animation.

If you prefer, you can build each keyframe as a complete pose, including every object at once. It does not matter in what order you build your keyframes, as long as everything is specified at each key by the time you have finished. In some systems you need not specify everything in every keyframe. If you leave a model out of a keyframe entirely, then its parameters at that key are interpolated from the nearest keys at either side. So if you want to show a character riding a motorcycle, you build the complete position of the character and the motorcycle at the first and last frame in the scene. Assuming nothing else moves, you could animate only the eyes and mouth at the keyframes, and they would stay on the character's face as the motorcycle and the character moved.

Suppose for a moment that the computer is just going to linearly interpolate the two keyposes in Figs. 14-15 and 14-16. The ball will move down and to the left, and the board will tilt into position. But the ball won't necessarily stay on the board! After all, there is no explicit connection between them; the ball just happens to be on top of the plank at the extreme poses. So you get a smooth sequence of in-between frames, but they won't necessarily make physical sense.

There are several ways around this problem of keeping the ball on the board. One way is to make use of a *constraint system*, which is a special modeling system that works with *constraints* (or *rules*) in addition to keyframes. Using a constraint system, you build both poses, and then add the rule that "the sphere must stay in contact with the board." The constraint system then generates in-between frames where this specification holds true. But you might find that the ball just remained in one spot on the board until the board straightened out, and then the ball rolled left. But how could the computer know that is not what you wanted? After all, this motion does satisfy the constraint you specified. So you add another rule, "the sphere must roll to the left as the board straightens out." Now the result will look better.

But this was a simple example; imagine trying to build rules that describe a walking person. Constraint systems can be powerful for mechanical assemblies, but they are very difficult to use when you try to make realistic-looking, organic motion.

Another approach to fixing the "ball on the plank" problem is to use a dynamics system, which is covered later in this chapter, but perhaps the most straightforward approach is to put in another one or two keyposes between the two extremes. The ball might float above the plank briefly between these keys, but it will not go up too far. Of course, that is an expensive solution to what seems like a simple problem, but aside from constraint and dynamics systems (or custom programming), there is no better answer thus far.

Kinematics Systems

Keyposing systems such as those discussed above are also called *kinematics systems. Kinematics* is a branch of physics that studies the position and orientation of objects. It essentially freezes them in time to study them. Likewise, in keypose systems you specify just where each object is at each keyframe and let the computer calculate in-between positions.

You can also ask the computer to interpolate the object properties in the model, in addition to position, to enable you to move the top and bottom bounds of a cylinder, or to slowly change the color or texture of a polygon as a scene progresses.

Note that a keypose interpolation system is really just creating the model descriptions at in-between frames. You can then adjust or modify those descriptions any way you like before rendering them.

When the camera is also part of a scene description, its parameters (position and orientation) are also interpolated frame by frame. Consequently, you can design the path of a camera through a scene as action is taking place and pull the focus back as the camera moves. When you render the animation, your moving camera will be used as the point of view for that scene at each frame.

There are two important points about kinematics systems that you should note in particular. First, if you have a model in one keyframe, that model must not change its structure in the next keyframe. The idea is that every node in every model tree at one keyframe must have a corresponding node in the next keyframe, in order for the computer to interpolate the parameters at that node. So if a character walks offscreen, you have two choices. One is to keep modeling keyframes in the scene, but place that character offscreen so it is not seen. The other choice is to decide that you have finished with that scene, and save it. Then start a new scene with only the models you want.

Second, observe that the type of interpolation used makes a big difference in how the animation appears. (Remember, you are interpolating the model characteristics and transformation parameters at the nodes, not the picture.) Linear interpolation usually results in motion that is choppy and unnatural. Most systems use splines of some kind that produce a more fluid motion. Spline-based interpolation usually produces animation with a very distinct look; different splines produce different "looks."

Your best approach to mastering a spline-based keypose system is probably to make several simple animations on your system to see how things move. A good test case is a ball bouncing on the floor. Make three keys: one of the ball in the air before the bounce, one of the ball bouncing on the ground, and a third of the ball springing back into the air. Check that the computer doesn't send the ball through the ground after the bounce! If it does, you should insert more keyframes of the ball as it nears the ground. Another solution is to repeat the same keyframe several times, but this can also look unnatural. Experiment with your system and learn its idiosyncrasies.

Once you have built the keyframes, then you tell the computer to calculate the in-betweens. Once the frames are built, the complete animation can be played back to you in real time. You can insert or delete keyframes, ask for more or fewer interpolated frames, or make many other modifications of the animation. In particular, you can hand-modify the interpolating splines, which can reintroduce a human touch, similar to the distortions introduced by conventional animators. You can also tweak individual frames if you like.

Imagine that you want to make an animation of a dog running through a field. Ideally, you could just make a keyframe each time one of the dog's legs hits the ground, and let the computer interpolate the keys.

One problem with this approach is similar to a problem noted before: there is nothing to stop the limbs of the dog from passing through each other as it runs. I said that constraint systems could solve the task, but that setting up the constraints would be very difficult. Fortunately, there is a special kind of system that combines some of the features of both constraints and keyframes to help produce this sort of motion.

When you design your dog model, part of your specification is the connection of the components. For example, you might say that where the neck enters the body is like a ball-in-socket joint, while legs are hinged at the knees. Then you specify the keyframes as previously described. An *inverse kinematics system* tries to use your specifications and keyframes to compute the individual keyframes that somehow make sense when the mechanical restrictions are taken into account. For example, the system will try to ensure that parts do not cross through each other, that hinged joints work correctly, and that connected pieces do not separate.

An inverse kinematics system is good for animating something like a walking or running character. But such an approach also has its drawbacks. These systems are often not easy to use; setting up the controls, limited as they are, can be a lot of work. Calculating the motion can take a long time. And sometimes there are many ways to create a motion that satisfies your rules so the system has to guess which way is best, the problem being that you might disagree. Then you have to try, and try again until you achieve the kind of motion you want. The inverse kinematics technique is powerful, but requires some sophistication on the part of the user to be practical for routine animation.

Dynamics

Just as kinematics describes where objects are, *dynamics* is a branch of physics that describes how objects move. Systems that create animation based on principles of dynamics use the physical properties of objects (for example, mass, size, and center of gravity) and the properties of the world in which they live (for example, air resistance and gravity).

A *dynamics system* is an animation system that tries to make your motion as physically correct or realistic as possible. Earlier in this chapter I used the example of keyframing a bouncing ball. If you wanted the ball to bounce a lot, you had to make many keyframes of the ball in the air, then on the ground, then in the air at a slightly lower position, then on the ground again, and so on. Using a dynamics system, you would simply describe the properties of the ball and the world and specify an initial configuration. The computer would figure out how the ball would move and bounce according to the laws of physics, and it would create the appropriate model description for each frame.

Once the calculations were complete, the computer would next produce descriptions of the individual frames. You would need only view this animation interactively and position the camera before rendering your final frames onto film or videotape.

To get a dynamics system to work properly you need to describe many of the physical properties of your objects. If you use a keyframe system to render an animation of a heavy bouncing ball made of hard rubber, your skill at animation would determine whether the ball appeared "heavy" and made of "hard rubber." With a dynamics system, you just specify the weight and bounciness of the ball as part of its material description, along with its color, reflectivity, and other material properties.

Once all the objects are described, you need to specify the environment, such as indicating how much gravity and how much resistance to movement there is (for example, things move more easily in air than in water).

When your models are built and your world specified, you supply an initial keypose. Then you simply tell the computer to simulate this mechanical universe you've built. You might ask for sixteen seconds of simulation, for example, and then put those right onto videotape.

This is an ideal technique for all sorts of applications. For example, suppose you want to illustrate a shot in a pool game. You set up the balls, specify the initial force applied to the cue ball, and watch the action. (Actually, you simulate the action and then watch it later.) Or imagine a scene in a film about mechanical structures. The scene begins with a shot of a bookshelf. The bookshelf shakes a bit, the top shelf breaks, and then the books on the top shelf fall, taking all the other books with them in a flying tangle. Finally all the books are in a heap on the floor. Creating this animation by hand would be difficult; you would have to position each book individually and make it fall realistically, while the pages flap in the wind. You can see it would quickly become a huge task. But a dynamics system can do it all for you: You build the books and the bookshelf, apply a shuddering force enough to break the top shelf (which you have specified as weak), and the rest happens automatically.

But, as usual, dynamics systems are not the answer to every purpose. Perhaps their biggest problem is also their biggest asset: The motion they generate is very realistic and physically true. Sometimes that result is just what you want. But over the years animators have developed many techniques that help make animation look fluid and smooth. These methods have little, if nothing, to do with physical reality; for example, a character (two- or three-dimensional) should have an easily understood silhouette. If the silhouette is unclear, the character's actions or intents may be unclear as well. Often an animator will move a character around until the silhouette "reads" well. This result may have nothing to do with the physical reality of the motion; it involves a tradeoff of animation art against physical reality. There are many such tricks that are a standard part of the animation repertoire; trying to model them with dynamics would be a very difficult task. So if your goal is mechanical motion, dynamics is an excellent time-saver, but if you are trying to make natural-looking motion, you may want to do some subjective things by hand that dynamics just will not produce.

Another drawback to using dynamics is that it may not be easy to specify the physical parameters for your objects. Intrinsic properties, such as moments of inertia, may be difficult to compute except with special programs, and material properties, such as coefficients of friction, may be difficult to choose to make the resulting action looks acceptable.

The advantage to dynamics systems is ease of achieving particular results. Imagine a parade scene where several bands are marching, each holding giant flags high in the air, each flag flapping wildly in the wind. You might specify most of this scene with keyframe techniques, but how much easier it is to simply tell the computer "Here, you make these flags flap in a realistic way as though there were a stiff wind," and have that effect appear in your animation.

If you want to create a scene that contains physically correct motion (such as a flag flapping in the wind) without creating the motion yourself, you may find that a dynamics system is your answer, even with the additional setup work it requires. But if you want motion that appears natural and fluid (such as a walking person), you may find that kinematics techniques are more useful.

Procedural Motion

There is another approach to three-dimensional animation that shares some properties of both keyframing systems and dynamics systems. This technique is actually a whole body of methods and systems for building animation according to a program and it is called *programmed* (or *procedural*) *motion*.

The underlying idea is that when you want a specific kind of behavior or action, you can write a program that makes that action for you. For example, if you want to make a wheeled vehicle that bounces as it traverses the surface of Mars, you write a program that takes your completed, keyframed animation and adds some bounce to the model as it rolls. This procedure is not simply keyframing, because the system is adjusting your frames for you. And it is not really dynamics either, because you are not really simulating anything; you are just writing a special program that does a single, particular task for you. It need not have any relation to the real world or anything else. It is just a program that does what you want simply because you want it.

Procedural motion is an open-ended subject, just like programming. Whatever kind of motion you can invent, you can program. Of course, "you" might mean a friend or colleague, but the idea is that the burden of doing some bit of animation is taken from your shoulders and transferred to the computer. For example, you might want to animate a character playing a guitar. You have built the animation so that the character picks the right strings at the right time, and then you turn over the complete animation to a special program. This program looks for string plucks and vibrates the string for the next few frames in response to the plucking.

The advantage to using procedural motion is that you don't have to do all the setup work needed for dynamics (specifying the properties of all the objects in detail), nor do you need to do it yourself by hand. You let the computer handle some of the details while you take care of other things. And you are the one who chooses who does what, and when, so that your final animation looks as good as you can make it.

SUMMARY

When frames of animation are shown in rapid succession, they appear to move because the eye retains each image for a fraction of a second before it fades. This phenomenon is called persistence of vision, and it is the effect that allows animation and film to mimic motion.

A two-dimensional animation begins with a script. Once the story is ready, the action is planned using a series of panels that form a storyboard, which gives a visual summary of the film. Then the soundtrack is recorded and timed.

The actual animation is begun by drawing pieces of characters on clear plastic sheets called cels. By stacking these cells you can make a composite image out of several independent pieces, and perhaps reuse those pieces to save time and labor.

A master animator prepares keyframes that give the opening and closing frame of each sequence of action. Assistants prepare the in-between frames (or in-betweens) to fill in the blanks between keys. Once all the frames have been drawn on paper, they are inked onto cels, the big areas are painted with color, and then the component cels are stacked and photographed.

Some complex animation can be traced from film shot live; this is called rotoscoping.

The computer's main contribution to computer-assisted animation is its help with interpolation (and to a lesser extent, painting and photographing). The animator enters keyframes as a collection of strokes, which are simply continuous strokes of the pen. The computer then performs stroke interpolation, which creates in-between frames by interpolating each stroke independently. Linear interpolation of strokes usually looks choppy, so nonlinear interpolation is often used instead.

When the cels are all built, the computer can paint them on a paint station and then stack the cels to create a final image, which is then transferred to videotape or film.

Three-dimensional keyframing is very similar to two-dimensional keyframing. But rather than specify an image for the keys, you provide poses, called keyposes, that identify the position and orientation of every object in the scene at an important frame. This technique is especially well suited for use with models built in the form of articulation trees. Using an interactive system, you can specify the value of every transformation at every node in the tree. The computer then interpolates these values to produce trees describing the objects at in-between frames; these can then be rendered to create in-between frames.

You can shift some of the burden for controlling the animation to the computer in several ways. One technique is to specify constraints on the objects from within a constraint system. The computer will try to create motion that satisfies the constraints.

Because keyposes and constraints describe where objects are at particular moments, they are called kinematics systems, based on the field of physics that studies orientations and positions.

If you only specify where objects are at keys, but provide some mechanical constraints (less general then those in a constraint system), an inverse kinematics system will try to create in-between frames that satisfy both the keys and the mechanical conditions.

An alternative to these techniques is the use of a dynamics system, based on the field of physics that studies how objects move. In a dynamics system each object is assigned additional properties that describe its physical make-up: mass, material, moment of inertia, and so on. You also provide a description of the environment that defines the physical world in which the objects move. You finally provides an initial configuration for every object. The dynamics system then applies the laws of physics to determine just how all the objects move and interact. One difficulty in using such a system concerns the selection of the correct values for the complex material descriptions required for the simulation. Another problem is controlling the motion; a dynamics system typically creates motion that is physically true, and that may not always be what you want.

A compromise between kinematics and dynamics is programmed (or procedural) motion. Using this technique you specify the motion of objects with a special-purpose program written only for that task. Such a system is extremely flexible, but you have to be a programmer to use it.

15 PRODUCTION TECHNIQUES

The final step in creating an animation involves combining the frames and scenes into a single film. Sometimes a single frame is created from many individual images, each independently rendered and saved; this approach can provide a great advantage in speed because some pieces (such as the background) of the frame can be reused again and again. When the frames have been created, they need to be combined into scenes, and then the scenes need to be combined into a film.

This chapter presents some of the techniques available to produce a complete film. It covers some operations that have direct analogs in the classic film industry, and other techniques that are new with the introduction of computers.

TRANSITIONS

In most animations there are times when you need to switch from one scene, or point of view, to another. In general, this kind of change is called a *transition*. The most basic transition is to simply switch immediately to the next scene, which is called a *cut* and is illustrated in Fig. 15-1.

The next scene can "push" the first scene out of the way, and this effect is called a *wipe* (Fig. 15-2), or the first scene can fade out as second scene fades in, creating a *dissolve* (Fig. 15-3).

Transitions can be very simple, such as the ones just discussed, or as complex as you like. The computer offers the versatility to design any kind of transition you care to have. For example, you can use the computer to retain information about some of the rendered shapes in the scene you are leaving and the scene you are going to. It can then use these shapes as surfaces upon which to texture map the two scenes, and then it can change one surface to the other.

Or, you can choose to cause each pixel to slowly run through a set of colors until it arrives at the correct color in the scene you are going to. Or you could map the scene onto the surface of a sphere, spin the sphere to reveal the next scene on the other side, and then unmap the new scene back onto the full screen (Fig. 15-4).

You might want to make the old scene drip down the face of the screen as if it were drawn with watercolors and splashed with water, and let the new scene drip down from the top of the screen in the same way.

Such transitions must normally be programmed by someone with computer programming experience. But you can create a transition and describe it in detail, and then ask a programmer to write the necessary programs. If the transition is well described, a programmer can usually make it happen.

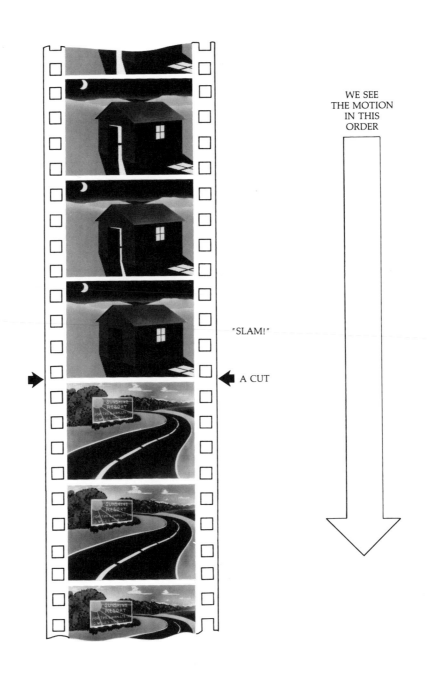

WE SEE
THE MOTION
IN THIS
ORDER

"SLAM!"

◀ A CUT

15-1. A piece of film showing a cut.

A. Horizontal wipe.

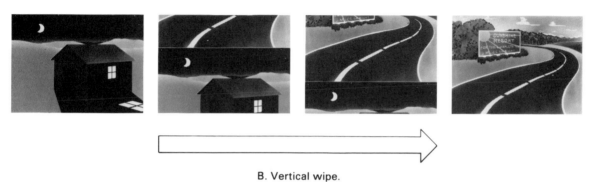

B. Vertical wipe.

15-2. Examples of wipes.

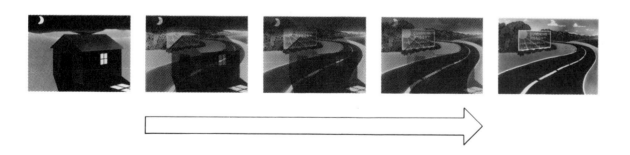

15-3. Example of a dissolve.

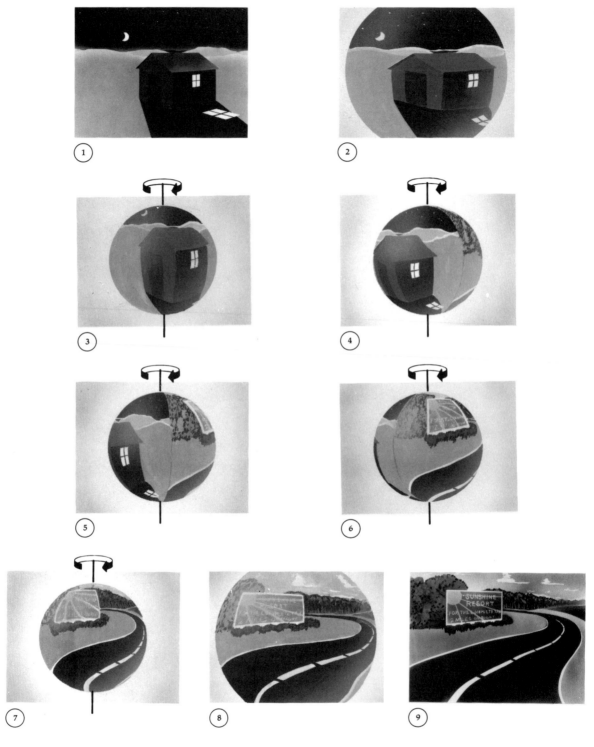

15-4. A complex transition.

PANS AND ZOOMS

Pans and zooms are standard cinematic techniques that can be emulated and embellished through the use of a computer. A *pan* is a slow move by camera across the face of a picture (Fig. 15-5). A *zoom* causes the camera to close in on a smaller part of the picture (called *zooming in*) or to pull back to reveal more of it (called *zooming out*), both of which are shown in Fig. 15-6.

With a computer doing the work, both of these techniques can be done at a constant rate, or at any speed and direction you choose. Some systems will even let you control the focus on a three-dimensional scene, as well as simulate different lenses on the camera taking the computer-simulated picture.

15-5. A pan.

A. Original image.   B. Zooming in.   C. Zooming out.

15-6. Zooming in and out.

MATTES AND COMPOSITION

Suppose you want to make an outer-space scene of a starship flying by in front of a background of stars. You might render just the starship (Fig. 15-7A), save the picture, then render just the stars (Fig. 15-7B), and save that. Now, you want to combine the two pictures (Fig. 15-7C).

You need some way to add the two pictures together in just the right way. The process of combining independent images to make a new composite is common in computer production, because full frames are often drawn in several different stages, as in the spaceship example.

One of the most useful methods for combining pictures is *transparency*, in which you specify some color (or colors) to be transparent, so that pixels of that color are not copied into the final image. Suppose you rendered the stars and spaceship, and currently have the stars sitting in a frame buffer. You might tell the computer to copy the spaceship image on top of the stars, except that black is transparent. So all black pixels are ignored, and only nonblack pixels are written over the stars. Fig. 15-8 shows the result.

Note that the star field comes through around the ship, which is what you wanted. However, the star field also comes through inside the ship through one of the windows! You told the computer that all black was transparent, and it simply did its job. Transparency is suitable for many tasks, but, as it turns out, not for this particular example.

An alternative solution for the starship production is to copy a technique used in film production called *matting*, or *image composition* (the use of the word matte here is not like that for describing a finish). The basic idea behind matting is that the editor cuts a *mask* (or *matte*) to be used for each frame that goes into the total picture. The mask instructs you to cut out only the pieces of the frame that are not covered. Then, you take the cutout pieces and lay them into the total frame.

This process can also be executed optically by making a mask out of some opaque material (such as heavy cardboard) for each frame. Then each frame is put in a slide projector with its mask and all the frames are projected onto one screen. Only those areas that are not covered by a mask appear on the screen. Sometimes a matte is just the same size as the picture it is

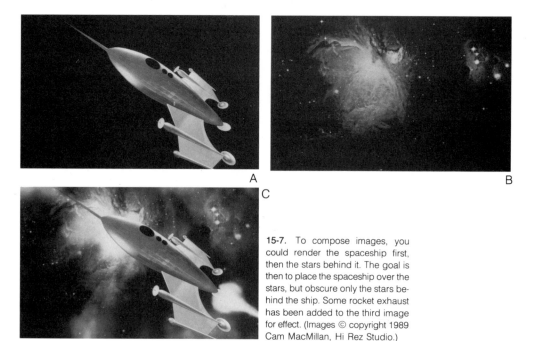

A

B

C

15-7. To compose images, you could render the spaceship first, then the stars behind it. The goal is then to place the spaceship over the stars, but obscure only the stars behind the ship. Some rocket exhaust has been added to the third image for effect. (Images © copyright 1989 Cam MacMillan, Hi Rez Studio.)

15-8. The images from Fig. 15-7 have been combined by drawing the spaceship over the stars, but any black pixels in the ship image were considered transparent. Now stars show through the black window of the ship. (Images © copyright 1989 Cam MacMillan, Hi Rez Studio.)

modifying. It is then sometimes called a *matte buffer* (or *alpha buffer*), and the matte value for a particular pixel is said to be that pixel's *alpha value*.

To make the image of a starship over the stars, you can create mattes for the two images that make up the picture. To create a matte in the computer, you draw the matte into a frame buffer, the matte buffer. When a pixel is copied from a *source picture* into the *composite*, its corresponding pixel in the matte buffer is checked. If the matte buffer is white, the pixel is not copied into the composite; if the matte buffer is black, then the pixel is copied. You can make mattes for both the spaceship and the star field and draw the two images into a new frame buffer, one after the other. The result of successful matting is shown in Fig. 15-7C.

Mattes need not be black and white. An optical matte might be made out of materials with different transparencies so that two images might blend into each other. In matte buffers you can use shades of gray to indicate transparency. You might say that 0 is black, 255 is white, and intervening levels are gray. If a pixel's alpha value is a shade of gray, then it is blended into the existing image in the frame buffer. The closer the matte pixel is to white, the more that pixel's color influences the composite color. The new value is a linear interpolation of the pixel in the image buffer and the pixel that is being drawn on top of it. Fig. 15-9 shows some examples of this kind of matting.

You can do some interesting things when a matte has many levels of control for merging two pictures. Using the term *alpha buffer* instead of matte, you can easily speak of a single pixel as having four values: red, green, blue, and alpha (usually written in the order [rgba]). Sometimes the four values are also called *channels*, so you might hear the term *alpha channel*. So far I have described using an alpha channel to put one picture on top of another. But you can take two pictures, both with associated alpha buffers, and merge them together to make a new, third image. There are many interesting ways to work with these two alpha values. In all, there are some sixteen different operations for compositing two pictures.

The advantage of matte buffers is that they can save you a lot of time. Remember that for two-dimensional animation, you can draw just the moving parts of a character and leave the others unchanged. So a character can walk across a background, and you do not have to redraw the background every time. That is exactly what you want to do with three-dimensional images. Matte buffers allow you to render pieces of an image at different times—even on different machines—and then combine all the pieces together into one composite frame. There are two major advantages to this procedure. One is that you can often make these many separate pictures faster than one large picture. The other is that you can use parts of the picture (the background, for instance) over and over without rerendering it.

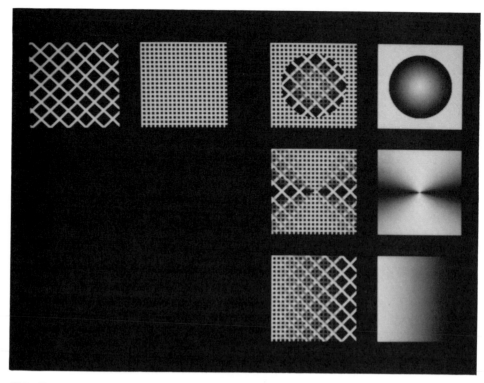

15-9. The two source images on the left, combined according to the mattes on the far right. The column to the left of the mattes shows the result.

The operating principle behind an alpha buffer is that it contains *opacity information* for every pixel in the image. Some pixels are not completely filled up by an object; that is, the object is only visible in part of the pixel. If you ignore this information, as described in Chapter 11, you get jaggies, because every pixel is either covered or not covered. Alpha buffers give you a powerful way to generate anti-aliased pictures and then to combine (or composite) them in a way similar to cinematic production, with results that are free from aliasing.

Suppose you are working with a twenty-four-bit frame buffer. Then each pixel contains eight bits that give the red intensity, eight for green, and eight for blue. If you are fortunate enough to have thirty-two bits, then you can use eight more bits for alpha. Now the alpha values are numbers, just like the red, green, and blue intensities. But to avoid numbers in this discussion, I will just say that the alpha buffer contains values from black to white, with grays in between. A black alpha value means that the pixel is completely empty, white means completely filled, and grays mean in-between coverage.

Here is a trick you can use. If a large, partly transparent object is on the screen, you know that it fills many pixels. But if you associate a gray alpha value with each of those completely filled pixels, then later operations will proceed as if those pixels are only slightly covered, and thus the background will show through. The more black the alpha value, the more the other image will show through, and the more transparent the object will appear.

Where do alpha buffers come from? If you are doing special effects, you might draw them by hand or have a special program make them for you. More typically, your rendering system will make them for you and save them as part of the image. So suppose you render a giant frog that you will later place on a lily pad. When you finish your rendering of the frog, the computer will have a record of which pixels are completely covered by the frog, and which are partially covered, and by how much. If you request it, the system can save this information for you in an alpha buffer associated with the image.

Binary Matting Operators

How can you use alpha buffers to combine images and create new ones? Suppose you have two source pictures (call them A and B), each of which has an alpha buffer. There are five popular methods for combining those pictures to create a new one. A common technique for specifying which method you want is to name one picture, then the name of the operation, then the other picture. The name of the operation is called the *operator*; because it works with two pictures it is called a *binary operator*. In most cases the order in which you name the pictures is important. The result is a new picture (with its own alpha buffer), which I will call picture C.

Each matting operation uses the alpha buffers in a different way. The results look different, so each operator has a name that reminds you how the result appears. The operators work by looking at the alpha channel in each picture, and modifying the colors in each source picture accordingly before adding them together. You can usually write the operations as though you were typing them into a program that understood your typewritten commands directly; your own system may actually use a different convention.

For these examples, refer to the images (and matte buffers) shown in Fig. 15-10, which are pieces of a farmhouse scene.

The first operator is called *only*, and it is unusual because it ignores the second picture. If we say A *only* B, then C is exactly the same as A. For this operation, you can omit the second picture entirely, so you could say A *only* for this example. This procedure is really just an easy way to make an extra copy of a picture.

The second operator is called *over*, which is written A *over* B. This procedure is useful for creating a picture where A is in the foreground and B is in the background, and A contains some object that you want to be completely visible in front of B. So if you say *House over Field*, you will see the opaque house sitting in the field, as in Fig. 15-11A. The edges of the house will be smoothly blended into the background to preserve that illusion, since the alpha values on the edges of the house are gray (indicating partial coverage), not black or white.

The third operator is called *in*, which is written A *in* B. The previous discussion assumed that you had only the two pictures *House* and *Field*, and that they contained all the matting information needed within them. Another typical situation involves wanting to put a foreground over a background, but the matte that controls the situation is a separate alpha buffer, independent of the two pictures. For example, suppose you want an animation where you see only the field, and then the house begins to grow: first the bottommost part, then the section above, and finally the roof. You could use your images *House* and *Field* again, and build a third image called *Growth*. *Growth* contains no picture; it is just an alpha buffer. At the beginning of the animation *Growth* is completely black, indicating that nowhere should the house be visible. Then you slowly start adding white lines from bottom to top, representing the growth of the house. So what you want is to first matte the house with *Growth* before putting it in front of the field. You could write that first operation *House in Growth*; the result is a picture that only contains *House* where *Growth* is white. To put that picture in front of *Field* you can give the complete operation (*House in Growth*) *over Field*. This procedure is demonstrated in Fig. 15-12. Note that you can use parentheses to give a more complex command, yet still indicate in what order the instructions are to be executed. This last example is very different from *House in (Growth over Field)*, so the parentheses make a big difference.

The fourth operator is called *out*, which is written A *out* B, and is the opposite of *in*. The idea behind the *out* operator is that you want to hide A behind B; you only want to see those parts of A that are outside of B. Suppose that you want to make a simple house in a field scene

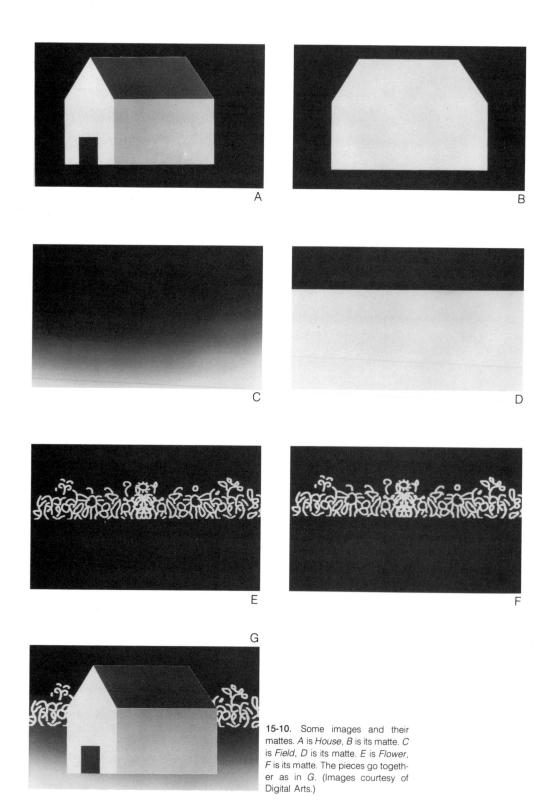

15-10. Some images and their mattes. *A* is *House*, *B* is its matte. *C* is *Field*, *D* is its matte. *E* is *Flower*, *F* is its matte. The pieces go together as in *G*. (Images courtesy of Digital Arts.)

again, but you want a field of flowers behind the house. Then *Flowers out House* is only that part of the flower field where the house is not, as in Fig. 15-11B. If you wanted the house in the picture, you could use *House over Flowers*, but then you must have the house in the scene. Use *out* when you want to get the image behind another, but you don't want the blocking image in the picture just yet.

The fifth operator is called *plus*, which is written *A plus B*. This operator merges the two images together according to their individual alpha buffers. Instead of using the matte buffers to control the transfer of a pixel, it is used to scale the pixel's brightness. White alpha pixels say leave the color unchanged, black means send the color to black, and in-between alphas scale the brightness of the color. On a pixel-by-pixel basis, each pixel in *A* and *B* is scaled and then added together to make the new picture. It does not matter whether you say *A plus B* or *B plus A*. Fig. 15-11C shows the result of using this operator to create *House plus Field*.

A

B

C

15-11. The result of using binary matting, or composition, operators. *A* is *House over Field*, *B* is *Flowers out House*, and *C* is *House plus Field*. (Images courtesy of Digital Arts.)

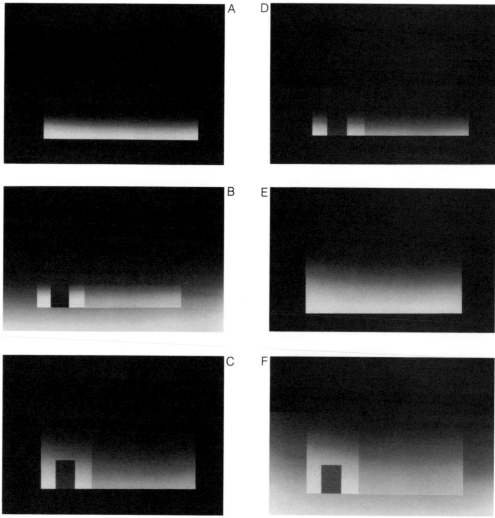

15-12. Using the *in* operator to control the application of a foreground to a background. *A* is the *Growth* alpha channel, *B* shows *House in Growth*, and *C* shows *(House in Growth) over Field*. *D, E,* and *F* show the same results. (Image courtesy of Digital Arts.)

Unary Matting Operators

There are three matting operators that modify a single picture to make a new image; because they take only one picture these are called *unary operators*. Each one takes a number that controls its effect, and I use the word *amount* here to represent that value. The value used by an operator is sometimes called its *argument*. Normally, *amount* will be an a number between 0 and 1. Each operator is written as *operator-name picture-name amount*.

The first unary operator is called *darken*, and it causes the whole picture to be darkened, without modifying the alpha value. If *amount* is 1, the picture is left alone. If *amount* is 0, the picture becomes completely black. In-between values darken the image accordingly, as shown in Figs. 15-13A and B. This operator is useful if you want something to appear behind something else, or lessened in intensity.

The next operator is called *dissolve*. It is similar to *darken*, but the alpha value is also changed. Thus, not only does the image get darker; it also gets more transparent, as shown in Figs. 15-13C and D. This operator is useful for making an image gradually fade from view during a dissolve between scenes.

The third single-image operator is called *opaque*. It is useful for glowing objects, such as sparks, that add color to a pixel but don't block objects behind them. When *amount* is 1, the object is opaque. When *amount* is 0, the object is completely transparent, but the color remains; in other words, the image is drawn into the final image without regard for any of the mattes involved in the operation, as shown in Figs. 15-13E and F. When you are building images including particle systems, which usually radiate light, but don't block anything behind them, *opaque* is the operator to use.

15-13. The results of using unary composition operators *darken* for *A* and *B*, *dissolve* for *C* and *D*, and *opaque* for *E* and *F*. A value of 0.25 was used for *A, C,* and *E,* and 0.75 for *B, D,* and *F*. (Image courtesy of Digital Arts.)

Combining Operators

With these five two-image operators and three one-image operators, you can reproduce almost any cinematic effect, as well as make many new ones. For example, suppose you want to dissolve from one scene A to another scene B over five frames. You could make the five frames this way:

$$
\begin{aligned}
\text{frame1} &= (\text{dissolve } A \ 1.00) \text{ plus } (\text{dissolve } B \ 0.00) \\
\text{frame2} &= (\text{dissolve } A \ 0.75) \text{ plus } (\text{dissolve } B \ 0.25) \\
\text{frame3} &= (\text{dissolve } A \ 0.50) \text{ plus } (\text{dissolve } B \ 0.50) \\
\text{frame4} &= (\text{dissolve } A \ 0.25) \text{ plus } (\text{dissolve } B \ 0.75) \\
\text{frame5} &= (\text{dissolve } A \ 0.00) \text{ plus } (\text{dissolve } B \ 1.00)
\end{aligned}
$$

So frame1 contains only A, and frame5 contains only B, and the in-between frames have intermediate values. Fig. C-28 illustrates another example of using several matting operators to create one complex image.

Matte production is sometimes challenging. Mattes can always be drawn by hand at a paint station, and can often be generated by the computer. Matte buffers that are generated according to a computer program can produce beautiful transitions.

SUMMARY

Many of the production techniques used in creating an animation with computer graphics are borrowed from classic film production. Standard transitions that are commonly used include the cut (an abrupt switch between frames), the wipe (where one scene slides in over another), and the dissolve (a fade between two scenes).

A pan is a movement of the camera across a scene. A zoom is a motion of the camera either closer to a subject (zooming in) or farther away (zooming out).

Partial images of three-dimensional scenes can be combined in a number of ways to create a single composite image. This process is similar to the use of cels in two-dimensional animation, so that some parts of the image remain constant while other change.

This job of image composition, or matting, can be accomplished many ways. The simplest is probably to use just transparency and not copy pixels of a particular color, but that approach has problems in many applications.

A more sophisticated method is to use a mask (or matte) to describe the transparency information for an image. Each pixel in the image has a corresponding pixel in the matte, which tells what fraction of the image pixel is actually covered by the object it represents. This information allows smooth and alias-free composition of images. Sometimes the matte value is called the alpha value, in which the contents of a pixel are often written (rgba). If the matte is stored in a frame buffer, it is often called the matte buffer, alpha buffer, or alpha channel.

 Each source picture is combined with its matte into a composite under control of a matting operator.

There are five popular binary matting operators, each of which takes two pictures. The binary operator *only* simply copies its first argument into the final image. Both the image and matte buffers are copied.

The binary operator *over* is useful for superimposing a foreground object on top of a background object. Where the foreground object is opaque, it has precedence in the image; where it is transparent, the background shows through.

The binary operator *in* is useful for combining two images under the control of an auxiliary matte buffer. This new buffer acts to select one image when that image is within a specific range, and allows the other image to show through elsewhere.

The binary operator *out* is the opposite of *in*, and allows one object to effectively block another.

The last binary operator, *plus*, simply merges two images using their respective alpha buffers for relative intensities.

Three unary matting operators help modify a single image, either in preparation for matting or on its own.

The unary operator *darken* causes an image to appear darker, without modifying its alpha values. The unary operator *dissolve* is similar to *darken*, but it modifies the alpha buffer as well and is useful for making an object fade from view. The unary operator *opaque* allows a picture to seem transparent as far as matting is concerned, but still have its pixels contribute color to the final image. It is a useful technique for images containing transparent, glowing objects.

BIBLIOGRAPHY

There are many books available on three-dimensional computer graphics. Most are for the programmer and geometer; these books cover the theory and principles behind the physics of light and surfaces, as well as the techniques and mathematics behind the computer programs that render surfaces.

For artists, designers, and animators, the selection is somewhat smaller. Below I have listed those books that I think will be useful and interesting to non-programmers. For the technically motivated I have included a few books that provide an introduction to the mathematics and computer principles behind computer graphics. These are indicated by an asterisk.

Editors of Time-Life Books. 1986. *Computer Images*. Alexandria, Va.: Time-Life Books.

*Foley, J. D., and A. van Dam. 1982. *Fundamentals of Interactive Computer Graphics*. Reading, Mass.: Addison-Wesley.

*Glassner, A., editor. 1989. *An Introduction to Ray Tracing*. London: Academic Press.

Greenberg, D., A. Marcus, A. H. Schmidt, and V. Gorter. 1982. *The Computer Image*. Reading, Mass.: Addison-Wesley.

Jankel, A., and R. Morton. 1984. *Creative Computer Graphics*. Cambridge: Cambridge University Press.

Kerlow, I. V., and J. Rosebush. 1986. *Computer Graphics*. New York: Van Nostrand Reinhold.

*Newman, W. M., and R. F. Sproull. 1979. *Principles of Interactive Computer Graphics*, 2nd ed. New York: McGraw-Hill.

INDEX

A

Algorithms, *See also* Rendering, algorithms
  painter's solution for hidden-surface problem, 51
  rendering, 131, 139-156
Aliasing, 131-134. *See also* Anti-aliasing
  flicker, 131
  jaggies (edge staircasing), 132
  temporal, 135
Angles, 24-25
Animation, 177-184. *See also* Animation, computer-assisted
  cels, 180-184
    in-between frames, 181
    keyframes, 181
  persistence of vision, 177
  rotoscoping, 184
Animation, computer-assisted, 184-193, 195-208. *See also* Animation
  production techniques, 195-208
    alpha buffer (channel), 201, 202-203
    mattes and image composition, 200-208
    matting operators, binary, 203-205
    matting operators, combining, 208
    matting operators, unary, 206-207
    opacity information, 202
    pans and zooms, 199
    transitions, 195
    transparency, 200
  three-dimensional, 187-193
    articulation tree, 187
    constraint system, 189
    dynamics system, 189, 191-192
    inverse kinematics system, 191
    keyframing, 187-190
    keypose, 189
    kinematics system, 190-191
    programmed (procedural) motion, 192-193
    spline-based interpolation, 190
  two-dimensional, 184-187
    linear/nonlinear interpolation, 185, 190
    paint stations, 186
    stacking, 187
    stroke interpolation, 184-185
Anti-aliasing, 132-134
  matte (alpha) buffers for, 202

  quick-and-dirty, 134
  and ray tracing, 147
  and stochastic ray tracing, 153
Apparent color, 53
  shading, 52
Articulation trees, 122-123, 187
Axis, 20-23

B

Bell Curve, 47
Bits, computer, 36
Body color, 56
Bump (normal perturbation) mapping, 92-94
Bytes, computer, 36-37

C

Calligraphic CRT, 8
Cartesian coordinate system, 21. *See also* Coordinate system
Cascading textures, 95
C curve, 104
Clipping planes, 128, 129
  hither (near) and yon (far), 128
Closed surfaces, 50
Color, 31-33, 53-57. *See also* Apparent color; Body color; Radiosity; Ray tracing; Shading; Surface color; Z-buffers
Color maps (or color tables), 41-44, 140
  gamma correction, 43-44
Color models
  hue, lightness, saturation (HLS), 32
  red, green, blue (RGB), 32-33
  spectral energy curve, 31-32
  textual, 33
Color raster CRT, 7
Color-shifting, 54-55
  metallic coefficient for specifying, 55
Complex (aggregate) surfaces. *See* Surfaces, complex
Computer-aided design (CAD), 166
Computer model, 1-2
Computer programs
  procedural motion, 192-193
  renderer, 3

  random-number generator, 47
  software, 6
  texture, 96-97
  transitions, 195
Coordinate system, 20-23, 28-30
  Cartesian, 21
  global (world), 28, 115
  manipulating of, 28-30
  nested, 115-116
    pop back up, 115-116
  orientation of, 22-23
    left-handed, 22
    right-handed, 22
  pushing, 116
  rotation, 22-23
    handed-rotation rule, 23
  viewing transformation, 129
CRTs, 7-8
  colors, 39-40
  electron guns, 37-38
  interlaced vs. noninterlaced, 39
  pixel, 41, 43
  scan lines, 39
    fields, 39
  triplet, phosphor, 38
CSG tree, 167-171
  formula, 170

D

Data tablet, 8-9
  pressure sensitive, 9
Degrees, 24-26
Derivatives, 27-28
Dimension, 15
Displacement mapping, 94-95
Displays, 7-8, 12-13
  open vs. closed, 12-13, 14
Distributions, numbers, 47
  bell curve, 47
  Gaussian, 47
Dragon curve, 104
Drawings, 3

E

Fractal geometry, 99
Fractals, 99-105

C curve, 104
  characteristics, 102
  database amplification, 100
  detail control, 102, 103-104
  dragon curve, 104
  generator, 102-103
  Koch curve, 102-103
  self-similarity, 102, 103
  subdivision (generation), 104
  in three dimensions, 105
  use in computer graphics, 102-104
Frame, 39. *See also* Frame buffer
Frame buffers, 37, 40-43. *See also* Z-
  buffers
  depth, 43
Free-form deformations (FFD), 171
Free-form modeling (FFM), 171

G

Gamma correction, 43-44
Gaussian distribution, 47
Geometry, applied, 15-31
  angles, 24-25
  axis, 20-23
  coordinate system, 20-21. *See also*
    Coordinate system
  degrees, 24-26
  derivatives, 27-28
  dimension, 15
  line, 19, 27
  motion, 15
  origin, 19
  plane, 19, 28
  point, 19
  radians, 25-26
  space, 19
  tangency, 27-28
  transformations, 28-30. *See also*
    Transformations
  vectors, 31
Geometry, constructive solid (CSG),
  167-171
Gouraud (smooth) shading, 81-82

H

Hand tracker, 11-12
  gesture interface, 12
Hardcopy, 8
  equipment, 8
Hardware, computer, 8
  graphics, 35-48
Head-mounted display (HMD), 12-13
Hidden surfaces, 51, 149
  problem, 51
    painter's algorithm solution, 51
Highlight, 54. *See also* Materials,
  roughness

I

Image digitizer, 8
Images, computer-generated, 3-5
  dynamic, 5
  interacting with, 12
  static, 4
Interpolation, 45, 184-185, 190

J

Joysticks, 10

K

Keyboard, computer, 7
Knot, 45
Koch curve, 102-103

L

Lambert (faceted) shading, 79-80
Light. *See also* Materials; Ray tracing
  reflected, 53-56, 58-59
    diffuse, 55-56
    specular, 54-55
  refraction, 58-59
    total internal reflection (TIR), 58
  transmitted, 53, 56-57
    diffuse, 59
    specular, 57
Lighting, light sources, 61-66. *See also*
  Shadows
  ambient (indirect), 65-66
  controls, 62-63
  darklights, 66
  goniometric color diagram, 62
  goniometric intensity diagram, 62
  infinite (remote), 64-65
  local, 64
  specifications, 62-63
Linear interpolation, 45
Lines
  curved, 27
    spline, 45
  normal, 53
    slope of, 27
    straight, 19, 27

M

Mach bands, 85
Mapping. *See* Texturing
Material mapping, 91
  multiplexing, 91
Material properties. *See* Materials
Materials, 53-59, 60, 91
  reflected light, 53-56, 58-59
    coefficients, diffuse and specular, 56
    diffuse, 55-56
    specular, 54-55
  roughness, 55
    highlight factor/exponent (roughness
      coefficient), 55, 57
    internal roughness, 57
  surface color, 54
  transmitted light, 53, 56-57
    coefficients, specular and diffuse, 59
    diffuse, 59
    specular, 57
Mattes, 187, 200-208. *See also* Animation,
  computer-assisted
  alpha buffer, 201, 202-203
  mask, 200-201
Memory, computer, 36-37, 40-43. *See
  also* Color maps; Frame buffers
  storage location, 36
  types, 37
Metallic coefficient, for specifying color-
  shifting, 55
Modeling, 2, 115-123. *See also* Fractals
  additive, 2
  advanced, 159-174
  articulation trees, 122-123
  constructive. *See* Modeling, additive
  free-form (FFM), 171
  interactive, 2
  instancing, 118-121

natural phenomena, 173-174
  prepared, 2
  primitives, 50, 159-174
  script, 118
  solid. *See* Modeling, additive
  subtractive, 2
  trees, 122-123
    self-referencing, 123
Models. *See also* Color models; Lighting;
  Polygon shading models; Shading
  articulated, 122-123
  dynamic, 5-6
  instancing, 118-121
  mathematical, 1-2
  scale, 1
  static, 5-6
Motion, 15
  vector components, 15
Motion blur, 134-135
  animating on fields, 135
  and ray tracing, 147
  simulated, 134-135
  strobing, 134
  temporal aliasing, 135
Mouse, 9
  relative positioning, 9
Multiple textures, 95

N

Natural phenomena, 173
Nested surfaces, 50
Nonlinear interpolation, 45
Nonlinearity, monitor, 44
Numbers
  as attributes of models, 35
  distributions, 47
  random, 47

O

Open surfaces, 49
Origin, 19

P

Patches, 107-109
  approximating (e.g., Bezier), 108
  interpolating (e.g., cubic), 108
Persistence of vision, 177
Perspective, 129
Phong (normal interpolating) shading,
  82-83
Photorealism, 157
Picture mapping, 87-90
Pixel, 41, 43. *See also* Z-buffers
Plane, 19, 34
  clipping, 128
  tangent, 28
Point, 19
  coplanar (planar), 71
Polygonal models, 71-73
  curved objects, 76-78
    face normals, 78
    vertex normals, 78
  flat objects, 76
  front and back facing, 72-73
  and patch-based models, 108
  problems with smoothing, 83-84
    Mach bands, 85
Polygons, 71-84. *See also* Polygonal
  models; Polygon shading models;
  Surfaces, complex
  concave, 76

convex vs. concave, 73
defined, 71
edge, 71
faces, 72
with holes, 76
planar vs. nonplanar, 74
self-intersecting, 75
surface normal of, 73
vertex, 71
Polygon shading models, 79-84
Polyhedron, 76
Positioning devices, 8-13
Primitive surfaces (primitives), 50, 159-174
Prototype, 115
Puck, 9
absolute positioning, 9

Q

Quadric surfaces, 109

R

Radians, 25-26
Radiosity, 154-156
balance, balancing loop, 155
converged system, 156
diffuse inter-reflection, 154
form factor, 154
Random-number generator, 47
Ray tracing, 147-153
bounding or world sphere, 151
depth, 149, 151
eye ray, 149
hidden surfaces, 149
illumination or shadow ray, 151
problems, 153
ray tree, 149, 151
stochastic ray tracing, 153
transmitted and reflected rays, 148, 153
Ray tree, 149, 151
Real time, 5
Refraction, index of, 58
Rendering, algorithms, 131, 139-156. *See also entries for individual types listed*
comparisons, 156-157
radiosity, 154-156
ray tracing, 147-153
realism, 156-157
types of, 131
Z-buffers, 139-145
Rendering, principles, 127-137. *See also Aliasing; Motion blur; Shadows*
clipping planes, 128, 129
frustrum, 129
projections, 129
object space, 127-128
viewing pyramid, 128
viewing transformation, 129
Rotation, 22-23, 30

S

Scaling, 30, 161
differential, 30

uniform, 30
Screen space, 127-128
Shading, 52-53. *See also* Polygon shading models; Radiosity; Ray tracing; Z-buffers
diffuse, 67-68
Lambert (faceted), 79-80
reflection and transmission, 67-69
smooth, 80-83
Gouraud shading, 81-82
Phong shading, 82-83
specular, 68-69
Shadows, 67, 87, 136-137
diffraction effects, 137
radiosity and, 156
ray tracing and, 147, 151-152, 153
umbra and penumbra, 136, 137
Z-buffers and, 144-145
Shear. *See* Skew
Simulation, 4
Skew (or shear), 30
Softcopy, 8
Software. *See* Computer programs
Space, 19
Space textures, 96-97
Space tracker, 11, 12
Spline interpolation, 45
Stochastic ray tracing, 153
Stylus, 8-9
absolute positioning, 9
tilt sensitive, 9
Surface color, 54
Surface normal, 53
Surfaces, 49-53. *See also* Surfaces, complex; Surfaces, curved
closed, 50
complex, 50, 159-167
hidden, 51, 149
matte, 56
nested, 50
open, 49
optical appearance. *See* Materials
quadric, 109
primitive, 50, 159-174
shading, 52-53
shiny, 56
visible, 51
Surfaces, complex, 50, 159-167
blends (fillets), 166-167
blobby and implicit surfaces, 163-165
blobiness, 164
implicit surfaces, 165
isodensity contours and surfaces, 164
cameras, 166
contour sets, 162-163
X-rays and CAT (computer-aided tomography), 163
manipulating, 167-173
constructive solid geometry (CSG), 167-171
free-form deformations (FFD), 171
free-form modeling (FFM), 171
global control, 171
local control, 171
natural phenomena, 173-174
particle systems, 165-166
advantages, 166
shading languages, 173

sweep surfaces, 160-162
generalized cylinders, 160-161
generalized prism, 160
surfaces of revolution, 161-162
surface sweeps, 162
twist, rotation, and scaling, 161
Surfaces, curved, 107-112
parameterization, 111-112
patches, 107-108
quadric, 109
shading, 107
texturing, 107, 111-112

T

Tangency, 27-28
Text CRT, computer, 7
Textures, 87-97. *See also* Texturing
cascading textures, 95
multiple textures, 95
space (spatial) textures, 96-97
Texturing (texture mapping), 87
bump mapping, 92-94
displacement mapping, 94-95
material mapping, 91
multiplexing, 91
modulation, 90
parameterization, 88
picture mapping, 87-90
shading and color, 89-90
texture alignment, 96
transparency mapping, 90
U and V axes, 88
Trackball, 11
Transformations, 28-30
rotation, 30
scaling, 30
skewing, 30
translation, 29
Translating, 29
Transparency mapping, 90
Triangulation, 76

V

Vector component, 15
Vectors, 31
surface normal, 53
Visible surfaces, 51

W

Words, computer, 36

Z

Z-buffers, 139-145
advantages, 144
illumination or shadow buffer, 144
image buffer, 140
problems, 143-144
shadows, 144-145
Z-depth, 140